SINKING THE BEAST

THE RAF 1944 LANCASTER RAIDS AGAINST *TIRPITZ*

JAN FORSGREN

FONTHILL

This book is dedicated to the brave aircrews of Nos IX(B) and 617 Squadrons who, despite overwhelming odds, managed to slay the Beast.

Fonthill Media Limited
Fonthill Media LLC
www.fonthillmedia.com
office@fonthillmedia.com

First published in the United Kingdom
and the United States of America 2014

Copyright © Jan Forsgren 2014

ISBN 978-1-78155-318-3

The right of Jan Forsgren to be identified as the author of this work has been asserted by him in accordance with the Copyright, Designs and Patents Act 1988

All rights reserved. No part of this publication may be reproduced, stored in a retrieval system or transmitted in any form or by any means, electronic, mechanical, photocopying, recording or otherwise, without prior permission in writing from Fonthill Media Limited

Typeset in 10.5pt on 13pt Minion Pro

Contents

	Acknowledgements	7
	Notes on Sources	9
	Introduction	12
Chapter One:	A Background History	17
Chapter Two:	Sink the Beast!	35
Chapter Three:	Operation *Paravane*	75
Chapter Four:	Operation *Obviate*	107
Chapter Five:	Operation *Catechism*	123
Chapter Six:	Aftermath	148
Appendix 1:	Avro Lancaster B. Mk I Specification and Data	163
Appendix 2:	RAF raids against the *Tirpitz* 1940–1942	164
Appendix 3:	Fleet Air Arm raids against the *Tirpitz* 1942–1944	165
Appendix 4:	Operation *Paravane* 15 September 1944	166
Appendix 5:	Operation *Obviate* 29 October 1944	170
Appendix 6:	Operation *Catechism* 12 November 1944	175
	Endnotes	179
	Bibliography	184
	Index	187

Acknowledgements

Although the process of writing is lonely work, a large number of people have contributed with information, photographs and sound advice. In particular, I would like to thank Christine Audis of the Roger Audis Estate for allowing me to include Roger's article on the '*Tirpitz* bulkhead'; Mats Averkvist for forwarding many valuable contacts; Even Blomkvist (Curator of the Alta *Tirpitz* Museum) for taking his time to locate suitable photographs; Bertil Boberg who pointed me towards sources on *Tirpitz*'s cruise into Finnish waters in September 1941; John Bryggman who has spent fifty years researching the final flight of Lancaster NF920—better known as 'Easy Elsie'—graciously gave his permission for me to use his 2002 interview with the navigator of 'Easy Elsie', Alex McKie, as well as supplying several photographs; Anders Eriksson for producing the maps; my old friend Pär Erixon who first visited the wreck of 'Easy Elsie' during the late 1970s and took his time to speak about his experiences of aviation archaeology as well as searching through his archives for photographs; the aviation historian and author Mikael Forslund who supplied good advice and encouragement on the writing process; Finnish aviation historian Carl-Fredrik Geust who provided invaluable information on the Soviet attack on the *Tirpitz* and Operation *Paravane*; Lars Gyllenhaal, the war historian and expert on the war on the Arctic Front, who kindly forwarded information on the use of *Tirpitz*'s armour as gunnery range targets in Sweden as well as information on the telegraphic messages sent from the site of 'Easy Elsie's resting place in 2011 and 2012; Chris Henderson, editor of *Après Moi*, the magazine of the 617 Squadron Aircrew Association, who kindly forwarded many valuable contacts and photographs; Bengt Hermansson of the Forced Landing Collection (FLC) who immediately made available several rare photographs of Lancaster LM448; the noted model builder Mats Johansson who kindly supplied photographs from his recent trip to northern Norway; Norwegian aviation historian Nils Mathisrud who provided several valuable contacts; Swedish journalist Bert Persson, who in 1946, made his way to Tromsø to visit the hulk of *Tirpitz*, kindly gave his time to speak about his experiences; John Shortland who kindly gave his permission to quote from his interview with Alfred Zuba that was originally published in *Après Moi*; Eva Svensson who took her time to search through the archives of Jokkmokk County; Michael Tamelander, the co-author of an excellent book on the *Tirpitz*, who kindly took his time to discuss various issues on the history of *Tirpitz*; Inger Wallbing, chairman of the Porjus Archival Committee, which maintains the wreck of 'Easy Elsie' at Porjus; and Margot ('Peggie') Ward for kindly allowing me to quote from her late husband Arthur Ward's article in *Après Moi* on Operation *Paravane*.

I would also like to thank my editor at Fonthill Media, Jay Slater, for having faith and trust in the project.

Apologies to anyone whom I have forgotten!

Jan Forsgren
Gävle, Sweden
January 2014

Notes on Sources

The Operational Record Books (ORB) of the relevant RAF Bomber Command Squadrons that flew raids against the Tirpitz have been referred to; these include the ORBs of 44 and 97 Squadrons for the raids in March and April 1942, and the ORBs of IX(B), 463 and 617 Squadrons for September, October and November 1944 respectively. The historical ORBs of the RAF are kept by the National Archives at Kew, being available online at www.nationalarchives.co.uk. The information contained in the ORBs include specific data on each operation, listing each participating aircrew member and aircraft (including serial numbers and code letters), time for take-off and return to base, and bomb load carried. Also included are brief abstracts of the raid from each individual crew and information on the target and other defences, altitude of bomb release, and estimations of damage incurred on the target. This first-hand information, compiled immediately following the conclusion of a bombing raid, provides invaluable insights into Bomber Command operations and the human effort required to bring the war to Germany.

Other materials used were several contemporary telegraphic messages, both from the Churchill Archives (www.churchillarchives.com) and the National Archives.

Other first-hand archival sources include data on RAF incursions into Swedish airspace during Operation *Paravane*, *Obviate* and *Catechism*, all provided by the Swedish National War Archives and National Archives. Interrogation reports with the crews of the two Lancasters that force landed in this neutral country were located at the National War Archives. The internment and eventual repatriation of several RAF aircrews in early May 1942 following the failed Halifax raids are described in great detail in Rolph Wegmann's *Brittiska nödlandare 1940–1945* while much information can also to be found in Nigel Smith's excellent *Tirpitz: The Halifax Raids*. The latter book also provided much relevant information on the RAF raids against the Beast during the spring of 1942.

A number of secondary sources have been used. Among the most important of these were John Asmussen and Kjetil Aakra's *Tirpitz: Hitlers siste slagskip* (*Tirpitz: Hitler's Last Battleship*). Originally published in 2006 by the Midt-Tromsø Museum, it is an excellent photographic record of the *Tirpitz* from her launch until the final scrapping during the late 1950s. The various attempts to sink the *Tirpitz* by submarine, FAA and RAF are presented in great detail as are the day-to-day life aboard the battleship.

General historical references to the *Tirpitz* are plentiful. One of the first of these to be published was Paul Brickhill's classic *Dam Busters* that was originally issued in 1952.

Patrick Bishop's recent *Target Tirpitz* and *Slagskeppet Tirpitz* by Michael Tamelander and Niklas Zetterling were the main sources both on the *Tirpitz* as well as a broader background of the war in the North Atlantic and on the Arctic Front. Alf R. Jacobsen's *Dödligt angrepp* (*Deadly Assault*) concentrates on the X-Craft raid, but also provides much insight into the German occupation of Norway and subsequent war operations against Russia.

Specific details on the *Tirpitz* such as weaponry and camouflage schemes were mainly culled from Peter Hore's *The World Encyclopedia of Battleships*, Steve Becker's *Bismarck and Tirpitz* and Gordon Williamson's *German Battleships 1939–1945*. The master's thesis *'Easy Elsie' och Nordens ensamma drottning* (*'Easy Elsie' and the Lonely Queen of the North*) contains interesting snippets of information on the planned construction of large battleships in Germany during the mid-1930s. Regarding the *Tirpitz*'s brief voyage into Finnish waters in September 1941, the best printed source for these events are *Ofredens hav Östersjön 1939-1992* (*Sea of War—The Baltic Sea 1939–1992*), while Harry Moyle's *The Hampden File*, and *Arctic Airmen: The RAF in Spitsbergen and North Russia, 1942* by Ernest Schofield and Roy Conyers Nesbit, add much information on RAF operations on the Arctic Front in 1942.

In regard to the various RAF and FAA raids against the *Tirpitz*, arguably the best book is John Sweetman's *Tirpitz: Hunting the Beast*. Alan W. Cooper's book *From the Dams to the Tirpitz* concentrates on 617 Squadron. Basic histories of IX(B), 463 and 617 Squadrons can be found in Philip Moyes' *Bomber Squadrons of the RAF*. Various Internet websites provided additional information. The quotes from the personal recollections of Arthur Ward and Alfred Zuba respectively were originally published in *Après Moi*, the magazine of the 617 Squadron Aircrew Association. Also thanks to Richard 'Dicky' James of IX(B) Squadron for his valuable input.

The Luftwaffe's view of the events of 12 November 1944 is briefly described in Werner Girbig's *Chronik Jagdgeschwader 5*. John Asmussen and Kjetil Aakra's *Tirpitz: Hitlers siste slagskip* also describes the events from the German point of view.

Regarding the rebuild and use of RAF Lancasters by the USSR, Vladimir Kotelnikov's article 'From Roundels to Red Stars' (originally published in *Aeroplane*, January 2007) provided much information. Additional data was supplied by Finnish aviation historian Carl-Fredrik Geust, the world's foremost expert in Soviet use of American and British aeroplanes supplied under the Lend Lease agreement. Carl-Fredrik also kindly provided details on the sole Soviet attempt to strike at the *Tirpitz* by air on 10–11 February 1944.

Regarding information on Kriegsmarine operations during the last two years of the war, V. E. Tarrant's excellent *The Last Year of the Kriegsmarine* has been referred to.

A number of websites also proved useful. The political situation in Germany and the political career of Alfred von Tirpitz is partly based on www.weimar.facinghistory.org/content/political-parties-weimar-germany. The best overall website on the *Tirpitz* and *Bismarck* is maintained by John Asmussen: www.bismarck-class.dk. The amazing history of the *Tirpitz* bulkhead can be found at: http://ixb.org.uk/2012/history/tirpitz-bulkhead/. This article was originally written by IX(B) Squadron historian Roger Audis who died in June 2013. The editor of *Après Moi*, Chris Henderson, added further information on this matter: www.lancaster-archive.com/bc_tirpitz2.htm. The background history of IX(B) Squadron was for the most part culled from the http://ixb.org.uk/2012/history/sep-1939-1945 website. The arrival of Lancaster LM448 in Sweden is described in detail at www.vannasberget.se/ormanget.html. Valuable pieces of information, including reminisces from participants of the 1944 Lancaster raids, from the following websites were used: www.467463raafsquadrons.com/TrueTales/sink_the_tirpitz.htm; www.historysite.co.uk/tirpitz.htm; www.bombercommandmuseum.ca/s,tweddle.html; and www.bombercommandmuseum.ca/tirpitz.html

Transmitted radio messages from the crash site of 'Easy Elsie' took place in 2011 and 2012 and can be found at www.sm2tos.se/easyelsie/swe/html/historia.html.

With regard to the use of measurements, two standard sets of measurements and weights have been used for imperial (pounds, inches, feet, miles and gallons) and metric (kilos, tons, kilometres, etc.) for such data pertaining to British and German sources throughout the book.

Introduction

The German battleship *Tirpitz* is still part of the public conscience. With the possible exception of her sister ship *Bismarck*, sunk in 1941 during her first cruise, the *Tirpitz* remains the best known German warship of the Second World War. Churchill referred to her as 'The Beast', an apt nickname as the battleship from her lair in northern Norway represented a very real threat to Allied convoys carrying vital supplies for the Soviet Union. Commissioned into service on 25 February 1941, the *Tirpitz* was deployed to Norway almost one year later in January 1942. However, the *Tirpitz* rarely left her northern port. Although taking part in regular exercises, she engaged in combat only twice during four operational cruises. The first operational cruise was a brief voyage into the northern Baltic Sea in September 1941. The first operational sortie, in March 1942, was a failed attempt to intercept the PQ 12 convoy. During the brief cruise, cut short by the need to conserve precious fuel, she was shadowed by the Home Fleet. No combat with the Home Fleet ensued, although two Fleet Air Arm Albacore torpedo bombers were shot down during a failed torpedo attack. *Tirpitz* suffered no damage.

The next cruise took place sixteen months later during a brief (little more than four hours) attempt at catching the PQ 17 convoy. The fear of having Germany's largest battleship attacking the hapless convoy caused the Admiralty to order the merchant vessels of PQ 17 to scatter with disastrous consequences. The *Tirpitz* did not fire a single round against the ships of PQ 17 with submarines and torpedo-carrying bombers accounting for many of the vessels. The final sortie, in September 1943, saw a weather station in the Spitzbergen islands attacked, but for the most part, *Tirpitz* spent most of her life at anchor with the Norwegians referring to the battleship as the 'Lonely Queen of the North'.

With *Tirpitz* firmly entrenched in Norway, numerous attempts to sink the Beast were made. RAF bombers, Fleet Air Arm carrier-based aircraft, human torpedoes and midget submarines were all sent against the battleship. It seemed as if many of the ideas on how best to sink the *Tirpitz* verged on the fanciful. Even though the battleship suffered damage in varying degrees during the raids, it was left to RAF heavy bombers to finish the job on 12 November 1944. The final blow was delivered by RAF Lancasters of Nos IX(B) and 617 Squadrons.

Even before the battleship had been finished, RAF bombers attempted to disable her at the Wilhelmshaven docks. Often bombing in extremely poor weather conditions, none of the RAF raids even scratched the *Tirpitz* (tentative plans also included attacking the docks area with carrier-based aircraft). After being officially commissioned into Kriegsmarine service, extensive sea trials in the Baltic Sea followed for the huge battleship and her crew. When Germany invaded the USSR on 22 June 1941, *Tirpitz* did not take part in the operations. Instead, training continued.

In September 1941, *Tirpitz* became the flagship of the Baltenflotte. The Baltenflotte was formed to stop the Soviet fleet, entrenched at Kronstadt and Leningrad since the beginning of the German invasion of the Soviet Union, to break out into the Baltic Sea. In the event, not a single shot was fired by the Baltenflotte.

The question of how to deploy the surface warships of the Kriegsmarine was the subject of intense debate among the German High Command. Following the loss of the *Bismarck* in May 1941, sending her sister ship *Tirpitz* on a similar and almost inevitably fatal voyage was out of the question. Losing the *Tirpitz* would raise serious doubts about the fighting ability of the Kriegsmarine and such a propaganda defeat was to be avoided.

Instead, it was decided to send the *Tirpitz* to central Norway where the battleship would function both as a deterrent against a feared Allied invasion of Norway, but also as a prime resource in attacking Russian-bound convoys. The latter, packed with aeroplanes, tanks and other vital war supplies, strengthened Russian forces against the Nazi invaders. Soon after the arrival of *Tirpitz* in Norway, the first RAF raid took place. In early March, the Home Fleet came close, joining the *Tirpitz* in a sea battle. This did not happen, although the battleship was unsuccessfully attacked by Fairey Albacore torpedo bombers. Further RAF raids during the spring failed to damage the *Tirpitz*. Several bombers, along with their crews, were lost. In June 1943, an aborted attempt was made to attack the PQ 17 convoy. A Soviet attempt of sinking the *Tirpitz* allegedly went unnoticed by her crew! Compared with the German forces fighting on the Eastern Front, the crew aboard *Tirpitz* enjoyed a fairly good life.

In September 1943, the *Tirpitz*'s third and last operational cruise took place. Codenamed Operation *Sicily*, this entailed the naval bombardment of an Allied stronghold at Barentsburg on the Spitzbergen islands. Shelling the small Allied garrison—mostly consisting of Norwegian troops—involved very little real danger for the *Tirpitz* and her crew. Nevertheless, the crew, as well as those other participating Kriegsmarine vessels, was liberally doused with decorations following the conclusion of Operation *Sicily*. This was, of course, a simple way of raising the spirits for the crew who longed for active combat.

On 24 September, British midget submarines managed to penetrate the underwater defences and place explosive mines under her hull. Although the midget submarines were sunk with some of their crews taken prisoner, the Beast suffered severely in the resulting explosions. In fact, the battleship remained out of action for nearly six months. Despite being based close to the Arctic frontline, few Russian attempts to sink the *Tirpitz* were made. Although several photo-reconnaissance sorties were flown, only one dedicated bombing raid by Russian aircraft resulted and occurred on 10–11 February 1944. Out of thirty-six Ilyushin Il-4 medium bombers that took off, only two managed to find their way to Kaa Fjord. None of the bombs hit the battleship.

With the repairs finally completed, sea trials were expected to begin on 3 April. In the early hours on 3 April, Fleet Air Arm Barracudas struck *Tirpitz*. This attack, codenamed Operation *Tungsten*, turned out to be the most successful of the many Fleet Air Arm raids that were to follow during the spring and summer. One major drawback was that the standard FAA strike aircraft, the Fairey Barracuda, could only carry one 1,600 lb armour-piercing bomb. This bomb was belatedly recognised as being incapable of penetrating the thick armour hull of the *Tirpitz*.

Despite the fact that the *Tirpitz* up to that time had never engaged any Allied convoy, the battleship was still regarded as a major threat to the vital supply line to Russia. As a result, efforts to disable or sink the *Tirpitz* continued unabated. With the Royal Navy having failed to sink her, the job was forwarded to Bomber Command. With the *Tirpitz* being holed up at Kaa Fjord and beyond the range of UK-based bombers, it was decided to deploy a force of Avro Lancasters to Russia's Kola Peninsula. This raid, Operation *Paravane*, went ahead on 15 September. The raid saw permanent damage to the Beast, which eventually made the Germans decide upon anchoring the battleship near Tromsø and convert her into a floating fortress. The extent of the damage to *Tirpitz* was not known to Bomber Command, which mounted a second raid, Operation *Obviate*, on 29 October. Yet again, this raid had inconclusive results. With the Arctic weather fast deteriorating, getting the job done of finally sinking the *Tirpitz* became a priority. The third raid, Operation *Catechism*, went ahead on 12 November. This, the third RAF raid during the autumn of 1944, saw the Beast finally slain.

One might argue that the *Tirpitz* was an obsolete behemoth and of little practical use to the German war effort. Indeed, the *Tirpitz* was far more valuable as a propaganda tool than as an operational warship, functioning as a weapon of deterrence and as an ever present threat against Allied shipping. In fact, she never sank any Allied battleships or merchant vessels, but several Fleet Air Arm and RAF aircraft were shot down during 1942 and 1944 raids.

Compared with the high-profile surface battleships, including the *Tirpitz*, the most effective part of the Kriegsmarine was its large fleet of U-boats that accounted for thousands of Allied merchant vessels and warships. Numerically inferior to the Royal Navy, the surface warships of the Kriegsmarine seldom engaged in naval combat. Naval historian Ludovic Kennedy poignantly wrote that the *Tirpitz* 'lived an invalid's life and died a cripple's death'. Nevertheless, the mere presence of the *Tirpitz* in northern Norway made it necessary to devote huge resources of men, ships and aircraft to cripple or sink the battleship.

Since the end of the war, much has appeared in print on the mighty battleship *Tirpitz*. Printed sources include numerous articles, books and freely available material on the Internet. This book mainly concerns itself with the three RAF Lancaster raids against the *Tirpitz*: Operation *Paravane* (15 September 1944), Operation *Obviate* (29 October 1944) and Operation *Catechism* (12 November 1944). The first of these raids saw the *Tirpitz* so badly damaged that the Germans realised she could no longer be considered a seaworthy warship. Instead, it was decided to tow her to Håkøya near Tromsø where the battleship would be used as a floating fortress in a last line of defence against advancing

Russian forces. At the time, the Allies were unaware of the heavy damage that had been inflicted on the Beast. A second and unsuccessful raid was flown on 29 October. The last raid, on 12 November, saw the mighty battleship capsize. The hunt for the Beast had finally ended in success.

Also included is a brief history of the battleship *Tirpitz* as well as the many efforts to disable or sink her by means of RAF bombers, Fleet Air Arm strikes, midget submarines and human torpedoes. The war on the Arctic Front was in large part shaped by the presence of the *Tirpitz*. Because of this, the history and eventual fate of the *Tirpitz* cannot be written without referring to battles and events connected to the battleship, the German presence in Norway and Finland, and operations against Allied Russian-bound convoys. This also includes briefly describing the overall Allied war effort in the Arctic.

A summarising chapter includes details on the war on the Arctic Front until the end of the conflict as well as the subsequent histories of Nos IX(B) and 617 Squadrons. A postscript has also been included, detailing the scrapping of the *Tirpitz*, the various physical surviving remains of the battleship and her opponents. Here, the remarkable story of the *Tirpitz*'s bulkhead can be found that spurred intra-squadron rivalry to reach previous unknown levels. The continued survival of a 617 Squadron Lancaster in northern Sweden and the risk that the wreck stands at succumbing to the elements and thoughtless souvenir hunters can be found in this final chapter. Also included here are reminiscences of surviving members of Nos IX(B) and 617 Squadrons. Six appendices complete the book. Among these are details of every Lancaster and the aircrews who manned them that took part in Operation *Paravane*, Operation *Obviate* and Operation *Catechism*.

CHAPTER ONE

A Background History

Following the end of the First World War, the German armed forces were largely disbanded. Britain, France, Italy, the US and a number of other countries had finally defeated Imperial Germany and the double monarchy of Austria-Hungary. Negotiations for a peace treaty began at Versailles and the German High Seas Fleet was ordered to sail to Scapa Flow in December 1918. Protracted negotiations on the final fate of the German warships continued until mid-1919 when, as conditioned in the Versailles Treaty, it was decreed that they would be handed over to the Allies. In defiance, the sailors of the High Seas Fleet scuttled their warships, including ten battleships and forty-one other vessels, at Scapa Flow on 21 June 1919.[1]

Several remaining German naval vessels were subsequently handed over to the Allies in recompense to the ones sunk at Scapa Flow. Commanded by Admiral von Trotha, the much reduced Reichsmarine of the Weimar Republic that was established in April 1919 had eight capital ships in service: the *Braunschweig, Lothringen, Preussen, Hessen, Schleswig-Holstein, Schlesien, Elsass* and *Hannover*. According to the Versailles Treaty, this was more than enough to protect German coastal waters, particularly in the eastern Baltic Sea against any threat posed by the Russian Bolsheviks. The remaining capital ships were designated as Linienschiffe (Line Ships). Any new-build warship was to be limited to a displacement of 10,000 tons.

German warship designers soon came up with a solution to this problem with the Deutschland-class of naval vessels, which were referred to as Panzerschiffe (Armoured Ships). Exceeding the 10,000 tons displacement limit by a handsome margin, these armoured ships were commonly referred to as pocket battleships. Of the Panzerschiffe, only *Deutschland* met the restrictions of tonnage. Both the *Admiral Scheer* and *Graf Spee* were substantially larger.

In this context, it must be said that the battleship had since the late 1800s been the largest surface warship of the world's fleets. It was the ultimate symbol of naval power. However, with the introduction of the aeroplane and the aircraft carrier, the hitherto unchallenged hegemony of the battleship on the high seas was put into question. However, for many high-ranking naval officers, having small aeroplanes with their limited range and bomb-carrying capability, attack, let alone sink, a battleship was a ridiculous notion.

In July 1921, the US air power advocate Billy Mitchell did just that, bombing the former German battleship *Ostfriesland*. Several difficult questions regarding the sinking by aeroplane were subsequently raised. First of all, the *Ostfriesland* was anchored and lacked on-board damage control parties. Also, Mitchell and his bombers had the distinct advantage of not having to endure being shot at by the warship's flak. Thus, wartime conditions had obviously not been completely reconstructed for the bomb tests. Nevertheless, the sinking of the *Ostfriesland* showed that air power would ultimately spell the end of the large battleship.

Post-war Germany

The immediate post-war years in Germany were marked by a record-high inflation, huge unemployment, social unrest and political polarisation. The democratic Weimar Republic was weak and lacked popular support. The small NSDAP political party, led by Adolf Hitler, attempted to seize power in 1923 and the *coup d'état* was quickly put down with Hitler sentenced to prison. Here, Hitler formulated the idea that the Germans had lost the war through the Jews and cowardly politicians, which had thrust a dagger in the back of the Imperial forces. Hitler and the NSDAP soon gained support from large sections of the German population as well as several influential industrialists. The promise was to avenge the humiliation suffered by Germany following the signing of the Versailles Treaty. After Hitler's ascent to power in January 1933, the preparations for German rearmament by land, air and sea began in earnest. Only three of the Great War capital ships, *Hessen*, *Schleswig-Holstein* and *Schlesien*, remained in service. The former was soon taken out of service, albeit being retained as a training vessel and later seeing use as a full-scale target.

New battleships for the Kriegsmarine

In May 1935, the Kriegsmarine was officially established. On 18 June, Germany and Great Britain signed a naval treaty that allowed Germany 35 per cent of the warship tonnage of the Royal Navy, including the exact number of submarines. Later the same year, the pocket battleships *Gneisenau* and *Scharnhorst* were ordered. According to the treaty, both *Gneisenau* and *Scharnhorst* were supposed to have a displacement of 26,000 tons. In reality, the displacement of the respective warships was 32,000 tons with the full load being 38,700 tons; however, the treaty did not provide any real obstacles against further rearmament of the Kriegsmarine. In reality, building additional naval vessels boiled down to economics. According to Hitler, the naval treaty eliminated the risk of war with Great Britain for the next ten years until 1945.

Three years later in 1938, Hitler had once again changed his mind, considering Great Britain as a high-risk potential enemy in a future war. The threat posed by the Royal Navy was detailed in Plan Z, which developed by the German Naval High Command, included a sharp increase in the strength of the Kriegsmarine. According to Plan Z, the Kriegsmarine would have an additional six battleships, four pocket battleships and four battle cruisers to the four battleships and three pocket battleships in service or under construction. Four aircraft carriers were also to be built.[2]

However, the construction and introduction into service of these warships would take years and consume resources needed elsewhere. As a result, Plan Z did not indicate that the strength of the Kriegsmarine would in any way be comparable to that of the Royal Navy until the late 1940s. In fact, the only comparison between the Royal Navy and Kriegsmarine on the eve of war was that both navies could field fifty-seven submarines. In all other respects with battleships, cruisers, destroyers and aircraft carriers, the Royal Navy was numerically superior to the Kriegsmarine. Regarding aircraft carriers, due to military indecision and changing requirements, the Kriegsmarine failed to bring any such surface warship into service.

The outbreak of war in September 1939 saw Plan Z scuppered. The commander of the Kriegsmarine considered that the force of surface warships 'are so inferior in numbers and strength to those of the British Fleet that even at full strength, they can do no more than show that they know how to die gallantly'.[3] Indeed, during the war, the Kriegsmarine would be allocated far less resources in material and manpower than the Luftwaffe and Wehrmacht. Overall, the Kriegsmarine was the loser in the German rearmament race. It was decided, though, that the battleships under construction would be completed, but no additional naval vessels of such large displacement ordered, thus negating the intentions of Plan Z. The emphasis would be placed on submarines.

Numerically, the Kriegsmarine was at a clear disadvantage to the Royal Navy, something which was reflected in the war strategy. Following the outbreak of war, Grossadmiral Erich Raeder stated that the Kriegsmarine 'was in no way adequately equipped for the great struggle with Great Britain'.[4]

The primary function of the new heavy warships was as surface raiders, i.e. to chase down and sink enemy cargo ships in the Atlantic, Indian and Pacific Oceans. This was essentially the same tactic that had been successfully employed during the First World War. One might also refer to the surface raider tactic as naval guerrilla warfare. The armament of the battleships and pocket battleships was to be heavy enough to provide a fighting chance against the battleships of other navies, particularly against the French Navy and Royal Navy. Prior to the outbreak of war, two pocket battleships with support vessels were dispatched to the Atlantic. Both of them, the *Graf Spee* and *Deutschland*, were successful in sinking a number of cargo ships. However, the *Graf Spee* met her fate off Montevideo in neutral Uruguay, being scuttled on the orders of her commanding officer, Hans Langsdorff, after being damaged in an encounter with three Royal Navy cruisers, HMS *Exeter*, HMS *Achilles* and HMS *Ajax*. Meanwhile, the *Deutschland* returned to Germany to avoid being hunted down and sunk by the Royal Navy. Hitler subsequently insisted in changing the name of *Deutschland* to *Lützow*, fearing a huge loss of face if a battleship named after the nation were to be sunk by the British.

The largest battleships in the world

In 1936, two battleships in the new large Bismarck-class were ordered for the Kriegsmarine; these were *Bismarck* and *Tirpitz*. While *Bismarck* was to be built at the Blohm & Voss dockyards at Hamburg, *Tirpitz* would be built at the Kriegsmarinewerft at Wilhelmshaven. The chief designer for the new *Bismarck*-class of battleships was Otto Reidel.

The formal contract for the battleship *Tirpitz* was placed on 14 June 1936 with the battleship being described as New Construction 'G'. *Tirpitz* was to replace the old *Linienschiff Schleswig-Holstein*. Construction of the new battleship began immediately at the lengthened and strengthened Slipway 2 with the keel being laid down either on 24 October or 2 November.[5]

Grossadmiral Alfred von Tirpitz

The new battleship was named after Alfred von Tirpitz (1849–1930). Having joined the Imperial Navy at the age of twenty in 1869, von Tirpitz quickly rose through the ranks. In 1877, he became responsible for the development of a new naval weapon, the torpedo. In 1892, von Tirpitz was promoted to become the head of the Imperial Naval Staff, reaching the rank of Grossadmiral (Rear Admiral) three years later in 1895. In 1898 when Germany began a programme of expanding the Hochseeflotte (High Seas Fleet), von Tirpitz was the Minister of Naval Affairs, becoming known as the founder of the modern German navy. Balancing on the Emperor's enthusiasm for the navy as well as popular support, von Tirpitz was able to modernise and expand the Imperial Fleet.

Beginning in 1884, Imperial Germany began to build a colonial empire—despite the initial doubts held by the 'Iron Chancellor', Otto von Bismarck—acquiring territories in Africa and the Pacific. In order to protect the growing empire, a large navy was required. This was the era of gunboat diplomacy. The long term goal of the naval expansion was to challenge the Royal Navy's domination of the seas. The naval expansion programme was revised and expanded on several occasions. With the 1908 expansion programme, it was calculated that by 1920, the Imperial German Navy would have surpassed the Royal Navy, both in terms of quantity and quality. The importance attached in building a strong naval force—and the desire of the Second Reich in gaining a place as one of the dominant European powers—may be seen from the fact that Kaiser Wilhelm II once proclaimed himself to be the 'Admiral of the Atlantic'. Having a huge and powerful navy was one of the key factors in becoming a powerful nation with the battleship as the ultimate military symbol of power.

Britain reluctantly picked up the gauntlet in the naval rearmament race with the slogan 'Two keels to one' becoming popular. When war broke out in 1914, the Royal Navy had twenty dreadnought battleships against fourteen in the Imperial German Navy. By this time, von Tirpitz was named commander-in-chief of the Imperial German Navy.

On 7 May 1915 when the British liner *Lusitania* was torpedoed off the coast of Ireland, a furore was created both in Britain and the neutral United States. Of the 1,198 lives lost, 128 were Americans. As a direct result of the sinking, the US public's support for President Wilson's policy of neutrality evaporated. On the other hand, support for Britain increased dramatically (the United States would eventually enter the war in 1917). The Germans subsequently claimed that the *Lusitania* had carried war supplies and that the large ocean liner was a legitimate target. Nevertheless, the German High Command eventually stepped back on submarine attacks.[6] The sinking of the *Lusitania* eventually saw von Tirpitz resigning from his commission in protest when Wilhelm II refused to allow unrestricted submarine warfare. Instead, von Tirpitz assisted in the formation of the highly patriotic political party Deutsche Vaterlandspartei (German Fatherland Party).

After the war, von Tirpitz continued in the political field, representing the right-wing Deutsch Nationale Volkspartei (German National People's Party, DNVP) in the Reichstag from 1924 until 1928. The DNVP's electoral base was a mix of wealthy landowners and industrialists. Some support from protestant clergy was also forthcoming as well as small business owners. Opposing the attempts of the Weimar Republic to fulfil the reparations demanded by the Versailles Treaty, the DNVP was both militaristic as well as anti-Semitic. Alfred von Tirpitz subsequently left the political scene, dying on 6 March 1930, only twelve days before his eighty-first birthday.

Interestingly, in view of things to come, a small Norwegian island in the Svalbard archipelago, Tirpitzøya, was also named after Alfred von Tirpitz.

The battleship *Tirpitz*

Tirpitz was indeed an extremely impressive piece of naval military technology. Her displacement was 50,933 metric tons when loaded (41,700 metric tons less fuel and ordnance), some 1,700 tons more than the *Bismarck*. This was due to a larger number of flak guns and strengthened armoured deck. Her overall length was 248 metres with the length along the waterline being 241.20 metres. The beam was 36 metres and the draught 9.75 metres. The armour plating of the main deck was 8 cm thick. The thick armour plating was constructed by Krupp from Wotan C special steel and in all likelihood some of the metal came from the high-grade iron ore imported from Sweden. The three Brown-Boveri turbines developed 150,170 hp (maximum power output was 163,036 hp), which gave the battleship a top speed of 30.5 knots. The hull weighed 12,700 metric tons (or 27 per cent of the total displacement) and the armour plating no less than 18,700 metric tons (40 per cent). The hull consisted of twenty-two watertight bulkheads.

Tirpitz was, and still is, the largest battleship ever built in Europe. It has only been surpassed in size by the American Iowa-class (the battleships *Iowa, New Jersey, Missouri* and *Wisconsin*) and the Japanese Yamato-class (*Yamato, Musashi* and the uncompleted *Shinano*). Fuel capacity of the *Tirpitz* was 8,000 metric tons. At a cruising speed of 16 knots, *Tirpitz* had a range of 9,280 nautical miles and the maximum speed of the battleship was 30.5 knots. Initially, she carried a crew of 2,092, which was later increased to 2,608 (108 officers and 2,500 conscripts) when the battleship was commissioned into service. The cost of the *Tirpitz* and her sister *Bismarck* was enormous, rising to 200 million Reichmarks when fully equipped. In comparison, this price was roughly the same as 1,700 tanks.[7]

For its time, *Tirpitz* was fitted with a very heavy armament developed by the Krupp Company, including eight 38 cm guns in four twin-gun barrel turrets, two forward and two aft. The four gun turrets were named Anton, Bruno, Cäsar and Dora respectively. Each of the barrels had an elevation of 30 degrees and could fire two 800 kg projectiles per minute at a maximum range of 36.5 km. Incidentally, during the design stage, both triple and quadruple gun turrets were considered, but ultimately rejected. The main reason for choosing the twin gun turret mount was to simplify the storage of ammunition. Twelve 15 cm guns in six twin-turrets and sixteen 105 mm guns in eight twin-turrets completed the heavy armament. The latter had an elevation of 85 degrees and a vertical range of 12,500 metres and horizontal range of 17,700 metres. With a rate of fire of fifteen projectiles per minute, the 105 mm guns formed the heavy anti-aircraft artillery of the battleship. A number of flak guns of different calibres, including sixteen 37 mm and twelve 20 mm guns, also protected the *Tirpitz*. A FuMo 23 radar set was connected to the three main rangefinders.

As a means of providing an extended aerial eye, *Tirpitz* carried four Arado Ar 196A two-seat spotter floatplanes. (The importance of the naval spotter floatplane had been recognised during the First World War, particularly during the Battle of Jutland in 1916. As a result, all major navies had introduced floatplanes, which could be catapulted off battleships and cruisers.) Apart from being an excellent aerial observation post beyond the range of *Tirpitz*'s radar, the Ar 196s could also carry out limited offensive sorties, being armed with two 20 mm cannons, two 7.9 mm MG 17 machine guns and a 100 kg bomb load. Powered by an 880 hp BMW 132Dc radial engine, the Ar 196 had a maximum speed of 310 kph. All Ar 196As formally belonged to a Luftwaffe unit, 1./Bordflieger Gruppe 196, and all ship-based Ar 196s of the Kriegsmarine belonged to this unit. Between sorties, the Ar 196s were usually kept dismantled inside small hangars. Two Ar 196s were kept in a 120-m² large hangar with the remaining two stored in separate 60-m² large hangars. To conserve storage space, the wings of the floatplanes could be folded alongside the fuselage. A double catapult, 32 metres in length, was fitted amidships and it was possible to extend the double catapult telescopically to 48 metres. The Ar 196 was catapulted off *Tirpitz*, reaching a speed of 112 kph when the aeroplane left the catapult. Upon returning to the battleship, the Ar 196 crew landed alongside and was then lifted aboard by a 12-tonne crane. One major drawback was that this could only be carried out in calm seas. Also, recovery of the Ar 196 would be impossible during naval battles.

Tirpitz was the synthesis of decades of German warship development. Along with her sister vessel *Bismarck*, *Tirpitz* was the largest and most capable of all Kriegsmarine surface warships. Despite the construction of *Bismarck* and *Tirpitz*, the German process of rearmament devoted far more resources to the Wehrmacht and Luftwaffe, with the Kriegsmarine as a poor third. This state of affairs was reflected in the war strategy, and in the event, the subsequent Kriegsmarine operations following the initiation of hostilities. The German commerce raiders would be able to attack British shipping along the trade routes of the Atlantic and Pacific Oceans, but lacked the strength of taking on the Royal Navy on equal terms.

Launch of the *Tirpitz*

On 1 April 1939, *Tirpitz* was launched at Wilhelmshaven on the German North Sea coast. The launch was performed by Frau Ilse von Hassel, the daughter of Alfred von Tirpitz, with Hitler also being present. Marie von Tirpitz, the widow of Alfred von Tirpitz, had originally been offered to perform the launch of the battleship, but she declined due to old age and frailty. The offer had then been passed to Alfred and Marie's daughters, Ilse and Margot, who also declined. Nevertheless, Ilse ultimately agreed to perform the high-profile ceremonial launch. It was, after all, not an offer, but an absolute demand impossible to refuse by the Nazi dictator. Tens of thousands of cheering spectators, many of whom had been brought in by train from different corners of Germany, lined the harbour when the hull of the mighty *Tirpitz* slowly settled into the water. Although lacking a superstructure with no gun turrets or bridge being fitted, *Tirpitz* still instilled respect from workers and onlookers. Foreign naval observers noted the launch of *Tirpitz* with both fear and concern. It was as if the battleship represented the rebirth and rapid rise of German military might.

Initially, the hull was finished in an overall light grey colour. During the fitting-out *Tirpitz* was finished in what can only be described as a rather bizarre camouflage scheme. In an attempt to blend the huge battleship with the background of the city of Wilhelmshaven, the whole of the port side was finished in a red brick pattern, similar to a brick house. This pattern was also applied to parts of the superstructure.

Following the launch, the work on fitting-out *Tirpitz* and preparing the battleship for service began in earnest. Detailed British pre-war planning included Operational Order B2, which meant attacking German surface warships 'in the harbours or vicinity of Wilhelmshaven'. Low-level daylight attacks were 'to be made on targets which are well clear of residential areas'. Within six hours of declaration of war on 3 September, eighteen Hampdens of 44, 49 and 83 Squadrons were heading towards Wilhelmshaven; however, due to darkness, none of the bombers managed to locate their target. All aircraft made it safely back to base, a highly credible feat as few of the pilots had never performed a night sortie before.[8]

On 4 September, a solitary RAF Blenheim arrived over Wilhelmshaven to document the result of the raid by means of aerial photography. Similar photo-reconnaissance sorties to keep track on the progress of *Tirpitz* became a regular occurrence.

The bombing campaign against Germany had an inauspicious beginning. Following the declaration of war, the War Cabinet imposed an embargo on aerial attacks against Germany. Only strictly military targets were to be attacked, which meant that bombing warships while at berth in harbours was forbidden for fear of killing or injuring civilians. Attacks against warships on the high seas were allowed with numerous mines also being dropped by the RAF in German waters. The standard RAF twin-engine bombers of the day—the Armstrong Whitworth Whitley, Handley Page Hampden and Vickers Wellington—could not carry enough ordnance and were lacking in range and defensive capability. The RAF crews also lacked training in certain key respects. Setting out at dusk and finding the designated target in darkness, and then returning to base was a difficult and frustrating process. Many aircrews and bombers were lost with few results of the raids being available. Apart from bombs, thousands of propaganda leaflets were dropped over Germany.

One RAF daylight raid in December 1939 against Wilhelmshaven and the nearby naval base at Shilling Roads had disastrous consequences for the RAF. The force of twenty-four Wellingtons was discovered by German radar stations while over the North Sea and intercepted by Luftwaffe fighters over the island of Heligoland. Fighting their way towards their targets, the Wellingtons found all the warships at harbour, which, in accordance with the War Cabinet embargo, meant that no bombs could be dropped as non-combatant civilians risked being killed or injured. With heavy and accurate flak opening up on the hapless Wellingtons, the bombers turned for home. When they came out of range of the flak, the fighters returned. In the end, the majority of the Wellingtons were either shot down or badly damaged with four Messerschmitt Bf 109s claimed as shot down. This disastrous raid spelled the end for RAF unescorted daylight raids. Henceforth, bombing raids over Germany would be flown in the cover of night.

On 9 April 1940 Denmark and Norway were invaded as outlined in Operation *Weserübung*. Denmark was overwhelmed within a couple of days while Norwegian resistance proved more difficult to crack. After initial successes against the German invaders, the small Norwegian army was reinforced by French, British and exiled Polish forces. The Kriegsmarine suffered severely with cruisers *Blücher*, *Königsberg* and *Karlsruhe* sunk within the first few days of the invasion, with *Lützow* being seriously damaged.

By mid-May, fighting was concentrated around the northern city of Narvik. One of the main reasons for Germany to invade Norway had been to secure the supply of vitally important Swedish iron ore, which was exported through Narvik harbour. However, despite some successes, the Allied expeditionary forces soon withdrew from Norway. By early June, Norway had fallen, while on Continental Europe, the blitzkrieg had seen the Low Countries occupied with France on the verge of capitulation. Just before the fall of France, the majority of the British Expeditionary Force, as well as thousands of French soldiers, were evacuated from Dunkirk. Almost all of their equipment, including hundreds of tanks, other vehicles and heavy guns, had to be left behind.

Following a brief lull, the Battle of Britain began. Britain was standing alone against the German war machine. The invasion of Britain, codenamed Unternehmen *Seelöwe* (Operation *Sealion*), was to be the final stage of German victory in the west. Despite heavy air raids against military targets such as RAF airfields and radar stations as well as London and other cities, the Hurricane and Spitfire pilots of Fighter Command were the deciding factor in defeating the Luftwaffe. In Churchill's immortal words, 'Never in the field of human conflict was so much owed by so many to so few.'[9]

The RAF bombing campaign against Wilhelmshaven

Regular photo-reconnaissance sorties over Wilhelmshaven (twenty such sorties were flown between 8 April and 25 September 1940) kept track of the progress of *Tirpitz*.

Previous RAF raids against German shipping and military naval bases could be described as nothing short of disastrous with no hits being scored in air raids against Wilhelmshaven. By mid-1940, *Tirpitz* was nearing completion. Intelligence reports mentioned that the battleship appeared, at least externally, nearly complete. Delaying or even hindering the completion of the world's largest battleship became a priority for Churchill and the War Office.

The first raid specifically aimed at striking directly against *Tirpitz* took place on the night of 9 and 10 July 1940 when fourteen Hampdens bombed the Wilhelmshaven docks. Only eleven of the Hampdens, including six of 49 Squadron and five of 83 Squadron—including one flown by Fg Off. Guy Gibson who was to lead 617 Squadron on the immortal raid against the Eder, Möhne and Sorpe dams in May 1943—dropped their bombs, all of them missing the target entirely. Two further raids were conducted in July. During the night of 20–21 July, fifteen Hampdens of 61 and 144 Squadrons attacked the docks area. Six of the Hampdens (three from each squadron) were to attack *Tirpitz* with delayed fuse magnetic mines. The mines were dropped in the inner harbour area, exploding after some forty minutes. *Tirpitz* suffered no damage whatsoever. A third raid followed only a few days later, during the night of 24–25 July. The attacking bomber formation consisting of fourteen Whitleys found it difficult to locate Wilhelmshaven due to poor weather. In the event, only two Whitleys dropped their bombs in the Wilhelmshaven general area with the remaining bombers aborting the sortie.

In early August, Churchill wrote two separate memorandums to the Admiralty and the Air Ministry stating that both *Bismarck* and *Tirpitz* were 'targets of supreme importance'. At this stage, none of the battleships had been completed. Although no Royal Navy air strike against Wilhelmshaven ensued, the RAF would continue in their efforts to strike at the still uncompleted Beast in her lair.

The next RAF raid, during the night of 5–6 August, saw seventeen Hampdens attacking the docks area. Out of these, thirteen of the Hampden crews reported that they had dropped their bombs either on *Tirpitz* or *Bismarck* (also present at Wilhelmshaven at the time of the raid). However, neither of the battleships sustained any damage. Following this raid, RAF bombers did not visit Wilhelmshaven for two months. The reprieve lasted until the night of 8–9 October. Another four raids followed in October, all with the same negative results. The final raid of the year took place during the night of 25–26 November when five Whitleys of Nos 51 and 78 Squadrons bombed Wilhelmshaven in 'impossible conditions'. In all, RAF bombers raided Wilhelmshaven on no less than ten occasions from June until November 1940. No hits were scored on the huge battleship. In this context, it must be said that with the prevailing poor weather, locating *Tirpitz* during the night, no less managing to hit her, was extremely difficult. However, the RAF raids did manage to slow down the pace of construction work and fitting out of the battleship. These raids were, compared to the raids conducted in 1944, limited in several decisive ways. The bombers used, Hampdens, Wellingtons and Whitleys, all suffered from having a limited range and could only carry a limited amount of bombs. The bomber's defensive capability was also insufficient, also suffering from low speed. Only a small number of aircraft were involved, which considerably reduced the chances of hitting the *Tirpitz*. Had *Tirpitz* been struck by RAF bombs, it would have been through pure luck. Additionally, the tactics of RAF Bomber Command for night bombing raids against blacked-out targets had not yet been properly developed. All in all, the Bomber Command campaign against Germany was still in its infancy.

Nevertheless, Wilhelmshaven continued to be at the receiving end of RAF bombers, which tried to inflict damage to the battleship on several occasions. In January 1941 alone, Wilhelmshaven was bombed on no less than four occasions on the nights of 8–9, 15–16, 16–17 and 29–30 January. None of the raids managed to inflict any damage to the *Tirpitz*. The next RAF raid against Wilhelmshaven took place on 1 March when 116 Whitleys, Blenheims, Hampdens and Wellingtons paid the city a visit. Once again, *Tirpitz* escaped the attention of the bombers. The net result of the numerous RAF raids against Wilhelmshaven and *Tirpitz* can be described in one single word: failure. No less than 1,042 RAF sorties had been flown against the naval installations between September 1939 and February 1941. About 683 tons of bombs and mines had been dropped, two bombs striking *Prinz Eugen* and *Deutschland* being hit by a dud. *Tirpitz* survived unscathed.[10]

Shakedown cruise

Fitting-out the huge battleship was not completed until later that year with initial sea trials in the Baltic Sea being accomplished by February 1941. On 25 February, *Tirpitz* was officially commissioned into the Kriegsmarine with Kapitän zur See Friedrich Karl Topp being in command. Aged forty-five, Topp had a long career behind him, having served on U-boats and destroyers during the First World War and as the navigational officer aboard the cruiser *Emden*. In early March, *Tirpitz* left her birthplace for Kiel with Kapitän zur See Topp shortly afterwards on 9 March heading for Gotenhafen (present-day Gdynia in Poland) on the eastern Baltic Sea coast.

Tirpitz would be based at Gotenhafen for about three months before returning to Kiel during the early summer, an essential period for crew training as well as ironing out any problems with the battleship. Also of some importance was that Gotenhafen was outside the operational range of RAF bombers and with the non-aggression pact between Germany and the USSR in effect, this area of the Baltic Sea was a tranquil place, far removed from the war.

Following her entrance into service the 'red brick house' camouflage scheme of *Tirpitz* was replaced. Instead, the ship was painted light grey with the upper and side surfaces of the four main gun turrets finished in a darker shade of grey.

Norway: the new front?

By mid-1940, Norway had been occupied by Germany. With the German–Soviet non-aggression pact of August 1939, the Norwegian border with Russia was a peaceful part of Europe, seemingly far away from the war on the Continent. German and Soviet cooperation was such that as late as the autumn of 1940, plans to establish a permanent Kriegsmarine base at Molotovskij Fjord on the Kola Peninsula was still proceeding. At the same time, German ships were allowed to use Murmansk as an alternate harbour. All of this was just a ruse on the part of the Germans with an invasion of the Soviet Union being planned to begin in early 1941. By August 1940, the first of 12,600 troops specially trained in mountain warfare began to arrive in northern Norway. The German troops, the *Gebirgskorps Norwegen* (Mountain Corps Norway) and led by General Eduard Dietl, would less than a year later be part of the massive German invasion of the Soviet Union for Operation *Barbarossa*. The German soldiers were based from Narvik in the south to Varanger close to the border with the USSR, a distance of some 1,000 km.

In March 1941, British Commando forces raided the Lofoten Islands off the Norwegian coast. This small-scale raid, which was followed by other raids, raised concerns in the German High Command about the risk of a British invasion of Norway. Although little more than pinprick raids, Hitler became increasingly concerned about the weak German defences in northern Norway. Substantially increasing the German defences in Norway would mean that, as defined by the highest-ranking German admiral in Norway, Hermann Boehm, in a letter to Admiral Raeder, that the country would become 'a gun aimed at England's chest'. Norway would form the northern defence line against an invasion of the German *Festung Europa* (Fortress Europe). However, defending the entire Norwegian coastline with soldiers was impossible due to its numerous fjords, inlets and small islands. Instead, battleships were deemed a possible solution to the problem of defending Norway as well as fortified strongpoints with heavy coastal artillery.

Bismarck ventures into the Atlantic

On 5 May 1941, both *Bismarck* and *Tirpitz* were anchored at the Gotenhafen naval yard. On this date, Hitler made an official visit and inspected both battleships. Previously, the decision of allowing *Bismarck* to sail into the North Atlantic had been taken by the Naval High Command. During Hitler's brief visit aboard *Tirpitz*, Kapitän zur See Topp attempted to receive permission to accompany *Bismarck* on her impending Atlantic voyage. Having Germany's two largest and most powerful battleships sailing together would surely strike fear into the Royal Navy. This was refused as *Tirpitz* had not yet completed the necessary sea trials.

On 18 May, *Bismarck* left Gotenhafen, passing through the Kattegat strait before dropping anchor at Grimstad Fjord close to Bergen. However, *Bismarck*'s journey northwards had not passed unnoticed. The battleship had been observed by the Swedish aircraft cruiser *Gotland*, which duly reported the sighting to the Swedish Naval High Command. Within hours, the report that *Bismarck* had left port reached Britain. After replenishing supplies in Norway, the battleship sailed for the North Atlantic.

While *Bismarck* was in Norway, a pair of Bf 109 fighters circled overhead to protect her from British air attacks. Nevertheless, Flying Officer Michael Suckling managed to fly his Spitfire directly over the German flotilla at a height of 8,000 m (26,000 ft) and took several photographs of *Bismarck* and *Prinz Eugen*. Upon receipt of the information, Admiral John Tovey ordered the battle cruiser HMS *Hood*, the newly commissioned battleship HMS *Prince of Wales*, and six destroyers to reinforce the pair of cruisers patrolling the Denmark Strait. The remainder of the Home Fleet was placed on high alert in Scapa Flow. Eighteen bombers were dispatched to attack the Germans, but weather over the fjord had worsened and they were unable to find the German warships. The British squadron spotted the Germans at 05.37 on 24 May 1941 and the engagement commenced shortly after dawn. The British opened fire at 05.52 with *Hood* engaging *Prinz Eugen*, the lead ship in the German formation, and the Germans returned fire at 05.55, both ships concentrating on *Hood*. Just before 06.00, while *Hood* was turning 20 degrees to port to unmask her rear turrets, she was hit again on the boat deck by one or more shells from *Bismarck*'s fifth salvo, fired from a range of approximately 16.7 kilometres (10.4 miles). A shell from this salvo penetrated down into the vessel and a huge jet of flame burst out of *Hood* from the vicinity of the mainmast, followed by a devastating magazine explosion that destroyed the aft part of the ship. This explosion broke the back of *Hood* which then sank in just three minutes. Out of the crew of 1,418, there were only three survivors.

HMS *Prince of Wales* had created some damage to *Bismarck* which led to it having to curtail its cruise and head for St Nazaire for repairs.

The Royal Navy ordered all warships in the area to join the pursuit of *Bismarck* and *Prinz Eugen*. In all, six battleships and battle cruisers, two aircraft carriers, thirteen cruisers, and twenty-one destroyers were committed to the chase. Even with this massive naval force it was feared that the Kriegsmarine battleship would manage to escape and reach the safety of a French port. In the event, the British fleet located the *Bismarck* following an intense chase. On 26 May, Fairey Swordfish torpedo bombers from HMS *Ark Royal* managed to hit the *Bismarck*, damaging the propellers and rudders. This meant that the huge battleship had to reduce speed and also became difficult to manoeuvre. *Bismarck* was eventually sunk to the west of the Bay of Biscay, about 650 km (400 miles) west of Brest on 27 May 1941 through the concentrated efforts of both warships and torpedo-carrying aircraft of the Royal Navy. Fighting alone until the end, barely 100 of *Bismarck*'s crew survived the sinking of the battleship, her brief voyage lasting a mere nine days. During the hunt for the *Bismarck*, the Royal Navy had to devote many warships and aircraft in their efforts to sink the German battleship. Having *Bismarck*'s sister ship, *Tirpitz*, also reaching the Atlantic would put British shipping at serious risk. Thus, disabling or sinking *Tirpitz* became a priority for the Admiralty.

How to best make use of the *Tirpitz*

However, in the immediate wake of losing the *Bismarck*, deploying *Tirpitz* to the Atlantic was simply out of the question to the German Naval High Command. Considering the huge British effort to chase and sink the *Bismarck*, Grossadmiral Raeder made no illusions that if the *Tirpitz* was deployed to the Atlantic in the same manner as her ill-fated sister, the British would not rest before she had been dispatched to the bottom of the sea. Losing the mighty *Tirpitz* so soon after *Bismarck* would be a huge propaganda loss to Nazi Germany, which would have far reaching implications for the Kriegsmarine. Losing the *Tirpitz* as well would show that high-profile battleships—costly to build and operate—were useless heaps of armour.

The strategy of utilising the Kriegsmarine battleships as commerce raiders was proving to be a costly one. At the other end of the spectrum, the Kriegsmarine submarine fleet was causing serious damage to Allied shipping with several surface warships, including battleships and aircraft carriers, being sunk. Indeed, the U-boat was proving to be a far more economical warship, being cheaper to build than a battleship as well as requiring a smaller crew to operate. At this stage of the war, anti-submarine warfare had not yet been fully developed. As a result, U-boats were able to operate with considerable success against Allied shipping. (Until mid-1943, when long-range B-24 Liberators had been introduced into service, no Allied aircraft had the range to reach the centre of the Atlantic. This meant that U-boats could act with impunity along these sea lanes.)

In this context, it must be said that there existed a certain degree of inter-service rivalry between the Kriegsmarine and Luftwaffe, mostly due to the mutual loathing of Erich Raeder and Hermann Göring, the service's respective commanders. Göring berated the inferiority of the Kriegsmarine with its large, expensive and vulnerable surface warships, boasting that the Luftwaffe was the war-winning weapon of the German armed forces. Raeder on his part tried to get Hitler to devote more resources to the Kriegsmarine as well as allowing for more aggressive tactics to be adopted. Göring did not want any units of the Luftwaffe to be subordinated to the Kriegsmarine for maritime operations, despite constant pleas from Raeder. As a result, co-operation between the Kriegsmarine and Luftwaffe was limited at best and non-existent at worst. It must be said that the Luftwaffe also lacked the necessary resources to provide sufficient aerial cover for the Kriegsmarine surface warships with fewer than 300 four-engine Focke-Wulf Fw 200 Condors and a few dozen Junkers Ju 290 long-range maritime reconnaissance aircraft being built.

Additionally, despite much effort being invested into building aircraft carriers, the only warship that entered an advanced state of completion, *Graf Zeppelin*, was never finished. The lack of co-operation during operations between German naval and air forces during the war was glaringly obvious when compared with the naval and air arms of Great Britain and the United States.

First combat cruise of *Tirpitz*

Shakedown training of the *Tirpitz* crew continued throughout this period, which included gunnery training on 3 June 1941 against the obsolete Imperial German Navy *Linienschiff Hessen* which had been converted into a full-scale target vessel. During this time, the impressive armament aboard the *Tirpitz* was strengthened by adding quadruple 50 cm torpedo tubes. An unconfirmed source claims that these torpedo tubes had been recovered from the wrecks of ten Kriegsmarine destroyers sunk during the Battle of Narvik in May 1940. Supplementing the heavy guns with torpedo tubes meant that valuable ammunition for the former could be saved during a battle. However, the torpedo tubes aboard the *Tirpitz* were to remain unused during the battleship's entire career.

On 22 June 1941 when Germany invaded the Soviet Union, the *Tirpitz* did not take part. Instead, crew training along the southern Baltic Sea coast continued. In fact, the crew aboard the *Tirpitz* felt a degree of frustration in not being actively involved in the German thrust into the Soviet Union. However, German pre-planning of the invasion had considered the option that the Soviet fleet would break out of the confined waters of the Gulf of Finland (disparagingly referred to as the 'bathtub' by German submariners) and head for neutral waters, i.e. Sweden.[11]

During a meeting with Hitler on 9 July, Raeder assured him that the Kriegsmarine would hinder such attempts. However, saving his fleet and sailors through such measures was completely alien to the Soviet dictator. In the event of the huge base at Kronstadt falling into German hands, the naval installations would have been destroyed by Soviet forces in accordance with the scorched earth strategy. Nothing of value would be left to the Nazi invaders.

On 17 September, the question of the remaining Soviet fleet attempting to break out was raised again. Raeder stated that as the Gulf of Finland was heavily mined and around 80,000 Soviet naval personnel had been transferred to serve as naval infantry in the defence of Leningrad, such a breakout was highly unlikely. However, Hitler was not entirely convinced by Raeder's assurances. The result of Hitler's hesitancy with the continued assurances of Raeder was that *Tirpitz* was for the first time prepared for combat.

Sailing for the Aaland Islands

When German forces reached the suburbs of Leningrad two days later on 19 September, Hitler ordered the formation of a Baltenflotte (Baltic Fleet) that would be based at the Aaland Islands. It was thought that as the Soviet fleet risked losing their bases at Kronstadt and Leningrad, the warships would attempt to break out into the Baltic Sea. Although not yet combat ready, *Tirpitz* was assigned the role of flagship of the Baltenflotte which also consisted of the pocket battleship *Admiral Scheer*, the cruisers *Köln* and *Nürnberg*, three destroyers and several torpedo boats. The light cruisers *Emden* and *Leipzig*, as well as some torpedo boats, were kept as an operational reserve at Libau. All in all, the Baltenflotte was a very impressive armada.

Following hasty preparations, the Baltenflotte left Swinemünde on 23 September and headed north. The following day, *Tirpitz* (with the Finnish Master Pilot Laine aboard) and *Admiral Scheer* dropped anchor at Rödhamn Fjord near Mariehamn. The remaining vessels dropped anchor at Föglö Fjord.[12]

Tirpitz Baltic Sea Cruise September 1941

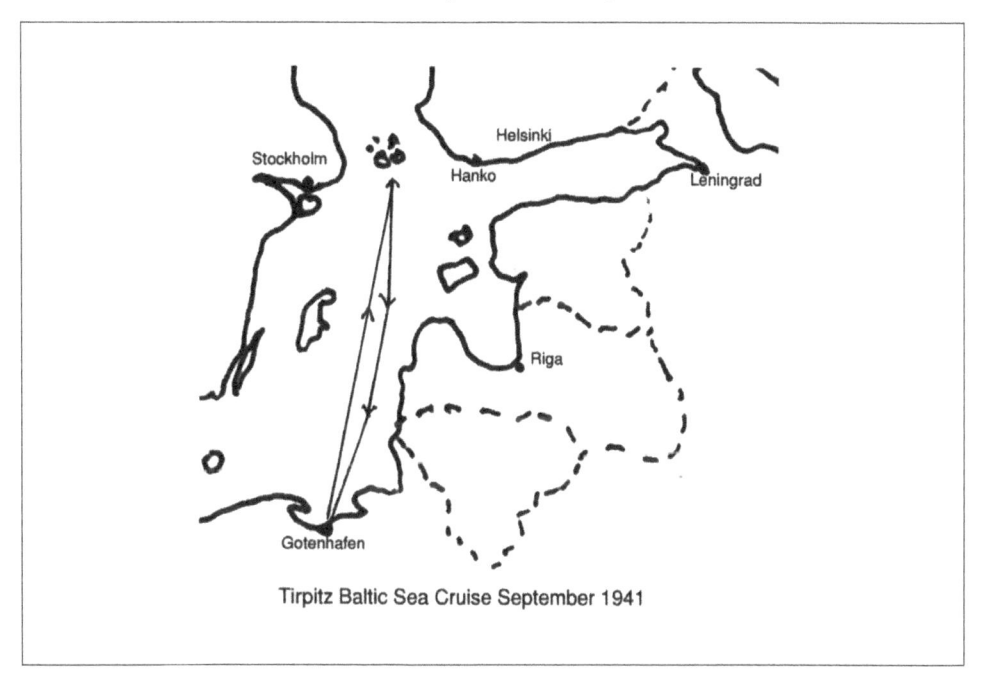

In September 1941, *Tirpitz* made her first combat cruise into the northern Baltic Sea without firing a single shot. (*Anders Eriksson*)

However, it was quickly established that the largest Soviet warships, the battleships *Marat* (named after the eighteenth-century French revolutionary Jean-Paul Marat) and *Oktiabraskaya Revolutia* (*October Revolution*) both remained at Kronstadt and Leningrad after being damaged in Luftwaffe air raids.[13] The Soviet Naval Command feared that the Baltenflotte would be used to bombard Kronstadt and Leningrad. The coastal gun batteries at Hanko, which had been ceded by Finland to the Soviet Union following the end of the Winter War on 13 March 1940, were put on full alert. Additionally, six Soviet submarines were available for any possible attempt to sink the ships of the Baltenflotte. However, on 25 September, the majority of the Baltenflotte was ordered to return to German waters. Before ordering back the remaining ships, Hitler stated that the Soviet battleships and cruisers did not pose any threat to the Germans. On 27 September, the last ships of the Baltenflotte returned to Gotenhafen. Apart from submarine operations, which included attacking Swedish cargo ships carrying iron ore destined for Germany, the Soviet fleet failed to break the blockade of the Gulf of Finland by German and Finnish forces.

Dispatching the largest and most powerful Kriegsmarine battleship to the confined waters of the Central Baltic Sea and Gulf of Finland can, in retrospect, be considered as highly risky due to the presence of Soviet submarines and coastal artillery. Also, one must take into account the German forces which were closing in on Leningrad, a quite unnecessary venture. The brief tenure as flagship of the Baltenflotte and deployment to Finnish waters may be considered as the first combat cruise of the *Tirpitz*. Not a single shot was fired by the *Tirpitz* or any of the other warships within the Baltenflotte. It was seen as an exercise for bigger things to come.

Following the brief deployment to Finnish waters, operational trials continued. Anti-torpedo trials were conducted from 10 to 18 October. Naval exercises with other Kriegsmarine surface vessels followed after which the battleship returned to Kiel. Further fleet exercises followed, which included anti-mine degaussing trials at the end of December 1941. On 6 January 1942, Raeder made a formal inspection of the *Tirpitz* to mark the end of operational trials.

By this time, Churchill was becoming increasingly worried that the *Tirpitz* (or as he more frequently came to call 'the Beast') would follow *Bismarck*'s example and venture out into the North Atlantic. Given the events during *Bismarck*'s brief cruise, a considerable number of warships and aircraft would have to be taken off other duties to hunt down *Tirpitz*.

Into Arctic waters

Following the German invasion of the USSR, Churchill promised immediate and extensive military aid to Josef Stalin. Getting the military aid, including tanks and aeroplanes, to the USSR included two main routes: via Iran and by cargo ship to the Kola Peninsula. (After the United States entry in the war, thousands of aircraft were transferred via the Alaska–Siberian route.) Establishing an Arctic convoy route would mean risking attacks from German air and naval forces based in Norway. The first convoy, codenamed PQ 1, sailed for Murmansk on 28 September. Only eleven ships were part of PQ 1 which carried twenty tanks and 139 fighters, however no German attacks were directed against this convoy.

This apparent ignorance from the Germans was soon to change when larger convoys sailed for Russia. Losses in crews, ships and cargo were high. Of the 1,038 merchant vessels that sailed an Arctic route between July 1941 and April 1944, seventy-nine were sunk, including thirty-four by U-boats. This represented a loss rate of 7.6 per cent.[14] No less than 399 Hawker Hurricane fighters out of nearly 3,000 supplied were lost on the Arctic route when the ships carrying the dismantled aircraft were sunk—a loss rate of 13 per cent. Another example of the high loss rate experienced was of 265 P-39 Airacobras dispatched aboard British merchant ships, fifty-four were lost at sea. Initially the British convoys were deemed to be of little importance by the Germans. The war material carried by the convoys was a mere trickle compared with the thousands of aeroplanes and tanks lost by the Russians since the beginning of the invasion. With German forces on the brink of reaching Moscow, it appeared as if a Soviet collapse was imminent.

On the Arctic Front things did not go entirely as planned. Due to the rugged terrain and arduous conditions in northern Norway and the Kola Peninsula, German forces found it almost impossible to advance. The elite mountain troops under command of General Dietl found it extremely difficult to break through the Russian front line. Despite large scale aerial support, the German advance came to an abrupt halt at Litza, some 45 km from Murmansk. According to the pre-invasion plans, Murmansk would fall on 20 July with invitations for the victory banquet—to be held at Hotel Arktika—having already been printed. The front line would remain static for the next three years.

Tirpitz is deployed to Norway

At this time, finding an efficient way of employing the heavy cruisers and battleships of the Kriegsmarine, including *Tirpitz*, was the subject of much debate within German High Command. At one point, Hitler suggested the radical idea of dismantling the warships and instead employing their heavy artillery pieces in strengthening the coastal defences in Norway. Needless to say, this suggestion by Hitler did not find favour with Admiral Raeder. However, Norway was seen with some justification as the weakest link in the German line of defence against an Allied invasion. Continued small-scale British raids against the Norwegian mainland and islands created a feeling within the German High Command, and Hitler in particular, that any forthcoming Allied invasion of Fortress Europe would begin in Norway.

Instead of dismantling the battleships, Admiral Raeder put forward a plan on 13 November to deploy *Tirpitz* to Norway. The battleship was to be based at Trondheim in central Norway. From this location, the Beast would, apart from protecting the northern flank, be able to intercept Allied convoys heading for Murmansk or Arkhangelsk (Archangel) on the Russian Kola Peninsula. The harbours in both northern Norway and on the Kola Peninsula were largely free of ice during the winter due to the warm water currents of the Gulf Stream, which considerably eased naval operations. A second reason for sending *Tirpitz* northwards was to try to tie down as many Allied air and naval forces that were sorely needed elsewhere. Hitler reluctantly agreed with Raeder's suggestion, but strictly forbade the use of *Tirpitz* in attacking convoys escorted by an aircraft carrier.[15]

At the same time, on 7 December 1941, the war became global when Japanese carrier-based aircraft attacked the United States naval base at Pearl Harbor. Within six months, American, British and Dutch forces had been driven out of the Philippines, Burma, Malaya, Singapore and the Dutch East Indies. Australia was under serious threat of Japanese occupation. In a manner similar to that in which Hitler had not apprised the Japanese of Operation *Barbarossa*, the Japanese had not informed the Germans of their intention of attacking American and British targets in the Pacific. Nevertheless, the Japanese actions were supported by Hitler who showed his approval by unilaterally declaring war against the United States on 11 December. The German High Command confidently expected that the Americans would not be able to make an impression in Europe until 1943. Unbeknown to the Germans, the American and British had already agreed on the principle 'Germany first' in case of such a scenario occurring.

Following completion of the shakedown cruise in early January 1942, Kapitän zur See Karl Topp declared *Tirpitz* to be finally ready for combat on 10 January. (Apparently, one of the battleship's engineers reported that a faulty generator would need replacing before she was declared operational.) The next day, *Tirpitz* sailed for Wilhelmshaven. This was a ruse to hide the real destination of the battleship. At 23.00 hours on 14 January—four days later than originally planned—*Tirpitz* left Wilhelmshaven and headed northwards, escorted by the destroyers *Richard Beitzen*, *Paul Jacobi*, *Bruno Heinemann* and *Z-29*. The secret operation was named Unternehmen *Polarnacht* (Operation *Polar Night*). The battleship passed via the Kiel Channel to avoid being noticed by Swedish ships or aircraft, and remove the risk of the whereabouts of *Tirpitz* reaching the British.

British intelligence were soon made aware of the fact that *Tirpitz* had left Germany, but incessant bad weather prevented the RAF from detecting the battleship and making any attempt to sink her.

Arrival at Fætten Fjord

The Commander-in-Chief of the Home Fleet, Admiral John Tovey, did not learn that *Tirpitz* had headed north for Norway until 17 January, the day after the battleship had arrived at Trondheim, safely anchored at Fætten Fjord. It was not until six days later on 23 January that British Intelligence were informed that *Tirpitz* was safely at anchor at Fætten Fjord, 65 km from the open sea.[16] With the largest and most powerful Kriegsmarine battleship present at Trondheim in central Norway, this created a looming threat against the Russian convoys. However, the risk of attacks from the air against the Beast meant that shortly after arriving at Fætten Fjord, four quadruple 20 mm anti-aircraft mounts were added to the already impressive flak defences aboard *Tirpitz*, along with two single-mount 20 mm guns mounted on the bridge. Furthermore, additional flak units were placed on various ships as well as ashore. To reduce the risk of a torpedo strike, torpedo nets were mounted in the water adjacent to the battleship. The existing FuMo 23 radar set was supplemented by a FuMo 27 mounted on the forecastle. Later, the larger FuMo 26 was added to the battleship's range detection gear.

German plans of further strengthening their naval presence in Norway began on 11 February when *Gneisenau*, *Scharnhorst* and *Prinz Eugen* left the French port of Brest on the first part of the journey to Norway, codenamed Operation *Cerberus*. Despite large-scale British efforts during what would become known as the 'Channel Dash', all three vessels made it to Wilhelmshaven, but both *Gneisenau* and *Scharnhorst* were damaged by mines. Only *Scharnhorst* and *Prinz Eugen* would reach Norway, the latter being seriously damaged by British torpedoes off Trondheim.

CHAPTER TWO

Sink the Beast!

Churchill was acutely aware of the danger that *Tirpitz* represented to the Arctic convoys. In a letter to General Ismay, he stated that *Tirpitz* offered the biggest single target of the naval war. He even mentioned that sinking or disabling the German battleship would mean that the Allies would be able to regain naval superiority in the Atlantic. Thus, *Tirpitz* was a high priority target, tying down several battleships and cruisers of the Home Fleet. Sinking the *Tirpitz* would mean that the strength of Kriegsmarine would be much reduced. On 25 January, Churchill wrote to the Chiefs of Staff Committee: 'The presence of *Tirpitz* at Trondheim has now been known for three days. The destruction or even crippling of this ship is the greatest event at sea at the present time.' Something had to be done and quickly. The best and quickest means of striking at the Beast while at anchor at her Norwegian hideout was by air power.

The first RAF bombing raid

The first RAF raid against the Beast's hideout in Norway was not long in coming. The task went to No. 3 Group, Bomber Command, based at Mildenhall. On 26 January, four squadrons—Nos 15 and 149, flying Short Stirlings, and Nos 10 and 76 with Handley Page Halifaxes—were ordered to fly north to Lossiemouth to prepare for Operation *Oiled* as the raid had been codenamed. 44 Squadron, the first unit to equip with the new Avro Lancaster four engine bomber, almost became involved in the raid as well. On 25 January, orders were received to transfer to Wick from where 44 Squadron was to be placed in readiness to drop mines along the mouth of Fætten Fjord; however, this was not to be.

The presence of *Tirpitz* at Fætten Fjord was confirmed on 29 January by a photo-reconnaissance Spitfire. In the early hours of 30 January, seven Short Stirlings of 15 and 149 Squadrons and eight Handley Page Halifaxes of 10 and 76 Squadrons took off from Lossiemouth in cloudy conditions. The bombers carried two different types of bombs, the 2,000 lb armour-piercing bomb and the 500 lb SAP. It was believed that the armour-piercing bombs would be able to penetrate the deck of *Tirpitz*, hopefully damaging the boilers and/or triggering explosions in fuel tanks or the ammunition storage compartments. The topography of Fætten Fjord was well suited to hide a battleship, being quite narrow and lined on three sides with steep hills. This made the job of the RAF airmen even more difficult.

The raid was a complete failure. Due to poor weather, the RAF bombers failed to locate the battleship. The presence of the Stirlings and Halifaxes in the area was discovered by the Germans with air-raid sirens wailing continuously in the nearby town of Trondheim between 05.12 and 06.45 hours. Aboard the battleship, flak crews readied themselves for the impending attack. At 05.57 hours, six bombers were observed from *Tirpitz*. However, no bombs were observed from the battleship as dropped by the RAF Stirlings and Halifaxes. Only one 76 Squadron Halifax (L9617) piloted by FS Herbert carried out an attack. After returning to Lossiemouth, FS Herbert reported:

> The target was not observed, but a barrage of light flak indicated the position of the target. Bombs were dropped from a height of 8,000 feet at 06.05 hours and bursts were seen between the ship and shore. Visibility was good but 10/10ths cloud cover over the target.[1]

A Halifax and Stirling were lost, albeit not to enemy action. Despite persistent poor weather, preparations began for a second raid against the battleship the following night. However, the raid was cancelled for the next week as poor weather hindered further RAF attacks. On 6 February, the Stirlings and Halifaxes left Lossiemouth and headed south for their respective bases. The take-off from the grassy airfield proved somewhat troublesome as a thaw had set in with large puddles of water forming on the runway. The failed raid may, in retrospect, be seen as a sign of utter desperation carried out without much planning or afterthought. However, the influence of *Tirpitz* on the naval war in the North Atlantic was such that the battleship simply had to be disabled or sunk. The Beast constituted a very real danger to the Allied fleets and later, when the importance of *Tirpitz* had been overshadowed by other the events in the war, sinking the battleship was still viewed as an extremely important target. Churchill in particular developed an obsession about sinking *Tirpitz* that at least during the latter stages of her active career, went beyond the overall importance of the battleship. *Tirpitz* was a symbol of the Kriegsmarine as well as Nazi Germany.

Following the failed RAF raid, the anti-aircraft artillery aboard *Tirpitz* was further strengthened in February 1942 when six quadruple 20 mm anti-aircraft guns were mounted in various locations, replacing four single-mount 20 mm guns. The latter guns were brought ashore. The overall grey camouflage colours made *Tirpitz* easy to spot from the air while at anchor. As a result, some of the snow that fell was left on the deck while huge canvas sheets covered the main gun turrets. To further increase the illusion of camouflage, evergreen trees were placed on the quarterdeck and forecastle.

One-way raid proposal

With the RAF raid having failed to damage the battleship, brief consideration was given to using Bristol Beaufort torpedo bombers instead. Beauforts of three squadrons—42

Squadron based at Leuchars, 86 Squadron based at St Eval, and 217 Squadron based at Thorney Island—were selected for the task of attacking *Tirpitz*. One serious problem was that the twin-engine Beaufort lacked the necessary range of making the return flight to the UK. Instead, following the attack, the Beaufort crews would head west for the British coast. It was estimated that fuel would run out about 60 miles from the coast. Ditching in the North Sea meant facing slim prospects of being picked up by rescue boats before succumbing to the ice-cold water.

Another alternative considered was for the Beauforts to continue eastwards towards Sweden. Having reached neutral Sweden, the crews would then bale out of their aircraft. The nature of such a one-way sortie was near suicidal, but planning continued until March 1942. The raid was codenamed Operation *Ship*. On 7 March, fifteen Beaufort crews (six from 42 Squadron, three from 86 Squadron, and six from 217 Squadron) received orders to fly to Sumburgh in the Shetlands in preparation for the raid.[2] Torpedoes were to be used in preference of bombs. What kind of effect the torpedoes would have had against the *Tirpitz* is uncertain. It must be remembered that anti-torpedo nets had been anchored close to the battleship. Also, in order to detonate as intended, the torpedoes needed to be dropped from a specific height and distance from the battleship. For a while, the raid was postponed as the Beast left Fætten Fjord on 5 March, sailing north with an escort of destroyers. The aim of the German flotilla was to attack the PQ 12 convoy. A large part of the Home Fleet was escorting the convoy and the British plan was to lure *Tirpitz* into action. In the event, the British and German warships did not engage in combat, although carrier-based Albacore torpedo bombers did unsuccessfully attack *Tirpitz* on 9 March.

The *Tirpitz* returned south, which meant that plans for the Beaufort raid were resumed. After arriving at Sumburgh, the Beauforts were lightened with much equipment being removed with the aim of carrying as much fuel as possible. Following the failed Albacore torpedo strike, the Beaufort crews were placed at one hour's readiness with the raid on the Beast due to take place on 10 March when it was expected that the battleship would reach the Trondheim area. The Beaufort crews (in all, about a dozen aircraft were involved) were ready for take-off, anxiously waiting for the go-ahead signal. The raid was cancelled at the last minute, however, with a red Very light being fired from the control tower to the utmost relief of the Beaufort crews. Aerial reconnaissance showed that *Tirpitz* was not anywhere near Trondheim and had replenished fuel from a tanker off Narvik. *Tirpitz* remained at Narvik for four days before returning to Fætten Fjord on 18 March. The weather was so poor that there was no opportunity of attacking *Tirpitz* during her journey south. In such circumstances, the high-risk Beaufort raid was cancelled altogether.

Setting a trap for the Beast

The German strategy was to strengthen the co-operation between the Kriegsmarine, Luftwaffe and Wehrmacht. More Luftwaffe aircraft were to be based in northern Norway while the operational activities would be co-ordinated. It was even intended that the aircraft carrier *Graf Zeppelin*, construction of which had been resumed in early 1942, would form part of an enlarged naval flotilla in Norway. In the event, *Graf Zeppelin* was never finished, being surrendered to Soviet forces in 1945.[3]

During the winter of 1941–42, three further convoys, PQ 9, PQ 10 and PQ 11, reached the Kola Peninsula without any interference from German forces. The Arctic route appeared to be a relatively safe way of transporting supplies to Russia. The next convoy, PQ 12, left Iceland in early March and headed for Russia. This time around, things would be different. On 5 March, a Luftwaffe Focke-Wulf Fw 200C Condor[4] maritime reconnaissance aircraft spotted PQ 12 cargo ships off Jan Mayen, a small Norwegian island, some 563 km off Iceland. The Condor crew immediately relayed a message to Berlin of the position of the convoy. Raeder sought and received Hitler's approval in attacking the Allied convoy. Here was the opportunity to give the mighty *Tirpitz* its long awaited baptism of fire. The crew of the *Tirpitz*, having suffered the ignominy of not seeing action, was jubilant for this opportunity for finally taking on the Royal Navy.

Later the same day, *Tirpitz*, along with an escort consisting of three destroyers, left Fætten Fjord. Operation *Sportpalast* had begun. Commanding the flotilla was Vice Admiral Otto Ciliax who made the *Tirpitz* his flagship. The British submarine HMS *Seawolf* spotted the German warships heading north and immediately relayed the information to the Admiralty. HMS *Seawolf* stayed on the surface long enough to catch a brief glimpse of *Tirpitz*. However, no attack was attempted with HMS *Seawolf* being ordered to keep a close eye on the Beast. Yet again, the *Tirpitz* camouflage scheme had been changed. The overall light grey colour scheme was altered with the sides of the bow and stern painted in a darker shade of grey. This created the illusion that the warship was smaller than it actually was.

Admiral Tovey had already anticipated *Tirpitz* leaving Fætten Fjord. Apart from providing escort to PQ 12, Tovey, with superiority in numbers, wanted to bring *Tirpitz* within range of the Home Fleet guns. Tovey left Scapa Flow with a formidable force consisting of the battleships HMS *King George V* and HMS *Duke of York*, the cruiser HMS *Renown*, one heavy cruiser, twelve destroyers and the aircraft carrier HMS *Victorious*. Aboard *Victorious* were two squadrons of Fairey Fulmar fighters and a squadron of Fairey Albacore torpedo bombers.

The Fairey Albacore torpedo bomber

The Albacore had been designed to replace the venerable Fairey Swordfish which had formed the mainstay of the Fleet Air Arm's airborne strike force. Some considered the Albacore an improvement over the Swordfish as it was faster and also had an enclosed cockpit. Others, occasionally referring to it as the Applecore, complained that the Albacore was not as sturdy and manoeuvrable as its older stable mate.

On 6 March, while steaming towards the northwest at a speed of 23 knots, Ciliax ordered the Arado Ar 196 crews to take-off and search for Allied cargo ships. However, it turned out that the wings of the spotter aeroplanes were covered in thick ice. Apart from adding weight, ice disturbs the aerodynamic flow over the wing, making it far more difficult for the pilot to control the aircraft. Along with the freezing cold, the ice made catapulting off *Tirpitz* an impossible venture. As a result, Ciliax had to send the escorting destroyers to locate the convoy—his mission being to sink as many cargo ships as possible. On the other hand he had also received strict orders not to engage British warships unless he considered the opposing force equal or inferior to *Tirpitz* and her escorting destroyers.

One major drawback of Kriegsmarine operations concerned a constant lack of fuel and black fuel oil. In all, Operation *Sportpalast* would consume some 8,000 metric tons of oil, a considerable drain on available stocks. In this context, the stocks of oil consumed by the Kriegsmarine during the 'Channel Dash' in February 1942 amounted to 21,000 metric tons. On 1 April 1942, Grossadmiral Raeder reported that the total stocks of oil available to the Kriegsmarine were 150,000 metric tons. In fact, the allocation of black fuel oil to the Kriegsmarine for April 1942 had been cut from 97,000 metric tons to 61,000 metric tons due to the pressing needs of the Italian Navy. At the time, the Rumanian oil fields delivered some 13 million barrels of oil to the German war machine. The vast majority of this oil was allocated to the Wehrmacht and Luftwaffe with the Kriegsmarine coming out as a poor third. This led to severe difficulties in planning operational voyages for the *Tirpitz* and due to the constant lack of oil, the deployment of *Tirpitz* called for careful planning. The mighty battleship was not to be wasted against the first available target.[5] In the event, only one cargo ship in the PQ 12 convoy was sunk: the Russian steamer *Izhora*. However, it was not *Tirpitz* that finished off the cargo ship. Instead, it was torpedoed by the destroyer *Z 14 Friedrich Ihn*. The radio operator aboard *Izhora* managed to send a final message that enabled the Home Fleet to narrow down the position of the German warships.

On 7 March, the weather was so poor that even though the British and German ships passed within 15 km of each other, no visual observation or combat (the Fairey Albacore torpedo bombers of HMS *Victorious* were within range) was possible. However, sending off the Albacores in the extremely poor weather in a desperate hunt for *Tirpitz* would most likely have resulted in losses of both crews and aircraft. The following day, however, the Albacore crews would get their chance of striking at the Beast.

As the three destroyers were running low on fuel, Ciliax ordered them to return to Norway. *Tirpitz* continued the search for the convoy, eventually reaching a position north of the small island Bjørnøya (Bear Island). Here, Ciliax expected to find PQ 12 coming within range of *Tirpitz*'s guns. With its superior armament and speed, *Tirpitz* would not have any problems in picking off the cargo ships one by one. Having never fired a shot in anger, the crew of the Beast was eagerly expecting this opportunity to meet the enemy, but naval combat was to elude *Tirpitz* on this occasion. Due to the encryption work performed by Ultra at Bletchley Park as well as the report from the Russian cargo ship *Izhora*, PQ 12 was made aware of the presence of the Beast. The convoy thus took a more northerly route to avoid her. Having failed to intercept the convoy, Ciliax broke off the hunt during the evening of 8 March. He then proceeded to send an encrypted message to the naval command at Kiel about his decision. This message was snapped up by Ultra and quickly deciphered. Five hours and forty minutes after Ciliax had sent the message its content had reached Admiral John Tovey, who immediately ordered the Home Fleet to change course and head southeast. The chase was on. At 06.40 hours, the first of six Albacores staggered into the air. The weather was cloudy with the occasional snowfall. Finally and just after 08.00 hours, Lt Tommy Miller sighted the battleship. Miller reported over the radio that the sighting meant a 'fantastic opportunity' for the fleet that could lead to 'significant results' if the battleship was disabled or sunk. None of the spotter Albacores had been observed from *Tirpitz*, which was then steaming in a south easterly direction off the Lofoten Islands. The attacking force, consisting of twelve Albacores from 817 and 832 Squadrons, lifted off from the deck of HMS *Victorious*. The battleship immediately sprang into action. One of its Arado Ar 196s was catapulted off the deck, its pilot scoring a few hits on an Albacore and injuring the observer Lt A. G. Dunworth.

Divided into four groups of three aeroplanes each, the Albacores prepared to attack the Beast. The first group dropped their torpedoes at too great a distance, but the other Albacores closed to within 900 metres before attacking the battleship. It seemed as if every weapon aboard *Tirpitz* opened fire on the tiny biplanes. Amazingly, even the huge 38 cm cannons went into action, firing off a couple of salvoes against the hapless Albacores and throwing up huge cascades of water. This was the first time that the heavy artillery of *Tirpitz* had been used in anger. In all, seven torpedoes were launched against *Tirpitz* and no hits were scored with one of the torpedoes passing a mere 10 metres aft of the stern. Two of the Albacores, one from 817 and 832 Squadrons, were shot down. A pilot on one of the Albacores managed to ditch his stricken torpedo bomber. Despite the fixed undercarriage and heavy engine, the Albacore did not flip over when it struck the water. Having survived the ditching, one of the three airmen then climbed out onto the wing and calmly sat down. With *Tirpitz* passing very close to the ditched Albacore, the British aviator was observed sitting on the wing of his downed aeroplane. *Tirpitz* did not stop or slow down and no attempt was made to rescue the Albacore crewman. His prospects of surviving for more than a couple of minutes in the freezing water were virtually nil. All six airmen in the two Albacores died.[6]

When the surviving Albacore crews returned to HMS *Victorious*, they were severely reprimanded for not damaging the battleship. The commanding officer of a Fairey Fulmar squadron, Lt Cdr E. G. Savage, is said to have suggested a 'head-on' attack by the Fulmar pilots against *Tirpitz*. Quite what damage the .30-calibre machine guns of the Fulmars would have caused to the heavily armoured battleship is open to debate. Understandably, the Fulmar pilots were not particularly keen on making such an attack.

German losses were limited to three sailors killed when Albacore gunners sprayed the deck of the battleship with machine-gun fire. In all, 4,614 rounds of ammunition had been fired by the flak guns during the attack.

Churchill subsequently demanded to know why twelve Fleet Air Arm Albacores had failed to inflict any damage to *Tirpitz*. Just three months prior on 10 December 1941, the battleships HMS *Repulse* and HMS *Prince of Wales* had been sunk by Japanese carrier-based aircraft off Singapore, but in comparison with the Japanese Nakajima B5N 'Kate' torpedo bomber, the Fairey Albacore was inferior in all respects. The B5N was a three-seat monoplane featuring a retractable undercarriage. First flown in January 1937, the first production examples were delivered to the Imperial Japanese Navy during the last weeks of the same year. For its day, the performance of the B5N was very good, it had a maximum speed of 368 kph at 2,000 metres, a service ceiling of 7,400 metres, and a maximum range of 2,259 km. The Nakajima B5N could carry an external war load (bombs or a torpedo) weighing 800 kg . First flown nearly two years later (in December 1938), the Albacore was a three-seat biplane with a fixed undercarriage capable of carrying a war load of 2,000 lb. The Albacore had a maximum speed 161 mph at 4,500 feet, a service ceiling of 20,700 feet and a maximum range of 930 miles. The first Albacores entered service in March 1940 and although designed to replace the Fairey Swordfish, the Albacore was outclassed in frontline service by its predecessor. Aircraft performance characteristics are only one of several factors that have to be taken into account when comparing actual success during specific operations. The aircraft of the FAA were, when compared with the Japanese and United States navies, both obsolete and lacking in performance. However, it must be emphasised that the bravery and tenacity exhibited by FAA aircrews was second to none.

Even though the FAA torpedo attack was unsuccessful, it made a huge impact on Hitler and Raeder. The fact that *Tirpitz*, as well as any other surface warship, was vulnerable to attack by aircraft was brought home to the German leadership.

More RAF raids

A second RAF raid against *Tirpitz* was flown on 30–31 March and it had been recognised that the tactics used during the first raid would have to be revised. In fact, it was implicitly acknowledged that the first RAF raid had proved lacking both in tactics and ordnance used. To put it more bluntly, the January raid had been a dismal failure, brought on by desperation and an urgent need to damage the *Tirpitz*.

The armour-piercing bombs of 2,000 lb and 500 lb available to the RAF were thought to be too small and lack the capacity to penetrate the deck armour of the Beast. High-explosive bombs would certainly do some damage to the superstructure, particularly the bridge, as well as killing or injuring the crew of *Tirpitz*. However, no lasting damage to the battleship would be done by using conventional bombs. Using torpedoes was also out of the question, due to the topography of Fætten Fjord and the way *Tirpitz* was anchored, furthermore the anti-torpedo nets would prevent any torpedoes reaching the battleship. The final option was to use mines. In the event, the Mk XIX anti-submarine mine was judged as being the most suitable weapon against the Beast. The mines would be dropped close to *Tirpitz* and explode while submerged, causing damage to the underwater hull of the battleship. As a result, a batch of 100 mines was transferred from the Royal Navy. Following delivery, the 31 inch diameter mines were strengthened for air dropping as well as changing the type of explosives from the original 100 lb of amatol to 770 lb of Minol, i.e. amatol mixed with aluminium powder in order to increase the blast. Due to its bulky appearance, the mine received the nickname 'Roly-poly'.

With the bomb bay of the Short Stirling being too small and constricted for carrying the mines, the Handley Page Halifax was the obvious choice. However, with the large mine having a diameter of about three feet, the bomb-bay doors of the mine-carrying Halifaxes were modified accordingly. In fact, a hole was cut into the doors to accommodate the mine. With the mine hanging halfway out of the bomb bay, this increased the air resistance and fuel consumption, and also reduced the speed of the bombers.

Operational trials by 10 Squadron based at RAF Leeming were flown during the first half of March 1942 to establish the optimum method of inflicting as much damage to *Tirpitz* using the modified mines. In order to breach the hull, one or several mines would have to be dropped in the confined water between *Tirpitz* and the side of Fætten Fjord, a mere 50 feet distance, creating a formidable task and risk for the RAF crews.

The training flights had their moments. One crew suffered a hung-up mine over Filey Bay and returned to base with the mine still in the bomb bay. Upon landing, the mine came loose and fell onto the runway, chasing the Halifax down the runway for some distance before coming to a halt. All activity at RAF Leeming was stopped while the errant mine was defused. During the training flights, it was established that the optimum altitude of dropping the mines was at an altitude of between 4,000 and 10,000 feet.

On 9 March, a number of 10 Squadron's Halifaxes were flown north to Lossiemouth. Lancasters of 44 Squadron were also due to take part in the forthcoming raid. The intention is not entirely clear, but it may have been as part of preparations to attack targets in Norway or possibly *Tirpitz*. Poor weather, as well as the fact that *Tirpitz* was out of range for the bombers, saw the return of the detachment to RAF Leeming on 13 March without flying any operations.

Keeping the Beast in Norway

With *Tirpitz* operational, the risk of having the battleship return south from its Norwegian hideout had to be removed. This risk was greatly reduced when on 27–28 March, British Commandos made a spectacular raid against the French Atlantic port of St Nazaire. The dry dock at St Nazaire was the only one large enough with the ability to repair any damage below the waterline sustained to *Tirpitz*.

In late March, thirty-six Halifaxes from three squadrons, including 10 Squadron (eleven bombers), 35 Squadron (thirteen bombers) and 76 Squadron (twelve bombers), were flown north to Scotland in preparation for taking on the Beast. Prior to the raid, it was necessary to make sure that *Tirpitz* remained anchored at Fætten Fjord. On 28 March, a photo-reconnaissance Mosquito made an attempt of doing just that, but upon crossing the coast, the Mosquito was discovered by German air defences. Five Messerschmitt Bf 109 fighters were dispatched from Værnes airbase close to Trondheim to take care of the lone intruder. The Mosquito crew had to abort the sortie, encountering flak before turning westward ahead of the Luftwaffe fighters. Later the same day, a reconnaissance Spitfire, flown by Flt Lt Fane, took photos of *Tirpitz*. Fane managed to capture the attention of Kriegsmarine sailors by passing over the battleship at very low level and unopposed taking one solitary picture of *Tirpitz*.

It was intended that two Lancasters of 97 Squadron would take part in the operation. Temporarily based at Tain, their task was to make a diversionary attack against the Luftwaffe airbase at Værnes. However, one of the Lancasters, flown by Fg Off. Hallows, was written off on 26 March in a take-off accident at Woodhall Spa when the undercarriage was retracted too soon. The second pilot, FS J. M. Smith, was injured with the crew unhurt. Although the second Lancaster, flown by Flt Lt Coton, arrived safely at Tain, it remained in Scotland until 28 March when Coton and his crew returned to Woodhall Spa when their participation in the forthcoming raid was cancelled.

The weather forecast during the pre-raid briefing stated that cloudy conditions were to be expected but it was expected that the Halifax crews would be able to locate the target. Twenty Halifaxes led by Group Captain Graham were to carry four mines each as well as small bomb containers and liquid phosphorous flares. The mine-carrying bombers were to drop their charges at low level, having first marked the battleship with the flares. Ten of the bombers carried 4,000 lb High Capacity (HC) bombs (called 'Dustbins' or 'Dangerous Cookies' due to their shape) and a number of 500 lb or 250 lb General Purpose (GP) bombs. Two of the bombers carried incendiary bombs. At 18.07 hours on 30 March, the first of the heavily-laden Halifaxes trundled off Lossiemouth's grass runway. When the first RAF bombers arrived over Fætten Fjord some five hours after take-off, they found *Tirpitz* completely covered by a low cloud base. Out of the thirty-three Halifaxes, many failed to locate the *Tirpitz* and those that did failed to hit the Beast. The only damage sustained by the battleship was a flare that was dropped from one of the bombers—the flare struck the funnel and caused insubstantial damage. The flak guns aboard *Tirpitz* fired off some 300 rounds in the attack that lasted about thirty minutes, during which six Halifaxes were lost. The Halifaxes lost were serial numbers W1043 and W1044 of 10 Squadron; R9438, R9496 and W1015 of 35 Squadron; and R9453 of 76 Squadron. All forty-two aircrew aboard the six Halifaxes died. A second 76 Squadron Halifax, L9581, ditched while approaching the Scottish coast and all seven aboard were rescued. At least three bombers were claimed as shot down by flak, although none by the flak guns aboard *Tirpitz*. Also, the Luftwaffe did not make any attempt to intercept the raiders. The raid had been flown at the extreme range of the Halifax bombers with one aircraft returning to Lossiemouth with a mere eighteen gallons of fuel left in the tanks.

The following day, an RAF photo-reconnaissance aircraft made a post-raid damage assessment flight over Fætten Fjord. The Beast appeared to have suffered no damage at all. Several reconnaissance flights over the Trondheim and Fætten Fjord areas were flown during April 1942. Several crews, along with their aircraft, were lost.

After the return to Fætten Fjord following the failure of Operation *Sportpalast*, the camouflage pattern of Tirpitz was yet again altered with irregular patches of green added to the gun turrets and deck. Spring was coming and the surrounding hills would soon be covered with forests and vegetation. Despite the obvious difficulties in making the huge battleship less visible, this camouflage pattern was relatively effective.

The third RAF raid

The planning of further raids continued throughout the month. Five squadrons would carry out the next raid. This time around, Lancasters would be part of the strike force as well as Halifaxes. Nos 44 and 97 Squadrons, both of which had recently re-equipped with Lancasters, deployed to Lossiemouth. The three Halifax squadrons, Nos 10, 35 and 76—all veterans of previous raids against the Beast—flew to Lossiemouth, Kinloss and Tain with mechanics packed into every available space aboard the bombers. The ferry flight to Scotland was largely incident free with the bombers hugging the coast. Flying some two miles off the coast, one 10 Squadron crew observed a convoy below them. The inexperienced pilot then decided to take a closer look and dived down towards the ships. The Halifax was greeted with a hail of gunfire, having failed to provide a correct identification signal. A mechanic aboard the bomber panicked and attempted to bale out before he was restrained. It may well be that the trigger happy gunners misidentified the Halifax for a Luftwaffe bomber as the twin fins were a notable feature on the Dornier Do 217 (twin-engine) medium bomber. Amazingly, a number of the crew and passengers did not notice the gunfire from the convoy below. One engine was hit and had to be shut down, and the propeller feathered. Having finally cleared the convoy, the flight northwards was resumed. Upon reaching Lossiemouth, the crew was told to circle to use up the remaining fuel. Some sixty holes were counted in the fuselage of the Halifax. Following a change of propeller and two radiators, the bomber was declared operational.

The third raid occurred during the night of 27–28 April when Halifax bombers of 10, 35 and 76 Squadrons and Lancasters of 44 and 97 Squadrons attacked the Beast. Several Halifaxes of 10 and 35 Squadrons carried mines, which if hit the steep slopes of the fjord, would then roll down into the water and still cause some damage. In order to drop the mines, the Halifax crews had to make the attack run at very low level, some 100 metres above the surface. However, this method of attack was considered downright idiotic by some Norwegians belonging to the Resistance movement. With high cliffs and dense forests surrounding Fættenfjord, any mine that hit the slopes would explode before entering the water. The RAF bomber crews suspected that the Germans had, apart from large numbers of flak guns, added one novel way of defending the battleship by stretching a cable across the fjord. However, apart from the flak guns, the best defence available was an artificial smokescreen. The smoke would belch out and cover *Tirpitz*, making it extremely difficult for the RAF bombers to locate the battleship. An artificial smoke generator was located in the stern of the battleship and when operational, the smoke was discharged via two funnels through pressurised air. The extremely toxic smoke consisted of chlorosulfuric acid and could be emitted for twenty minutes.

The bombers would use Salt Island, about one-and-a-half miles from *Tirpitz*, as a landmark and turning point. The raid was divided into two waves with the first wave dropping high-explosive bombs. The Halifaxes of the second wave would attack from low level and dropping mines. During the final briefing, messages from both the King and Churchill were read aloud. The King's telegram read: 'Good Luck, we will be waiting up for your safe return.' Churchill stated: 'This mission you will be proud to tell your grandchildren (about).'[7] It had been intended to go ahead with the raid on 25 April. However, due to the Trondheim area being covered by thick clouds, the raid had to be postponed. The following day, poor weather in the target area hindered the bombers yet again.

On 27 April, a photo-reconnaissance aircraft reported: '*Tirpitz* present at her berth with boom closed and 'A' turret still to starboard. She is emitting smoke but most of the camouflage arranged round her stern and bow.' Preparations for a possible raid were gathering pace. By 16.50 hours, the decision was taken: *Tirpitz* would be hit that evening. The first bomber took off at 20.01 hours and the last at 21.15 hours. In all, forty-two bombers set course for Norway and the Beast. The four-engine bombers were not the only RAF aircraft operating off the Norwegian coast that night. Shortly before the first of the Halifax bombers took off, a Coastal Command Catalina of 210 Squadron left Sumburgh. The intention was to divert attention from the main bomber force by flying at extreme low level along the coast. Additionally, two Lockheed Hudsons, one from 48 and 608 Squadrons, operated near the Norwegian coast to confuse the German radar stations. Furthermore, eight Bristol Beaufighters were to attack Luftwaffe airfields in the area while ten Hudsons would attack shipping.

The first wave consisted of twelve Lancasters of 44 and 97 Squadrons, and 76 Squadron carrying 4,000 lb high-explosive bombs as well as 500 lb bombs which would, it was hoped, clear the deck of *Tirpitz* as well as silencing the flak units. Orders had been received to document the raid by taking photographs using photo flashes. The Halifax and Lancaster crews would attack the Beast singly with the first bomber to attack *Tirpitz* being one of 44 Squadron's Lancasters, R5515. Heavy flak was encountered in the target area with the bombers dropping their bomb loads from an altitude of between 6,000 and 8,000 feet. The artificial smoke generators soon came into action, hiding the giant battleship from view. Out of the six Lancasters put up by 44 Squadron, the one flown by FS Jones (L7581) encountered engine trouble immediately after take-off: 'Liquid seen emitting from engine on take-off. As engine heated, liquid became steam and engine obviously unserviceable.' The crew had no choice but to jettison their load of bombs into the sea and return to Lossiemouth where they returned at 20.53 hours, thirty-five minutes after take-off.

The RAF bombers arrived over the target area just after midnight. The weather was fine with no clouds with good visibility due to the prevailing moonlight. It was the same story all over again with heavy flak being encountered over the target area. The first of the five 44 Squadron Lancasters to reach the target area was R5515 flown by W/op Stott. Flak positions were attacked at 00.06 hours with the bomb run (or rather dive) being initiated at 12,000 feet ending at 7,500 feet. Stott reported:

Several large explosions were seen in fjord by ship, one particularly bright during 10 mins, succeeding our dropping of bombs. Considerable flak experienced all the time. Set course for home at 00.40 hours. Trip home uneventful.

Plt Off. Nicholson of 44 Squadron flying L7584 attacked at 00.20 hours, dropping the bombs from 8,000 feet. He later reported that the bombs were:

> ... seen to have burst by 2nd pilot and W/opptr directly over target. Impossible to say if target actually hit, but if not direct hit, was very close. All bombs burst in a stick. First 2 x 500 bombs seemed to burst past the ship. Flash of 4000 bomb seen after and appeared directly over the ship.

The much reduced visibility and heavy flak over the target area forced the crews to drop their bombs over the general area with some bombing by means of dead reckoning. As a result, no hits were observed. One of the Lancasters of 97 Squadron, L7572, flown by Flt Lt Mackid, DFC, was shot down at 00.27 hours, most likely by the *Tirpitz*, crashing in flames into mountains near Kaldadammen. The loss was recorded in 97 Squadron's ORB:

> No fix was received and no news from the other crews beyond several aircrews having seen a ball of flame shoot down over the target and crash, which may have been the missing aircraft.

The entire crew was killed.

The first mine-carrying Halifax bombers of the second wave arrived over Fætten Fjord just after midnight. Dropping to tree-top level, the Halifaxes roared over Fætten Fjord against *Tirpitz*. The flak was very intense and forced several bombers to break off their attack runs. The heavy and accurate flak aboard *Tirpitz*, *Admiral Scheer* as well as other ships and land-based units accounted for four of the Halifaxes. W1037 and W1041 of 10 Squadron, and W1020 and W1048 of 35 Squadron, were shot down or suffered substantial damage to cause them to crash. It is believed that the flak guns aboard *Tirpitz* shot down at least three of the RAF bombers. Out of the twenty-seven aircrew, eight were killed, nine became prisoners of war, and nine managed to evade capture and cross the border into neutral Sweden. One of the RAF aircrews that managed to walk across the border was Wing Commander Don Bennett, something that will be described in more detail below.

Tirpitz suffered no losses during the raid with more than 2,000 rounds of ammunition being fired. One flak gun was damaged when its barrel burst and a German soldier was killed when a bomb landed on a road. The ORB of 97 Squadron rather optimistically noted that: 'The actual results are not yet known but considerable damage in the target area seems to have been done.'

The last RAF bombers left the area at 01.37 hours, the all-clear signal sounding a few minutes before midnight. According to a report sent from *Tirpitz* detailing the raid and intercepted through Ultra, the Germans felt admiration for the British aircrews for having managed to attack *Tirpitz* in force. Indeed, words such as 'most courageous' described the Germans' feelings about the raid, which, it was said, was carried out 'without regard to defence'.

It became painfully clear that the mines, to which such high hopes had been held, had failed miserably. No less than eight unexploded mines were found by the Germans. The mines were destroyed on 28 April, but not before one had been carefully hoisted up on a wooden frame alongside *Tirpitz* with its mechanism and war load carefully documented by the battleship's chief gunnery officer.

The last RAF raid of 1942

Thirty-six of the bombers staggered back to Scotland, the last to arrive being a 10 Squadron Halifax, W1056, which landed at Lossiemouth at 06.21 hours. The crew had spent nine hours and seventeen minutes airborne, most of it in darkness. Five of the aircraft had been lost. During the debriefing, it was noted that thirty-two crews had attacked *Tirpitz* with three other crews attacking diversionary targets. Four of the crews had for various reasons been forced to drop their bombs or mines prematurely.

Preparations for a second follow-up raid against *Tirpitz* began immediately with the bombers due to take-off during the evening of 28 April. During the briefing, it was apparent that 'there was an ominous quiet compared to the previous day'.[8] Once again, the Lancasters of 44 and 97 Squadrons were to attack with conventional bombs to destroy the shore-based flak positions, thus clearing a path for the mine-carrying Halifaxes. Some of the crews attacked the pocket warships *Prinz Eugen* and *Admiral Hipper* (briefed as secondary targets) at Aasen Fjord. Among these crews was W/op Wright in Lancaster L7545. Dropping the 4,000 lb 'Cookie' on *Tirpitz* from 8,000 feet at 00.35 hours, they continued to Aasen Fjord where *Admiral Hipper* and *Prinz Eugen* were the recipients of four 500 lb GP bombs.

> The main target was located and attacked in perfect visibility. The large bomb was seen to burst 100–150 yds. from the ship. We then turned right and did a bombing run with 4 x 500 lb bombs across the alternative target. Two were seen to burst between the two ships anchored in mid-stream off Lo Fjord. The remaining two bombs were not observed. Attack in each case was shallow dive, release at 8,000 feet. Heavy flak—little seen. Light flak moderate.

W/op Osborn, flying Lancaster R5492, stated during the debriefing that: 'One bombing run was made (at 00.29 hours) and all bombs in one stick with 4000 bomb in centre of stick.' The results of their bombs were noted by the crew as a 'dull red explosion' and 'Rear gunner and Navigator confirm large burst seen close to ship and percussion felt in aircraft.' The battleship was engulfed by the artificial smoke with the bomb aimers releasing their loads blindly or through dead reckoning. Despite that, several of the

Halifax and Lancaster crews had observed fires, no bombs had hit *Tirpitz*, *Admiral Hipper* or *Prinz Eugen*. There were some near misses, however, with debris from the shoreline hitting *Tirpitz*, but no real damage was done to the battleship. In all, the crew of *Tirpitz* counted eleven separate attacks with at least twenty-five bombs or mines falling nearby. Two of the bombers, both Halifaxes of 35 Squadron (W1053 and W7656), were shot down with all crews killed in action.

Aftermath

Post-raid reconnaissance photographs showed that the bomb that had fallen nearest the battleship had come down over 500 metres away. Despite the fact that 117 tons of ordnance had been dropped during the two raids, *Tirpitz* had not been hit once. In retrospect, it may be asked that if *Tirpitz* had been disabled or even sunk during these winter/spring bombing raids, the almost mythical status that the German battleship acquired later in the war and in the post-war years would have been substantially reduced. The five RAF raids in the three-month period resulted in the loss of eighteen bombers out of 126 committed, an unacceptably near 15 per cent loss rate. Following the last raid, *Tirpitz* briefly left the safety of Fætten Fjord before returning on 1 May.

However, *Tirpitz* would not remain at Fætten Fjord for long. In July 1942, the Beast would head for Bogen Fjord near Narvik. But before that, the camouflage pattern was altered yet again. The entire superstructure was repainted in a dark colour, either dark grey or green, and some parts were finished in brown. The upper surfaces of the gun turrets were painted dark green. Additionally, the port quarterdeck was covered with the symbol of Nazi Germany, the swastika-emblazoned flag. If this was painted on or was a huge flag is uncertain. Before leaving Fætten Fjord for good, the hull was covered in irregular patterns of grey, green and brown.

Internment and repatriation

As mentioned earlier, nine of the RAF aircrews managed to evade capture. The Swedish border was a mere 65 km away; however, with German troops on the lookout for British fliers in inhospitable and mountainous terrain including deep snow, it was fortunate that as many as nine of the downed British crews reached Sweden. Help was also received from ordinary Norwegians who always assisted in getting the British out of harm's way. The nine that made an unscheduled arrival in Sweden were Wing Commander Bennett, Flight Sergeant Colgan, Sergeant Forbes, Sergeant Walmsley (all from Halifax W1041), Sergeant Pierre Blanchet, Pilot Officer Hewitt, Pilot Officer MacIntyre, Sergeant Perry and Sergeant Ron Wilson (all from Halifax W1048). Bennett and Forbes made contact with a Swedish army patrol during the evening of 30 April. Following a brief initial interrogation, they were sent by train to the Främby internment camp near Falun. Both Colgan and Walmsley also arrived in Sweden on 30 April. On the train journey to Falun, they met Blanchet and Wilson for the first time since leaving Scotland. Bennett was appointed as senior officer at Främby; however, his tenure at Främby was brief as he managed to convince the Swedish authorities that he had been captured by a German patrol and subsequently escaped. Because of this, Bennett's status was that of an evaded prisoner of war, being eligible for immediate repatriation.[9] Bennett successfully argued his case with the Swedish authorities, and along with Walmsley, left Sweden in a BOAC Lockheed Lodestar on 26 May. Bennett went on to have an illustrious RAF career and formed the Pathfinder Force that marked targets for the main bombers. Post-war, Bennett continued to fly for a civilian airline. Forbes and Colgan remained in Sweden until 21 September when they were also repatriated. MacIntyre and Hewitt left Sweden on 1 June 1942. Perry was repatriated on 30 March 1943 while Blanchet remained in Sweden until 5 May, just over a year after he had arrived after being shot down over Norway. Incidentally, Blanchet would later take part in Operation *Paravane* on 15 September 1944.

Small tactical air raids or saturation bombing?

For the time being, no further RAF raids against *Tirpitz* took place. With the bombing campaign against Germany gathering pace, the Halifaxes and Lancasters returned to their bases to recommence operations. Shortly after the RAF raid on 28–29 April, *Tirpitz* sailed north for Alta Fjord that at the time was out of reach for UK-based bombers; however, she soon returned to Fættenfjord. On 7 May, 'Bomber' Harris discussed the possibility of mounting a raid using Lancaster bombers and further meetings ensued. Initial deliveries of a new type of bomb, the 5,500 lb 'Capital Ship' bomb had been made and it was thought that this type of ordnance would cause much damage to the Beast. It was planned that the Lancasters would avoid detection by German radar by making a very low level approach. However, it soon became apparent that the new bomb did not work 'properly' below 8,000 feet in conjunction with the new Mk XIV bombsight—this meant climbing for altitude before reaching the target to make a high-level approach. At this altitude, the bombers would also be relatively safe from light flak. Only a dozen aircraft would be used in the raid, making it the smallest yet since *Tirpitz*'s arrival in Norway.

There were a number of problems, however. Due to the summer solstice, there would be precious little darkness during the night hours for the bombers to use as cover, particularly during a full moon. A more practical issue was the lack of trained aircrews. If such an operation were rushed, the net result would most likely be failure, a repeat of the earlier late winter and spring raids. In order to train more aircrews, the Air Officer Commanding (AOC) suggested initiating training against a dummy target vessel. Such aircrews would have to be removed from regular operations and that meant a temporary reduction of Bomber Command's campaign against Germany. But the chances of hitting *Tirpitz* with such a small force while facing Luftwaffe fighters and flak were, to say the least, slim. A request for using more bombers, some of which would make diversionary attacks against airfields and flak positions, was initially turned down. Nevertheless,

Tirpitz remained firmly entrenched in the minds of Bomber Command which meant that the plans to strike at the battleship were further refined during the summer. The plans to use a small force were abandoned. Instead, a force of between forty and fifty bombers was seen as a minimum to ensure that the *Tirpitz* was damaged or sunk.

According to a plan put forward on 1 July, fifty Lancasters drawn from five squadrons (61, 83, 97, 106 and 207) were to deploy to Lossiemouth, Kinloss, Tain and Fearn, and one squadron was held in reserve. The Lancasters of one squadron were to carry the heavy CS bomb with the other three carrying the 2,000 lb armour-piercing bomb. The raid was planned to take place between 11 and 18 July. Coastal Command Beaufighters were to attack Luftwaffe airbases at Lade and Værnes while Royal Navy destroyers and Air Sea Rescue Hampdens carrying dinghies were to cover the flight path across the North Sea. However, the raid was postponed with the planned approach and return routes for the bombers being put into question. On 19 July, an amended plan was put forward. According to this plan, seven Lancaster squadrons of 5 Group (Nos 44, 50, 61, 83, 97, 106 and 207) were to deploy to Lossiemouth, Kinloss and Wick as well as the Coastal Command's airfields at Dyce and Tain. One of the previously intended forward Scottish airbases, Fearn, was declared unsuitable for use by four-engine bombers as late as 25 July, which showed a definite lack of 'liaison and preparation' between the different RAF Commands.

The changed plan called for five squadrons supplying nine Lancasters each with two squadrons held in reserve. In the event, the planned raid was put on hold yet again, this time due to *Tirpitz* having left Fætten Fjord. It was feared that the battleship was to intercept the PQ 17 convoy, but this did not happen, and instead of returning to Fætten Fjord, she made anchor at Bogenfjord off Narvik. In early August, another plan to attack the Beast at Bogenfjord was put forward. This included the possibility of deploying Lancaster squadrons to Iceland—a plan which had been mooted in May—or Sumburgh in the Shetlands. These proposals were eventually rejected, being referred to as 'impractical', with another proposal to continue to Russia after bombing the battleship. This idea had some definite drawbacks, however. The risk of early detection by German radar stations was too great, which gave the *Tirpitz* ample time to be completely covered in artificial smoke. Also, the nearest available Russian airfield, Vaenga, was a mere 15 km from the frontline and was the target of almost daily Luftwaffe air raids. Having over fifty Lancaster bombers on the ground so close to the frontline would surely provoke a massive reaction from the Luftwaffe. Vaenga was also within range of German artillery. Additionally, although RAF detachments were about to deploy to Russia (Operation *Orator*), precious little information on Russian airfields, including runway conditions and available ground-support equipment, was available. In fact

> . . . to stage an attack against *Tirpitz* at Narvik at the present time would accomplish nothing and would throw away almost all of the aircraft taking part.

The risk involved was simply too great. Although the raid was cancelled, the notion of using Russian airbases in attacking the Beast would feature prominently almost exactly two years later.[10]

However, *Tirpitz* did not remain anchored at Bogenfjord, for on 23 October, the Beast returned south to Fætten Fjord. Three days later, Churchill dispatched a personal minute to the First Sea Lord and Chief of Air Staff:

> The movement of *Tirpitz* and *Scheer* (*Admiral Scheer*) to Trondheim calls for every effort to strike them while there. Pray let me know in writing, or if you prefer orally, what you have in mind.

The reply was that sending a massive force of no less than 100 Lancasters carrying 4,000 lb 'Cookie' high-explosive bombs was under consideration. Continued planning included using Beaufighters of Coastal Command as escorts or being used to cover the return flight of the Lancasters. An intelligence officer wrote:

> I do not consider either of these roles necessary except to hoist the morale of the bombers, which should hardly be necessary with Lancasters.

Further planning saw a revision in the ordnance to be carried from the heavy Capital Ship bomb to the 500 lb semi-armour-piercing bomb. No less than nine Lancaster squadrons (9, 44, 49, 50, 57, 61, 97, 106 and 207) were to carry out the raid. In all, a maximum effort would involve ninety-nine Lancasters, i.e. eleven bombers from each squadron. If the reserve aeroplanes remained unused, the attacking force would be reduced to eighty-one bombers. In the event, the raid was cancelled.[11]

It was not until Operation *Tungsten* on 3 April 1944 that British aircraft would attack *Tirpitz*. This time, the RAF would not be involved. Instead, a massive strike force of carrier-based aircraft was to attack the battleship. However, *Tirpitz* would still cast a dark shadow on naval operations in the Arctic Sea. No better example of the deeply felt fear of the Beast and her capabilities by the Admiralty can be found through the fate of the PQ 17 convoy.

The tragedy of PQ 17

The fact that the most modern and heavily-armed battleship of the Kriegsmarine had safely arrived in Norway provided a huge amount of worry for the British. The five RAF raids against *Tirpitz* had failed to inflict any damage to the battleship. Alternative ways of striking at the Beast had been put forward only to be cancelled for various reasons. The convoys sailing for Russia would now require large numbers of Allied warships for protection. In the event, the fate of PQ 17—the best known convoy of the war—boiled down to the terrifying reputation and fear of the Beast. The mere presence of *Tirpitz* in northern Norway provided the Admiralty with many sleepless nights.

By mid-June, PQ 17 was assembling in Iceland. In all, thirty-five merchant ships carrying hundreds of aircraft, tanks, and other vital war supplies to the hard-pressed Russians were being readied for the journey across the Arctic Sea. Admiral Dudley Pound suggested that in the event of an attack against PQ 17 by *Tirpitz*, the convoy would scatter with the merchant vessels sailing for the Russian ports singly. The reasoning behind this was that the cargo ships would stand a better chance of survival in case of naval and air attacks. The Germans would find it more trouble than it was worth in locating and picking off the cargo ships one by one. Of course, this spoke against everything that had been learned the hard way. The method of assembling single merchant vessels into larger convoys in order to dissuade an enemy attack was a practical view of the old adage 'strength in numbers'. Dispatching convoys of merchant vessels was an invention of the First World War, but it worked just as well more than twenty years later. Having safety in numbers was a logical and well-established way of doing things. Admiral Tovey was 'shocked' about hearing Pound's suggestion of scattering the convoy.

However, in spite of Tovey's doubts, he had worked out a plan to lure the Beast out into the open sea. Tovey's plan called for providing false information to the Germans that a convoy was preparing to leave Iceland. Simultaneously, a second convoy was to assemble at Scapa Flow. It was vaguely hinted that these convoys would carry troops for the invasion of northern Norway. Dangling two troop-carrying convoys in front of *Tirpitz* was tempting bait that, it was hoped, would prove impossible to resist for the Kriegsmarine. Only one of the convoys, PQ 17, was the real deal. The information would be passed on by a German agent, who, upon arriving in Iceland, immediately revealed himself to the British authorities where he agreed to become a double agent. In short, the gist of Tovey's plan was that when *Tirpitz* and other Kriegsmarine warships left the safety of the Norwegian ports, the Home Fleet would attack in force west of Bjørnøya (Bear Island). The British would finally be able to dispatch *Tirpitz* to the bottom of the Atlantic Ocean. The plan was codenamed Operation *Tarantula*.

Tovey's plan was based on information provided to the Admiralty from the naval attaché in Sweden, Henry Denham. German telegraphic communication between Norway and Germany had one major drawback as the coded messages had to pass through the Swedish telegraphic net. Swedish cryptographic experts had, unbeknownst to the Germans, cracked the German code. One Swedish intelligence officer, Carl Björnstierna, contacted the British naval attaché in Stockholm, Henry Denham, with some interesting news on the *Tirpitz*. What Björnstierna provided was accurate information on both the *Tirpitz* and forthcoming Kriegsmarine operations on the Arctic Front. Immediately seeing the value of the information, Denham forwarded the message to the Admiralty on 18 June. According to Björnstierna's information, one pocket battleship, along with six destroyers, would transfer to Alten Fjord with *Tirpitz* transferring to Bogen Fjord off Narvik. *Tirpitz* would be the flagship of a huge force that would be ready to attack the next convoy. Finally, this information provided an excellent opportunity of taking on the *Tirpitz*.

On 27 June 1942, convoy PQ 17 left Hvalfjord, Iceland, and headed for Murmansk, and was the first joint Anglo-US naval operation of the war. Almost immediately, PQ 17 was sighted by a German U-boat that continued to shadow the convoy. Luftwaffe long-range flying boats based at Skattøra near Tromsø also shadowed the convoy on 1 July. The following day, PQ 17 was unsuccessfully attacked for the first time by the Luftwaffe. On 4 July, the first ship to be sunk was damaged by a torpedo-carrying Heinkel He 111, eventually being scuttled by an escort vessel. A second aerial attack later the same day saw another ship being sent to the bottom of the sea. At 21.36 hours, PQ 17 was ordered to scatter due to the risk of Kriegsmarine warships closing in on the convoy. This Admiralty directive was interpreted that the *Tirpitz* had left its lair and was heading out on the open sea towards the convoy. However, it was not the *Tirpitz* or any surface warship that was to wreak havoc on PQ 17. Of the thirty-five merchant ships, no less than twenty-four were sunk by Kriegsmarine U-boats and Luftwaffe torpedo bombers during a battle that raged on and off for one week. In all, 153 Allied sailors lost their lives. Of the valuable cargo carried by PQ 17, 3,350 trucks, 430 tanks, 210 aircraft and nearly 100,000 tons of other items went to the bottom of the sea. The Luftwaffe flew in excess of 200 sorties and claimed eight ships as sunk. Only five German aircraft were lost: two Blohm & Voss Bv 138 flying boats and three torpedo-carrying Heinkel He 111s. It was a small price to pay for the Germans.

Although the grievous losses suffered by PQ 17 was through U-boats and torpedo bombers, the Kriegsmarine had originally intended to field two battle groups of surface warships against the convoy. The operation was codenamed Operation *Rösselsprung* ('Horse's Leap'). The first of these battle groups, based at Fætten Fjord, consisted of the *Tirpitz*, *Admiral Hipper*, a number of destroyers and support vessels. The first vessels of Operation *Rösselsprung* left Norway on 2 July, the intention being to make a concerted attack on the convoy east of Bjørnøya, i.e. a different place than expected by Admiral Tovey. *Tirpitz* left port on 5 June at 15.00 hours. German intelligence subsequently intercepted a message from the British submarine HMS *Unshaken* that *Tirpitz* was heading for PQ 17. The element of surprise was gone.

The Russians were well aware that the Kriegsmarine ships had left port and were heading northwards. One Russian submarine, *K21*, claimed to have damaged the *Tirpitz* with a torpedo strike. Amazingly, the Russian attack was reportedly not even noticed by the *Tirpitz*! On a more serious note, the Kriegsmarine U-boats tracking Tovey's escort vessels lost contact with the aircraft carrier HMS *Victorious*. Losing the element of surprise and not knowing the whereabouts of HMS *Victorious* was deemed as extremely serious by Raeder. As a result, after having been at sea for a mere six and a half hours, *Tirpitz* was ordered to abort the hunt and return to Norway as Raeder thought that the risks were too high; however, the other surface warships continued the operation. But when several support vessels developed technical malfunctions as well as the constant lack of fuel, Operation *Rösselsprung* was finally aborted on 6 July.

No surface warships of either battle group encountered any of PQ 17's cargo ships. Although the Germans had clearly won the battle, the crew of the *Tirpitz* stared disappointment in the face. Yet again, they had been cheated from entering naval combat. It seemed as if the *Tirpitz* was destined to elude combat.

Operation *Orator*

The tragic fate of PQ 17 had made it abundantly clear that future convoys would require aerial protection. Carrier-based aeroplanes would be able to mount anti-submarine patrols as well as intercepting Luftwaffe aircraft. While various options were investigated, the next Russian-bound convoy was delayed for two months. The matter of how to get the convoys through to Russia without risking an encounter with *Tirpitz* had to be resolved as quickly as possible. One solution was to provide a strong naval escort, including carrier-based aircraft.

The next convoy, PQ 18, consisted of forty merchant ships and was provided with a strong naval escort. The escort included the destroyers HMS *Malcolm*, HMS *Achates* and HMS *Amazon*, four corvettes, three minesweepers as well as a small number of other vessels and left Iceland in early September. For the first time, an aircraft carrier, HMS *Avenger*, protected an Arctic convoy. Aboard the carrier were about a dozen Hawker Hurricane fighters and three Fairey Swordfish torpedo bombers. This relatively weak aerial strength was deemed insufficient, but it was the only Fleet Air Arm carrier and aircraft available. Apart from providing an aircraft carrier for aerial protection of PQ 18, it was also decided to dispatch an RAF detachment to the USSR. This detachment was codenamed Operation *Orator*. The various aerial components of *Orator* consisted of Consolidated PBY-5 Catalina flying boats (*Orator Cat*), Handley Page Hampden torpedo bombers (*Orator Ham*) and Supermarine Spitfire PR IV reconnaissance aircraft (*Orator PRU*). The RAF detachment was commanded by Group Captain F. R. Hopps from a temporary headquarters at Polarnoye. (This was not the first time that RAF aircraft had been deployed to the Kola Peninsula. In September 1941, two Hurricane squadrons, Nos 81 and 134, were based at Vaenga. Successfully operating under arduous conditions for two months, the remaining Hurricanes were subsequently handed over to the Russians at the end of the RAF deployment.) The Spitfires were to photograph the *Tirpitz* and provide regular and necessary updates of the situation on the Arctic Front. The Hampdens were to attack any Kriegsmarine surface vessels, including the *Tirpitz*, if the Germans ventured out to the open sea.

Anti-submarine Catalinas

The Catalinas of 210 Squadron were to provide an anti-submarine aerial escort for PQ 18. One drawback was that due to the vast distances involved, extra fuel tanks were fitted and the Russian-based Catalinas did not carry depth charges. It was simply a question of choice: to increase the range or to carry depth charges. In the event of a submarine being spotted, the Catalinas would inform the escort vessels of PQ 18; however, Catalinas operating out of Sullom Voe *did* carry depth charges. On 23 September, *U-253* was sunk off Iceland by a Catalina of 210 Squadron.

The Catalinas had a second task to perform, namely to maintain continuous patrols with Kriegsmarine surface vessels which ventured within range of PQ 18. These patrols were flown within ten sectors along the Norwegian coast designated AA to KK respectively. Originally, the Russian-based Catalinas were supposed to be flying from Lake Lakhta. After thinking twice about the virtually non-existent infrastructure of the area, Grasnaya was chosen instead. One major disadvantage of Grasnaya was its relative closeness to the frontline. Lake Lakhta did see some use during Operation *Orator*, however. In all, nine Catalinas were temporarily based in Russia.

Hampden torpedo bombers

On 5 September 1942, thirty-two Hampden torpedo bombers of 144 and 455 Squadrons set off from Lossiemouth and bound for Russia. Although designed for use as a conventional bomber, several Handley Page Hampdens were subsequently converted to carry torpedoes. Only twenty-three Hampdens reached Russia with several crashing in Norway and Sweden. One Hampden was shot down by a Russian fighter north of Afrikanda during an on-going air raid, the Russian pilot apparently mistaking the twin-tailed Hampden for a Luftwaffe Messerschmitt Bf 110. The Hampden pilot was also flying in a non-pre-approved sector.

The Hampdens were based at Vaenga. In the event, the RAF Hampden crews only flew one sortie, an armed reconnaissance sortie on 14 September over the Narvik area. No trace of *Tirpitz* could be found during the seven-and-a-half hour sortie that created a huge sense of worry. If *Tirpitz* had left for the open sea, this would mean major trouble for the PQ 18 convoy. However, later the same day, *Tirpitz* returned to Narvik, having performed sea trials and both the RAF and Admiralty were extremely relieved upon learning this. The risk of *Tirpitz* intercepting PQ 18 had been reduced considerably.

However, PQ 18 received a considerable amount of attention from the Luftwaffe and U-boats, and the Hurricanes aboard HMS *Avenger* proved their worth. During the persistent attacks, the Luftwaffe sustained severe losses, including fifteen Heinkel He 111Hs, twelve Junkers Ju 88s and five Heinkel He 115 floatplanes. Most of these fell to the Hurricane pilots. On the other hand, ten merchant ships were sunk and five Hurricanes lost. Three of the latter were shot down in error by the anti-aircraft guns of escort ships and the pilots rescued.

With PQ 18 having reached Russia, the question arose what to do with the remaining Hampdens? The commanding officer of 455 Squadron, Wing Commander Grant M. Lindeman, thought it would be 'suicidal' to fly the Hampdens back to the UK. Apart from an expected strong headwind and a lack of range, which meant the risk of having to ditch in the North Sea, it was believed that the engines would not run safely on the inferior Russian fuel. On 1 October, the Russians made a formal request for the Hampdens to be handed over. Following some debate, it was eventually decided to pass the surviving Hampdens to the Russians. One of the Hampdens was converted into an *ad hoc* dual-control conversion trainer by cutting through the wing main spar and fitting a second set of controls behind the cockpit. The Russian naval anti-shipping Wing 24 MTAP operated the Hampdens with some success for about a year when the remaining aircraft were withdrawn from use due to wear and tear.

Aerial-reconnaissance Spitfires

Three Supermarine Spitfire PR IV(D)s of the 1 Photo-Reconnaissance Unit (PRU) were to be ferried to Murmansk during the autumn of 1942. Four Spitfires, including one held in reserve, were set aside for the Russian venture. The Spitfires were unarmed with their only means of avoiding flak and interception by Luftwaffe fighters being their speed. The 1 PRU ground crews and support equipment left for Murmansk on 13 August. Initially, it had been planned that the three Spitfires would leave the UK on 20 August; however, a late change of plan saw them leave Sumburgh on 1 September, arriving safely at Afrikanda airbase having covered the 1,300 miles distance in four-and-a-half hours. The three Spitfire pilots were Flt Lt Edward A. 'Tim' Fairhurst, Fg Off. Donald R. M. Furniss and Fg Off. Gavin William 'Sleepy' Walker.

With Afrikanda airbase being too close to the frontline, as amply demonstrated by continuous Luftwaffe air raids, the Spitfires were flown to Vaenga airbase on 2 September. However, Vaenga was also raided continuously by the Luftwaffe. The RAF markings were over-painted with the Soviet five-pointed red star insignia. The conditions at Vaenga were primitive for the narrow undercarriage of the Spitfire, making take-offs and landings hazardous. The British presence at Vaenga had not passed unnoticed. On 9 September, a Spitfire was damaged in an air raid and it was subsequently deemed beyond repair, instead being used as a source for spares. A replacement Spitfire soon arrived along with a de Havilland Mosquito, W4061—only the twelfth Mosquito built.

The following day, Fairhurst made the first reconnaissance flight. The inherent dangers of the photo-reconnaissance sorties did not only include the enemy, poor weather and technical difficulties. While returning from a sortie in mid-September, Walker was intercepted by a Soviet fighter and the Russian pilot fired off a salvo against the unarmed Spitfire, damaging the propeller. Walker managed to land the Spitfire in one piece and it was repaired and returned to service. The Russian pilot claimed that he had merely been testing his guns! That his intended victim had managed to survive the attack was very fortunate indeed.

Tragedy struck on 27 September when Walker was shot down and killed nine miles north of the Luftwaffe airfield at Alta. Walker was on a low-level sortie to Altafjord to photograph *Tirpitz*. Remarkably, it is said that upon reaching the wreck of Walker's Spitfire, the Germans replaced the Soviet stars with RAF roundels. Walker's body was buried close to the site where his Spitfire had come down and following the end of the war, Walker's remains were moved to Tromsø.

In spite of being escorted by surface vessels and aircraft, PQ 18 suffered serious losses. Of the forty merchant ships, thirteen had been sunk, ten by the Luftwaffe and three by U-boats. In return, the Germans lost three U-boats and several aircraft, both to flak and carrier-based Hurricanes. Operation *Orator* was deemed a success and the majority of merchant ships reached Archangel while *Tirpitz* had failed to make an appearance.

On 18 October (or possibly 20 October), the remaining three Spitfires (either AB132, BP889, BP891 and BP923) were handed over to the Russians with the Mosquito ferried back to the UK. (No records appear to exist of which of these four Spitfires had been lost prior to the end of the RAF detachment and were not transferred.) The Russians thoroughly tested the Spitfires and continued to use them for photo-reconnaissance flights over the Arctic Front. Following the end of Operation *Orator*, the remaining Spitfires were handed over to the Russians and the RAF ground crews returned to the UK in November 1942. Meanwhile, *Tirpitz* continued to be checked regularly by RAF photo-reconnaissance aircraft. Although the photographs taken during these daring sorties provided much needed data, valuable information was also provided via the Norwegian Resistance, Milorg, with photographs and visual observations finding their way to Britain. Another source of information was the steady stream of messages intercepted and deciphered by Ultra.

Naval chariots

Following the cancellation of Operation *Rösselsprung*, *Tirpitz* remained based at Bogen Fjord near Narvik. She was to remain here until mid-October when on 23 October, the battleship returned to Fætten Fjord. The move had been expected by the British with the arrival confirmed by a photo-reconnaissance Spitfire the following day. On 25 October, Operation *Title* was initiated.

Operation *Title* was arguably the most novel way of striking at the Beast and involved the use of manned torpedoes. The inspiration to use manned torpedoes was through similar raids performed by the Italian Navy against Royal Navy warships in Egypt during 1941. The torpedo, codenamed *Chariot*, weighed 4,000 lb and was 25 feet in length. Initially, it was planned to use a Short Sunderland four-engine flying boat to carry two Chariots to a pre-determined drop site off the coast of Norway. The Chariots were to be mounted on the sides of the Sunderland's hull. However, the trials showed many obstacles, including increasing the take-off weight of the Sunderland beyond its maximum. Additionally, having the pair of Chariots mounted would induce a heavy drag during take-off and cruise flight. Developing the release mechanism and establishing the best method for the crews to board the Chariots were also fraught with difficulties. The fact that the mission would have to be flown at night further complicated matters. Nevertheless, six Sunderlands were subsequently modified at Wig Bay and held in reserve.[12]

Following much deliberation, it was decided that using the Sunderland as a carrier platform for the Chariots was out of the question: the risks were too high. Instead, it was decided that a large fishing boat towing two Chariots would stand a better chance in producing successful results. The boat chosen as a mother ship was a Norwegian fishing boat named *Arthur*. Operation *Title*, as the raid had been codenamed, went ahead on 30 October 1942. However, the operation had to be aborted when both Chariots broke away from the mother ship only ten miles away from the *Tirpitz*. The disappointment among the crew was 'intense'. *Arthur* was subsequently scuttled near the island of Tautra on 1 November with her crew walking across the border to neutral Sweden. The Germans soon discovered *Arthur* and after raising the fishing boat, managed to put together a fairly complete picture of the intended attack. *Tirpitz* was to remain at Fætten Fjord until January 1943.

Life aboard *Tirpitz*

News of the attempt to sink *Tirpitz* by means of manned torpedoes came as a complete surprise to the crew of the battleship. Since being declared operational in February 1941, she had only fired her big guns once in anger in March 1942 against British torpedo bombers and it appeared as if the battleship was fated to elude combat. As a floating fortress, she was apparently immune to the many RAF raids which had barely made a scratch. Even underwater attempts to damage her had failed with a Russian submarine attack having passed unnoticed.

Serving aboard *Tirpitz* was comfortable. When the battleship was dormant, the wake-up call for the majority of the crew occurred at 06.00 hours followed by roll call and breakfast. Regular day duty began two hours later and ended at 16.00 hours. For the regular day shift, bedtime was at 22.00 hours with lights being turned off at midnight. The flak crews had a twenty-four hour shift followed by twenty-four hours off-duty. When the warship left its lair, the crew served in four-hour shifts.

The Russian Front, where death and destruction was always present, was not far away, but could not in any way be compared with the few and infrequent attacks against the battleship. Indeed, life aboard *Tirpitz* could be described as seriously monotonous and regular exercises and training could not fill the days of the Kriegsmarine sailors.

The crew number varied periodically between just over 2,000 and more than 2,600, and this was due to regular transfers to other warships.

The battleship had a cinema, library, bakery and five hairdressing saloons and the battleship's brass band provided music both for VIP visitors and as light entertainment for the crew. Food was not a problem with three meals being served each day; the food supply aboard the battleship was large enough to last for more than three months. In comparison, the food stored aboard could have fed the inhabitants of a large town with 250,000 inhabitants for a day. There was storage capacity for up to 1,000 barrels of beer and each barrel held fifty litres. Toilets, baths and showers with cold and hot water were plentiful. Even though *Tirpitz* was the world's largest warship, space for the crew was confined and cramped. However, the cramped quarters also made for good comradeship between the members of the crew.

Relations with the local Norwegian population were generally good and shore leave was a common occurrence. Football matches against teams from other Kriegsmarine warships were typical. One way of keeping the crew active was the constant change of camouflage schemes. Following arrival at Bogen Fjord, the camouflage pattern was amended to better suit the Arctic environment. To keep the crew both informed and entertained, a regular newspaper, *Der Scheinwerfer* (*The Searchlight*), was printed aboard. *Der Scheinwerfer* was only four pages thick and included articles and jokes. The propaganda articles and regular radio broadcasts as well as speeches from the battleship's commander made it all too clear to the crew of *Tirpitz* that the war was raging on every front, apart from Norway. However, serving aboard the world's largest battleship and being confined to what seemed like eternal idleness in a Norwegian fjord could be frustrating. As a result, combat was eagerly expected by the crew from the lowliest conscript to the battleship's commander.

The almost complete lack of action apparently spurred one young conscript, eighteen-year-old flak gunner Bernhard Turowsky, to attempt to desert. Turowsky went missing one morning in August 1942. Four days later, Turowsky was caught near the Swedish border, carrying a compass and pistol, both of which he had stolen from an Arado Ar 196 pilot. During the court martial, Turowsky stated that boredom had caused his defection and he was executed on 4 September by a firing squad from his own unit in the presence of the whole crew. It was intended that Turowsky was to be buried ashore, but local authorities refused this taking place. Instead, his body was put in a weighted-down sack and dispatched to the bottom of Bogen Fjord. Turowsky was the fourth casualty from the crew of *Tirpitz*—the three other casualties had occurred when Albacores sprayed the deck with machine-gun fire during a failed torpedo attack.

Overhaul and repairs

During the late summer, it had become obvious that *Tirpitz* was in need of a general overhaul and the repair or replacement of worn-out equipment. Among other things, the magnetic field of the hull needed to be neutralised in order to reduce the risk of sustaining damage from magnetic mines. This work could not be performed at Bogen Fjord and brief consideration was given to returning to Germany or France; however, this would put *Tirpitz* within range of the RAF. Having the battleship return to Germany or sail to France meant an increased risk of *Tirpitz* suffering damage at the hands of the RAF or the Royal Navy—or both. Instead, she would remain in Norway with the necessary overhaul and maintenance being undertaken at Fætten Fjord. On 22 October 1942, *Tirpitz* left Narvik and arrived at Fætten Fjord the next day. By mid-December, maintenance work commenced with the assistance of a pontoon crane and workers from Germany. On New Year's Eve, the crew was treated with a special dinner including a bottle of wine and an extra ration of tobacco and sweets for every sailor.

Further north, things were going badly for the Kriegsmarine during an attack on the convoy JW 51B. Based on the order issued at the outset of the operation to avoid action with a force equal in strength to his own, poor visibility, and the damage to his flagship, Admiral Kummetz decided to abort the attack. In the course of the battle, the British destroyer HMS *Achates* was sunk by the damage inflicted by *Admiral Hipper*. The Germans also sank the minesweeper *Bramble* and damaged the destroyers *Onslow*, *Obedient*, and *Obdurate*. In return, the British sank *Friederich Eckoldt* and damaged *Admiral Hipper*, and forced the Germans to abandon the attack on the convoy. When Hitler learned that the Kriegsmarine had failed to inflict substantial damage to the convoy, he flew into a hysterical rage. During a meeting with Raeder on 6 January 1943, Hitler proclaimed the Kriegsmarine surface warships to be virtually useless. The battleships were obsolete behemoths which consumed inordinate amounts of fuel, fuel that could be put to better use elsewhere. The only part of the Kriegsmarine that was proving its worth was the submarine fleet. The Nazi dictator decided to disarm the battleships and cruisers, and use their heavy armament in strengthening the coastal defences of Norway. The metal and armour of the battleships would be supplied to the war industry for the production of aeroplanes and tanks. Raeder subsequently resigned and was replaced by the commander of the submarine arm, Admiral Karl Dönitz.[13] With

Dönitz replacing Raeder as commander of the Kriegsmarine, *Tirpitz* also saw the arrival of a new commander, Karl Topp being replaced on 25 February 1943 by Kapitän zur See Hans Meyer.

A tentative list of when the warships were to be taken out of service and scrapped was drawn up by the OKM. The list included *Admiral Hipper* (to be withdrawn on 1 March 1943), *Schleswig-Holstein* (1 April 1943), *Schlesien* (1 May 1943), *Scharnhorst* (1 July 1943) and *Tirpitz* (autumn of 1943). Although Dönitz initially seemed to agree with the Führer in his wish to dismantle the battleships, he later changed his mind. After weighing the pros and cons, it was, with Hitler's reluctant approval, eventually decided that *Tirpitz* had an active role to play in the war. A not insignificant factor in the decision was that the necessary resources needed to scrap *Tirpitz* were sorely lacking. It proved more economical to repair *Tirpitz* and return the battleship to operational status than to scrap her.

With the repairs finished, *Tirpitz* was once again ready for combat; however, the officers and crew found being consigned to Norwegian fjords incredibly frustrating. *Tirpitz* was built for naval combat and not getting the chance of striking at the enemy evoked feelings of being unwanted and redundant. Trying to keep the spirit of the crew at the highest possible level was highly important. The following weeks were spent working up both crew and vessel. On 5 March, *Tirpitz* was ready for combat. Six days later, *Tirpitz*, *Prinz Eugen*, *Karl Gaister*, *Jaguar* and *Greif* left Fætten Fjord for Bogen Fjord where *Scharnhorst* and *Lützow* had already arrived. On 20 March, a gunnery exercise was completed. On the night of 22–23 March, *Tirpitz*, along with *Scharnhorst*, *Lützow* and six destroyers, headed north for Kaa Fjord, a small inlet of Alta Fjord where further exercises were scheduled to take place. During the voyage north, *Tirpitz* travelled at the cruise speed of 16 knots in order to conserve precious fuel.

In April and May 1943, several reconnaissance sorties were flown by the VVS over Alta Fjord at the request of the RAF. It is believed that a Spitfire, possibly one of the *Orator* PRU aeroplanes, was used to complete these sorties.

During the spring and early summer of 1943, the Allies finally managed to push the last remaining Axis forces out of North Africa. The preparations for the invasion of Sicily and the Italian mainland included the participation of many of the Royal Navy's surface warships. As a result, naval operations against the *Tirpitz* would not be possible. With the *Tirpitz* far out of range for RAF raids, the battleship appeared safe from attacks from the air. When 617 Squadron was training for a highly secret bombing raid during the spring of 1943, the squadron's commanding officer, Guy Gibson, believed that they were going to hit the Beast. Gibson was much relieved to learn that *Tirpitz* was not the intended target. Instead, three dams in the Ruhr, Eder, Möhne and Sorpe were hit by nineteen Lancasters of the squadron.

However another plan to sink the *Tirpitz* was introduced which involved modifying Mosquitoes to carry Highball rotating mines. The Mosquitoes would be based at Vaenga. The operation was cancelled when Air Marshal Sir John Slessor declared that the Mosquito crews would stand little or no chance of striking the Beast due to the confined waters of Kaa Fjord as well as the heavy flak.

During this time, *Tirpitz* remained under the watchful eyes of Norwegian SIS agents. Written reports as well as photographs were dispatched to Britain via Sweden. One agent, Torstein Petersen, was sent by submarine to Alta Fjord to keep track of German shipping. Arriving on 1 September, Petersen was to establish a secret radio station codenamed Ida. However, Petersen did not have enough time to become settled in prior to two fateful events in *Tirpitz*'s career.

Combat in the Arctic Ocean

In early September 1943, *Tirpitz* fired her heavy guns in anger for the second and only time during an attack against an Allied strongpoint on the island of Svalbard on the Spitzbergen Islands, some 720 km north of the northernmost point of mainland Norway. German forces had not occupied Spitzbergen and that meant that the Allies had managed to establish a weather forecast station on the island. Dönitz needed a target of convenience and Svalbard fitted the bill nicely. A large naval force consisting of *Tirpitz*, the cruiser *Scharnhorst* and ten destroyers was assembled for the attack and codenamed Operation *Sicily*. Approaching Svalbard on 7 September, which was defended by a small garrison based at the small village of Barentsburg, the crews aboard *Tirpitz* and the other warships prepared for combat. In all, the garrison at Barentsburg consisted of 152 soldiers, including 143 Norwegians and nine British sailors, with two 40 mm Bofors anti-aircraft cannons forming the main defence. When the *Tirpitz* and other Kriegsmarine vessels arrived off Barentsburg, the white flag was raised to show their intent to surrender. This ruse made it possible for the warships to get very close to Barentsburg and the garrison was subjected to a heavy bombardment. *Tirpitz* alone fired no less than fifty-two 38 cm and eighty-two 15 cm shells. Two Ar 196 floatplanes were catapulted off *Tirpitz* and joined in the attack on the hapless garrison. (Another reason for the Ar 196s to be sent into the air was so that they were not damaged by the shockwave of the heavy gunfire.) Desperately fighting back, the defenders managed to hit the destroyer *Z 33* with a few rounds; however, it was a case of David versus Goliath. A shore party, landed by the destroyer *Z 29*, destroyed various installations as well as capturing seventy-four Norwegian soldiers. The destroyers, which remained in *Tirpitz*'s line of fire, then moved away. The remainder of the garrison avoided capture by hiding in mineshafts and in the stark wilderness. Apart from destroying the shore installations and capturing as many Allied troops they could find, the Kriegsmarine sailors also raided food supplies, which included chocolate bars, cigarettes and butter. The Kriegsmarine warships did not remain for long at Svalbard, returning south to Alten Fjord before Royal Navy ships could intervene. When the attack on Svalbard became known, the Home Fleet did indeed set sail to meet *Tirpitz*; however, the British soon turned home as it would have been impossible to catch up with the Kriegsmarine warships.

Despite the meagre results of Operation *Sicily* as well as *Tirpitz*'s limited participation, more than 400 Iron Crosses and other decorations were handed out to her crew on 20 September. More than anything else, showering sailors in medals and honours was an attempt to raise morale aboard the battleship. Following *Tirpitz*'s return to Kaa Fjord, work on an extensive overhaul began for an expected four months. Unfortunately for the Germans, the intended overhaul of the battleship would also include extensive repairs following one of the most daring and unusual naval strikes of the Second World War.

Midget submarines

Having failed to sink the Beast by means of RAF bombers and Fleet Air Arm aircraft, a different method was attempted: midget submarine (the submarines were referred to as X-Craft). On 22 September 1943, Operation *Source*, which called for mine-carrying midget submarines to attack the *Tirpitz* at Kaa Fjord, went ahead. Kaa Fjord was a small inlet of the larger Alta Fjord. The preparations for the midget submarine attack called for an increase in aerial reconnaissance. Subsequently, three Spitfire PR IVs of 543 Squadron, AB423, AB427 and BR658, were ferried from Sumburgh to Vaenga on 3 September by Sqdn Ldr F. A. Robinson, Fg Off. Roy Kenwright and Fg Off. John Dixon.

During the flight across the North Sea, Robinson became lost and arrived at Vaenga after being airborne for five-and-a-half hours. Seconds after touching the runway, the Spitfire's Merlin engine cut due to fuel starvation. With the RAF Spitfires having safely arrived, a VVS Spitfire was lost on 3 September when Senior Lieutenant Solovkin went missing while on a reconnaissance sortie over Alta Fjord. In all, the RAF pilots flew thirty-one reconnaissance sorties over Altafjord, the majority being successful. The Russians rated the RAF pilots highly with Robinson receiving the Order of the Great Patriotic War and a pension; however, the latter only lasted for five years until the beginning of the Cold War. The photographs of *Tirpitz* obtained by the RAF and Soviet pilots proved invaluable in the planning and execution of the midget submarine attack on 22 September. On 1 November, Robinson, Kenwright and Dixon returned to the UK by sea and the Spitfires were subsequently handed over to the Soviets.

Out of the eight midget submarines that managed to reach Norway, only three—*X 5*, *X 6* and *X 7*—managed to breach the underwater defences. The first of these, *X 5*, was soon discovered and subsequently sunk. However, the crews of *X 6* and *X 7* managed to place four 2-ton mines on the bottom of Kaa Fjord, close to the battleship before being discovered. Both submarines were sunk with six of their crewmen, four from *X 6* and two from *X 7*, surviving. Four crewmembers of *X 6* were brought aboard the *Tirpitz*. The British sailors caused a sensation among the crew as only a few had seen their enemy counterparts before. Max Krause, then a conscript sailor, later recalled a conversation with one of his comrades: 'Have you seen an Englishman before? Now's your chance. There are four of them standing outside constable's office!' Interrogation of the British sailors began almost immediately. Two of them were brought below deck while Goddard and Kendall remained on deck. The mines detonated at 10.12 hours, causing serious damage to the battleship. The explosion caused *Tirpitz* to lift out of the water about one metre and utter chaos reigned aboard the battleship.[14] Some 1,410 tons of water entered the hull of the Beast, causing a 1 to 2 degree list. An oil tank ruptured with the majority of electrical generators being damaged by water. Leaking oil spread for 3 km around the damaged *Tirpitz*. Two Ar 196 floatplanes were destroyed, including the aircraft catapult. Far worse was that one of the four 38 cm gun turrets, Dora, was torn from its mount by the second explosion. With no heavy-lift crane available in Norway, the Dora gun turret was rendered unserviceable for the rest of *Tirpitz*'s existence. The material damage was severe with rangefinders (necessary to establish the distance of targets), engines, generators, main shafts, propellers and rudders. In the extremely daring X-Craft raid, *Tirpitz* had suffered far more damage than during the numerous air raids. However, the personnel losses were slight with one sailor killed and another forty injured. Thanks to the inspired attack by the X-Craft, *Tirpitz* was out of commission. The Ida radio transmitter run by Torstein Petersen began transmitting on 11 November. Even though Petersen was able to report that the Beast had suffered considerably in the raid, no specific details on the damage were available to the Norwegian agent.

The fact that *Tirpitz* had been severely disabled was highly satisfying to Churchill. The pressure against the Arctic convoys had in one stroke been eased considerably and Russian complaints that too little war supplies were reaching the besieged country lessened. In a telegram to the Foreign Secretary dated 18 October 1943, Churchill wrote:

> In your talks about the convoys and the treatment of our men in North Russia, you should keep up your sleeve the use of the argument about the *TIRPITZ* being disabled by the valour of our midget submarines. This undoubtedly makes it easier for us to undertake the convoys than at the time when my offer to Marshal Stalin was made, and consequently the probabilities of our being able to execute what we propose and intend to try to have been much improved.

In early October, a committee consisting of experts from various companies originally involved in the construction of the battleship, including the turbine makers Brown-Boveri, the optical equipment company Carl Zeiss as well as the Wilhelmshaven dockyard, were dispatched to Kaa Fjord to assess the damage sustained by *Tirpitz*. Members of the committee, which was named Commission Paul, were horrified when they saw the battleship. It was questioned if it would be possible to return *Tirpitz* to full operational status. In the event, 800 workers from the Blohm & Voss Company arrived at Kaa Fjord to initiate work on repairing the Beast. When the repairs began, operational readiness aboard was reduced. The crew was divided into three groups and rotated back to Germany on Christmas leave; the first group of 600 left Norway on 1 November. However, it was not until 28 November that work on repairing *Tirpitz* began in earnest and repairs would last for five months.

On 26 December 1943, the Kriegsmarine suffered a severe setback when the *Scharnhorst* was sunk by a Royal Navy force consisting of the battleship HMS *Duke of York* and cruisers HMS *Belfast*, HMS *Jamaica* and HMS *Norfolk* while preparing to attack the JW55B convoy. The sinking of *Scharnhorst* turned out to be the final battleship to battleship combat between the Royal Navy and the Kriegsmarine. Apart from the *Tirpitz*, *Scharnhorst* had been the only German battleship left in Arctic waters.

The only remaining threat to the Allied convoys to Russia was the *Tirpitz* which was being repaired. Active intelligence work, including decrypted Kriegsmarine reports, aerial-reconnaissance photographs and Norwegian underground observations, made it clear that work on returning the *Tirpitz* to a state of operational readiness was well underway.

After the RAF Spitfire pilots had returned home, VVS photo-reconnaissance sorties over Altafjord continued. On 3 November, a Soviet pilot went missing. By 1 January 1944, four Spitfire PR IVs remained on VVS charge. Within two months, this had been reduced by half, one Spitfire being posted as missing on 22 January and another one on 29 February. The latter Spitfire was recovered from the Vaddasgaisa Mountain in 1972 and it was discovered that the pilot (name unknown) had managed to take thirty-eight photographs.[15]

Despite the short distance between Kaa Fjord and Soviet airbases on the Kola Peninsula, only one Soviet air raid against the *Tirpitz* was made. On the night of 10–11 February 1944, thirty-six Soviet Ilyushin Il-4 medium bombers unsuccessfully tried to hit the battleship. The Il-4s belonged to two Air Regiments, the 42nd and 108th AP, part of the 36th AD, which was based at Vaenga near the White Sea. Due to poor weather, only two Il-4s managed to reach Kaa Fjord with the others dropping their bombs over alternate targets at Kirkenes, Heg Bay, Hammerfest, Bos Fjord, Laks River and Liinahamari near Petsamo. The Soviet bombers that did reach Kaa Fjord found the conditions ideal with a full moon and no wind, dropping a FAB-500 high-explosive bomb (which hit the water), two RRAB-220 armour-piercing bombs (which hit the shoreline), seven SAB-100 phosphorous bombs and six SAB-15 phosphorous bombs. (None of the bombs caused any damage to the *Tirpitz*. FAB-500 indicates a 500-kg bomb, RRAB-220 a 220-kg bomb, etc.) In this context, it may be said that the VVS lacked a strategic bombing capability unlike the RAF and USAAF. The only bomber with a similar capability of the RAF Lancaster and the American B-17 Flying Fortress was the Petlyakov Pe-8 (also designated TB-7). However, less than 100 four-engine Petlyakov Pe-8s were built with most having been withdrawn from use or lost prior to 1944. The Germans subsequently reported that 'one or two' unidentified aircraft were observed over Kaa Fjord. For various reasons, no further Soviet air raids against the *Tirpitz* took place, although more than a dozen reconnaissance sorties—the last one on 3 November 1944—were flown after the failed raid.

Repairs to the Beast continued unabated. Apart from repairs to the ship, the camouflage scheme was yet again changed to a green and grey ray pattern, involving both the hull and superstructure, and a large Nazi flag was painted on the forecastle. As a result, any Allied aircraft venturing near Kaa Fjord would have had little trouble in identifying the battleship.

Operation *Tungsten*

By late 1943 when the battleship was under repair, the issue of how to permanently disable the *Tirpitz* was still deemed to be of utmost importance by the Admiralty and

Churchill. Using submarines for a second attempt was ruled out as impractical. This was due to the improved underwater defence systems with additional anti-submarine nets and mines having been greatly expanded. With Air Chief Marshal Harris insisting that as the *Tirpitz* was beyond effective range, using RAF bombers was also out of the question. The only available option left was to use carrier-based strike aircraft. In this context it should be noted that operations against *Tirpitz* since 1940 had been an almost wholly-British quest. At one time, however, converting a B-17 Flying Fortresses to carry a smaller variant of the rotating bomb used during Operation *Chastise* was contemplated but not proceeded with. During the autumn of 1943, the US Navy aircraft carrier USS *Ranger* was briefly attached to the Home Fleet. USS *Ranger* took part in an abortive attempt in late September to sink the pocket battleship *Lützow* during her journey from Norway to the Baltic Sea. The following month, USS *Ranger* took part in Operation *Leader* during which the Home Fleet attacked shipping off Bodø. The ships involved in Operation *Leader* did not venture further north and returned to Scapa Flow.

Planning for the Home Fleet attack on *Tirpitz*, Operation *Thrustful* (soon renamed *Tungsten*) began in December 1943. Based on aerial-reconnaissance photographs and reports from the Norwegian Resistance, a full-scale replica of the German defences and *Tirpitz* position at Kaa Fjord was constructed at Loch Eriboll. The German defences, including artificial smoke generators and flak positions, were recreated as far as possible. The former was a double-edged weapon as the smoke also reduced visibility for the flak gunners. Using torpedoes was out of the question due to the confined waters of Kaa Fjord. Instead, the Fairey Barracuda bombers would carry a combination of 1,600 lb armour-piercing (AP) bombs as well as 600 lb anti-submarine bombs or 500 lb medium capacity (MC) bombs—the latter intended for taking out the ground defences.

Ungainly in appearance and burdened with less than excellent performance characteristics, the Fairey Barracuda entered Fleet Air Arm service in late 1943. More than 2,500 Barracudas were produced during the war, more than any other British-designed naval aeroplane. Also, the Barracuda was underpowered and suffered from a number of less than optimal design solutions. Among these were the large flaps which folded upwards—this meant that the forward main wing spar was lacking in strength, having to take too much stress during dives. As a result, the wings would occasionally be ripped off during diving attacks. Although designed as a dive bomber, the high-wing loading during recovery from dives of up to 70 degrees put too much strain on the airframe, particularly on the wings but also the fuselage. It was quite common for rivets to come loose during such high-G pull outs and was referred to in a song by 820 Squadron: 'Every time it rains, it rains rivets from heaven.' To add insult to injury, an American officer famously described the Barracuda as the 'finest piece of machinery I had ever come across, but that it would never replace the aeroplane'. Despite all of its faults, the Barracuda was the best strike aircraft available to the Fleet Air Arm and its performance was superior to that of its predecessors such as the Swordfish and Albacore biplanes. Powered by a Merlin 32 engine rated at 1,640 hp, the Barracuda had a maximum speed of 211 mph. Two Barracuda Torpedo Bomber Reconnaissance (TBR) Wings—No. 8, consisting of 827 and 830 Squadrons from HMS *Furious*, and No. 52, 829 and 831 Squadrons from HMS *Victorious*, would form the bomber component of the strike force.

Prior to Operation *Tungsten* taking place, RAF photo-reconnaissance Spitfires were to return to Russia on one final occasion. The Spitfires were to keep an around-the-clock watch and monitor the progress of repairs to the *Tirpitz*. These flights were not only necessary but of vital importance to the British. As a result, three Spitfires arrived at Vaenga on 7 March. Two of the Spitfire pilots were veterans of previous operations: Sqn Ldr Furniss (*Orator*), Fg Off. Dixon (*Source*) with Fg Off. Searle being the newcomer. Clear photographs of *Tirpitz* were subsequently obtained during several reconnaissance flights and in order to avoid flying directly overhead the battleship, the photographs were taken by oblique cameras. While on a sortie on 2 April, Furniss experienced severe engine cooling problems and managed to return to Vaenga where a pair of pliers were found lodged in the oil cooler air intake.

Initially, it had been planned that Operation *Tungsten* would take place between 7 and 16 March; however, due to HMS *Victorious* undergoing scheduled refurbishment, the operation had to be postponed.

On 17 March, a message sent by Kapitän zur See Hans Meyer was intercepted by the British. The message, which concerned a trial run of *Tirpitz* two days previously, was disconcerting: 'From a material point of view, the hull, guns and power supply are fully operational, apart from some unacceptable vibrations that emanated from the amidships turbines.' In late March, another intercepted message stated that the next trial run would take place on 3 April or sooner.

The departing of the support vessel *Neumark* in late March indicated that the Beast was almost ready for action. *Neumark* and her party of workers had assisted greatly in the repair of *Tirpitz*, which was finally completed on 2 April 1944. The following day, high-speed trials were scheduled to take place. Following completion of the high-speed trials, *Tirpitz* was due to begin sea trials before being declared operational. The future looked bright for *Tirpitz*. The time had come for the pride of the Kriegsmarine to wreak havoc against the Russian convoys and Home Fleet. Combat was eagerly expected by the crew, from the battleship's commander to the lowliest conscript. By this time the Kriegsmarine was, apart from its U-boats, quantitatively inferior to the Home Fleet. With *Scharnhorst* sunk and with the repairs of *Tirpitz* still not finished, only the pocket battleships *Lützow*, *Admiral Scheer* and the heavy cruiser *Prinz Eugen* remained. However, the latter three warships were all sheltering in the confined Baltic Sea where they did not pose a threat to the Allies.

The decision to proceed with Operation *Tungsten* was finally made by the Admiralty with the dress rehearsal for the raid taking place on 28 March. With a large Russian-bound convoy, JW 58, about to depart on 27 March, the warships of Operation *Tungsten* would appear to the Germans as a strong convoy escort. The strike force was divided into two parts, Force One and Force Two. The former consisted of HMS *Victorious*, the battleships HMS *Duke of York* and HMS *Anson*, while the larger Force Two consisted of HMS *Furious*, three smaller escort aircraft carriers, HMS *Emperor*, HMS *Pursuer* and HMS *Searcher*, three cruisers and four destroyers. The escort carrier HMS *Fencer* would bring up the rear searching for German U-boats. On 30 March, the huge British fleet left Scapa Flow. There was, however, some doubts regarding the possibility of success. Vice-Admiral Sir Henry Moore had expressed doubts that the armour-piercing bombs carried by the Fairey Barracuda would be sufficient to penetrate the hull of the *Tirpitz*. Additionally, Moore also considered the Barracuda too slow for the job. Nevertheless, the Home Fleet was steaming towards the Norwegian coast. It was a matter of wait-and-see what Operation *Tungsten*—the largest air operation mounted during the war by the Fleet Air Arm—would achieve.

Attack

In the early hours on 3 April, Operation *Tungsten* was finally launched. The first aircraft left the deck of HMS *Victorious* at 05.15 hours. In all, forty-two Fairey Barracuda bombers escorted by eighty-eight Seafire, Hellcat, Wildcat and Corsair fighters were launched from the decks of HMS *Victorious*, HMS *Furious*, HMS *Emperor*, HMS *Pursuer* and HMS *Searcher*. The Hellcats were to attack flak positions surrounding the *Tirpitz* while Wildcats were to spray the deck of the battleship with machine-gun fire. Top cover would be provided by the Corsairs while the Seafires and remaining Wildcats were to fly escort, both for the large naval task force as well as the strike aircraft.

The preparations for the forthcoming *Tirpitz* sea trials were completed. It had been intended to initiate the sea trials on 1 April, but this was cancelled due to poor weather. In the early hours of 3 April, the order to raise anchors was received and *Tirpitz* was to sail at 05.30. With the starboard anchor out of the water and only 25 metres of chain for the port anchor remaining, all hell suddenly broke loose. British aircraft appeared to be everywhere, literally clouding the sky above Kaa Fjord. The first report of the incoming British aircraft had reached the *Tirpitz* at 05.24 hours local time. The report, relayed by the Luftwaffe observation centre at Alta, had been severely delayed and a mere four minutes later, the first British aircraft dived against the Beast. The anti-aircraft crews aboard *Tirpitz* suffered many casualties when the fast and nimble Wildcats sprayed the deck with machine-gun fire. One casualty was Kapitän zur See Hans Meyer who suffered broken eardrums, internal injuries and shock. Indeed, Meyer's injuries were so severe that he was relieved of his command of *Tirpitz* two weeks later. One minute later, the first wave of twenty-one Barracudas arrived overhead, diving from 8,000 feet. Pre-raid planning had called for the armour-piercing bombs to be dropped from an altitude of 3,000 feet; however, many of the Barracuda pilots dropped their bombs from a considerably lower altitude between 600-900 feet. The shore-based artificial smoke generators began to produce smoke, but it was too little and too late. The attack had lasted only for three minutes. At 06.25 hours local time, a second wave of twenty-one Barracudas arrived over Kaa Fjord. Despite that the artificial smokescreen belched out smoke, the Barracudas managed to drop an additional five heavy bombs on *Tirpitz*. The escorting fighters made strafing runs against the shore-based flak positions as well as the battleship. Apart from attacking the main target, other vessels and shore-based defence installations were attacked. One patrol boat was sunk and another three damaged.

One of the fighter pilots circling above the carnage, Sub-Lieutenant Don Sheppard, saw many of the bombs strike *Tirpitz*. The battleship was burning and was seemingly unable to fend off the British aircraft. She appeared doomed with the FAA aircraft having little trouble in avoiding the flak bursts. During the two raids, fifteen bombs had struck the Beast, including eight on the main deck with another four near misses. Four 1,000 lb armour-piercing bombs, four 500 lb high-explosive bombs, one 600 lb anti-submarine bomb and six 500 lb semi-armour-piercing bombs had hit the battleship. The bridge was completely destroyed with the kitchen and officers' mess being substantially damaged. However, none of the bombs dropped by the Barracudas managed to penetrate the heavy deck armour and damage the generators or other internal machinery. The crew of the *Tirpitz* suffered greatly with over 113 killed and 284 injured, including Kapitän zur See Hans Meyer. (He did not succumb to his injuries sustained in Operation *Tungsten*. Meyer passed away in 1989.) This was the highest casualty rate suffered by the *Tirpitz* in all air attacks. The ship's surgeon was among those killed and only one out of two doctors was available as the second was on leave. Confusion and shock reigned aboard the *Tirpitz*, enhanced by a siren that could not be turned off that spread the occasional howling wail across the battleship. Efforts were made to put out the fires while the wounded were attended to by the meagre medical staff. Gradually, the fires were put out with damage assessments being initiated.

British losses were low with eight airmen killed and three Barracudas (including one during the first strike) and one Hellcat lost, of which only two of the former being shot down.[16] The Hellcat ditched when its pilot ran out of fuel. By 08.30 hours, the aircraft of the second wave had returned safely to their carriers. It was decided not to conduct further strikes with the weather rapidly getting worse precluding further operations. Another highly important aspect in this decision was that the aircrews were suffering from fatigue. Initially, Operation *Tungsten* was considered a great success by the Admiralty and was believed that the *Tirpitz* had been immobilised permanently. However, it soon turned out that the damage sustained by the Beast was superficial, being largely confined to the deck.

The air attacks and their aftermath were noted by the destroyer *Z 38*. Just after 09.00 hours, the commander of *Z 38* received a desperate plea for help from the battleship: 'All doctors and surgeons to *Tirpitz*.' The deck of the battleship was awash in blood and gore with dead and wounded sailors crowding every available space. The whaler, *C. A. Larsen*, which had been moored alongside, had suffered a direct hit and was burning fiercely as was the steamer *Dollart*. According to a Norwegian eyewitness, the ships were 'toasted'. It was not until the afternoon when the final fires aboard the *Tirpitz* and *C. A. Larsen* had been put out or brought under control.

A third strike due to be carried out on 4 April was cancelled following a thorough assessment of the damage sustained by the *Tirpitz*.

Poor weather did not permit reconnaissance flights until 7 April. It turned out that the *Tirpitz* was covered by shadows, thus making it very difficult to assess the damage and continuous poor weather largely hindered further flights. British reconnaissance pilots finally left Vaenga on 31 May, travelling via Moscow and Iran to Britain—a safer, albeit considerably longer and time-consuming route.

Following Operation *Tungsten*, German efforts in hunting down Norwegian Resistance members in the area greatly intensified. The Germans were well aware that reports on their military strength in Norway and the *Tirpitz* in particular were reaching Britain. With northern Norway being sparsely populated along with the inhospitable terrain, locating radio transmitters was not an easy task. In the event, the Germans brought several radio location ships to the area and by triangulating the transmissions managed to locate their whereabouts. During the summer of 1944, four radio transmitter stations were located with thirty agents arrested. The first transmitter located was codenamed Lyre. Operated through the British Secret Service, Lyre was based at Porsa. On 6 June, German soldiers stormed ashore at Porsa and arrested two Norwegian agents as well as recovering much material. While every inhabitant of Porsa was locked into a warehouse, the agents were brutally beaten before confessing to transmitting reports to the British. The newly appointed Kapitän zur See Junge subsequently wrote in *Tirpitz*'s war diary:

> Almost a year and a half after the arrival of *Tirpitz* at Kaa Fjord, the first (foreign) agents has been arrested. Judging by the material and the oral report by the Abwehr officer, the following can be said: a burning interest for *Tirpitz*. The counterpart was well informed regarding single cases. From the questions, it is particularly obvious that the transmitter had exaggerated the damages after the raid on 3/4. The transmitter has primarily been operational as a weather station.[17]

However, Norwegian secret agents continued to transmit radio reports to the British on the *Tirpitz*'s status.

Further FAA attacks

Following the conclusion of Operation *Tungsten*, further air attacks against the *Tirpitz* were considered. However, despite that the Admiralty eagerly expected further carrier strikes, the First Sea Lord Bruce Fraser thought such raids were unnecessary. This was due to the Russian convoys having been temporarily suspended due to the threat of German U-boats. Furthermore it was considered that the Germans would be better prepared the next time around. Following intense discussions, preparations began for a follow-up raid codenamed Operation *Planet*. The raid was due to take place on 21 April; however, Operation *Planet* was cancelled at the last minute due to poor weather.[18]

After a month of intensive repairs (an additional 200 repair workers arrived from Germany in early May), *Tirpitz* was again ready for action. On 9 May, the huge Brown-Boveri turbines were successfully tested. The on-board radar coverage was supplemented with the addition of a FuMo 30 radar set with an anti-aircraft radar FuMo 213 (also known as Wurzburg) also being fitted. Yet again, the camouflage was changed into a splinter camouflage consisting of dark grey and light grey rays. During the following months, *Tirpitz* was repainted with one level above the shelter deck becoming dark grey, including the forward Anton and rear Dora main gun turrets, as well as the barbettes of the Bruno and Caesar main gun turrets. The upper levels of the superstructure were light grey. During the summer, the deck received patches of green paint camouflage. The final change of the camouflage colours occurred during the autumn of 1944 when the upper levels of the superstructure was repainted in an unknown colour.

Although Operation *Planet* had been cancelled, further raids were to follow. On more than one occasion, persistent poor weather, particularly low clouds, caused raids to be aborted, but it was clear that the Admiralty would continue to send its aircraft carriers against the *Tirpitz*. The chance to strike against the *Tirpitz* took place on 14 May when twenty-seven Barracudas and twenty-eight Corsairs were launched from HMS *Victorious* and HMS *Furious*, along with four Martlets and four Seafires. The raid was codenamed Operation *Brawn*. However, as *Tirpitz* was completely obscured by clouds as low as 1,000 feet, the strike force was forced to abort and return to the carriers. Incessant poor weather meant that a further raid, Operation *Tiger Claw*, planned for 28 May, was also cancelled.

Feeling the ground beneath him getting hotter with the Germans seeking out secret agents, Torstein Petersen, who operated the Ida radio transmitter, reported to his British superiors on 16 May that he was leaving for Sweden. By this time, the Germans were on the defensive on all fronts. Allied troops gathered along the southern coast of England to begin an invasion of Hitler's Fortress Europe. In the event, Operation *Overlord*, the Normandy landings on 6 June 1944, caused further raids on *Tirpitz* to be put on hold, but *Tirpitz*'s continued existence was still considered as a potential threat.[19] The lack of Allied attention saw the continuation and completion of repairs, and caused the battleship to get ever closer to operational readiness. As it was certain that the Allies would return to Kaa Fjord, flak defences were strengthened with additional artificial smoke generators mounted along the fjord and radar coverage was improved. *Tirpitz* made several trial runs along the fjord. The increased activity at Kaa Fjord was interpreted by the Admiralty as planning for a major operation. On 12 July, a reconnaissance Mosquito returned with photographs that showed *Tirpitz* at anchor on the western side of the fjord. However, it was not until five days later that the next attempt, Operation *Mascot*, took place.

The large FAA strike force consisted of forty-four Barracudas, eighteen Corsairs, eighteen Hellcats and twelve Fireflies, the latter making its operational debut. The British aircraft reached Kaa Fjord at 03.04 hours local time. With the Arctic midnight sun above the horizon, light was not an issue. However, in spite of scoring two hits (minor), the raid was considered a failure, much due to the recent installation of artificial smoke generators. It was subsequently estimated that the battleship could be completely covered in artificial smoke within ten minutes. In fact, German radar had spotted the British aircraft while several miles from Kaa Fjord. As a result, *Tirpitz* had been completely covered in artificial smoke when FAA crews arrived over the target and only two Barracuda crews caught a brief glimpse of the battleship. The smoke was a double-edged sword, however, as the German flak crews fired blindly through the smokescreen and attempting to aim their fire towards the sound of aircraft engines. The Barracudas circled the Beast for twenty-five minutes in a desperate bid to get a glimpse of *Tirpitz*. No bombs hit *Tirpitz* although there were several near misses. In all, the raid lasted for thirty-three minutes. According to the post-action report, *Tirpitz* was undamaged '… except for a barrel in a right-hand gun of starboard IV 105 mm gun mounting, damaged due to a premature detonation of a shell. One man was slightly injured. Observation from the deck showed four near misses on the starboard side and three on the port side of the ship. Five men in the forward 150 mm turrets suffering from smoke and gas poisoning.'[20]

It had been intended to launch a second wave of Barracudas. This was cancelled when fog and low clouds covered the aircraft carriers. During the sole raid to take place, only one Barracuda was lost with the pilot making a successful ditching alongside HMS *Formidable*.[21] During the raid, flak defences had fired off no less than 34,888 rounds that consisted of 38 cm main guns (thirty-nine rounds), 150 mm guns (359 rounds), 105 mm guns (1,973 rounds), 37 mm flak (3,967 rounds) and 20 mm flak (28,550 rounds). The post-raid report stated that: The failure of the attack was due to the fact that *Tirpitz* had fifteen minutes' warning which gave her sufficient time to man her guns, clear the ship for action, and put the various smokescreen apparatus into action. The weather conditions were particularly suitable for the use of smokescreen. The concentrated barrage from guns of all calibres screened the ship with such a success as to ward off the attacker, whose task was made more difficult by this smokescreen.[22]

A day after the 17 July raid, Corsair JT404 of 1841 Squadron had to make an emergency landing in a field near Bodø and its pilot, Lt Matthodie, was captured by the Germans. The Corsair was intact and the Germans attempted to get Matthodie to explain how the wing-folding mechanism worked in order to transport the fighter to Narvik for a detailed examination. The Corsair—the only one of its kind to be captured intact by the Germans—eventually found its way to Germany and was later reported as being held at Rechlin where many captured Allied aircraft were tested, and under repair. It is unclear if it was ever air-tested.

The failure of Operation *Mascot* only increased the Admiralty's determination to sink the Beast once and for all. With the *Tirpitz* a constant threat to the convoys and Home Fleet, more raids, codenamed Operation *Goodwood*, were planned for late August. The Russian-bound convoys were postponed until mid-August with the JW 59 convoy due to leave Scotland on the 15th of that month. As with previous operations, the large number of warships was to arrive north of the Norwegian coast, supposedly escorting the JW 59 convoy. The first of two separate raids were flown just before noon on 22 August. The raid had originally been set to take place on 21 August, but this had to be cancelled due to poor weather. The raid, Goodwood II, was a maximum effort with eighty-four aircraft, including thirty-one Barracudas, eleven Fireflies, eight Seafires, twenty-four Corsairs and nine Hellcats taking off from HMS *Formidable*, HMS *Indefatigable*, HMS *Trumpeter*, HMS *Furious* and HMS *Nabob*. As had happened before with Operation *Tungsten*, the FAA crews had honed their skills during mock attacks against Loch Eriboll where the location of *Tirpitz* and her various defences were continually upgraded through continuously updated aerial-reconnaissance photographs and intelligence reports. Also aboard the carriers were a number of Grumman Avengers. It had been intended that these would sow mines at the entrance to Kaa Fjord and the fjord; however, the Avengers were not launched due to the poor weather. With dense cloud at 1,500 feet, the Barracudas and twenty-four escorting Corsairs had to break off the attack and return to their respective carriers. Upon reaching Kaa Fjord, the Fireflies made the first of several flak-suppressing runs at 12.49 hours. Only a couple of minutes later, the Hellcats, carrying one 500 lb armour-piercing bomb each, attacked. No hits were scored with two aircraft being lost. The attack saw two of *Tirpitz*'s Ar 196 spotter floatplanes destroyed by the Seafires as were six Bv 138s and a He 115. (The Ar 196s were not aboard the battleship as they were moored nearby.) The airfields at Banak and Kolvika were also attacked as were several smaller ships, including the U-boat *U-965*.

The afternoon nuisance raid, Goodwood II, consisted of a mere six Hellcats and eight Fireflies, which did not damage the battleship at all. One sailor was killed and another ten injured when the British fighters made low-level strafing runs across the battleship. During the two raids, the flak defences aboard *Tirpitz* had fired off an astounding number of rounds (nearly 37,000) against the FAA aircraft, including seventy-five 38 cm grenades, 487 150 mm, around 2,050 105 mm, 3,140 37 mm and no less than 31,000 20 mm grenades.

Another attempt, Goodwood III, was made on 24 August. In all, eighty-five aircraft, including thirty-three Barracudas, twenty-four Corsairs, ten Hellcats, ten Fireflies and eight Seafires took off from the aircraft carriers HMS *Indefatigable* and HMS *Formidable*. Apart from the Barracuda bombers, five Corsairs carried one 1,000 lb bomb each with the Hellcats carrying one 500 lb bomb each. The large formation was discovered by the radar station at Alta that relayed information on the impending raid. Yet again, the artificial smoke generators began to cover the *Tirpitz* with smoke. Although one direct hit was scored, the battleship was only slightly damaged. A bomb dropped by the Hellcats hit the Bruno gun turret, causing slight damage, but also blew a 20 mm flak quadruple gun position into the water. Only one of the flak crew members survived with a broken arm. A couple of minutes later, the Barracudas and Corsairs arrived over Kaa Fjord. By this time, *Tirpitz* was completely engulfed in smoke, which forced the Barracudas to bomb blindly. However, fate intervened and a bomb dropped from a Barracuda from an altitude of between 4,000 and 5,000 feet managed to penetrate the armoured deck. The bomb passed through eight floors before ending up lodged just below the waterline. Had the bomb exploded, it would surely have caused substantial damage to the battleship; however, it was not to be. Following the delicate process of disarming the bomb, it was discovered that it contained only 45 kg of explosives against the normal 98 kg. The personnel losses were slight with eight sailors being killed, thirteen wounded with an additional five suffering from gas poisoning. Two aircraft were posted as missing during the 24 August raid, including a Hellcat flown by Lieutenant Commander Archibald Richardson. Having survived three attacks against the *Tirpitz*, attacks which were carried out with an extraordinary amount of bravery and lack of concern for one's own safety, it was proposed that Richardson should receive a posthumous Victoria

Cross. This was denied, however, although Richardson was Mentioned in Dispatches (MiD).

Royal Navy vessels had been spotted by a U-boat, *U-354*, which during the afternoon of 24 August, sank the frigate HMS *Bickerton* and damaged the aircraft carrier HMS *Nabob*. The aircraft carrier HMS *Trumpeter* and the remaining escort ships were subsequently ordered to escort HMS *Nabob* back to Scapa Flow. With the mine-carrying Avengers being aboard HMS *Nabob* and HMS *Trumpeter*, the mine-sowing operation at Kaa Fjord was cancelled. During the evening of 24 August, two Fireflies flew an armed photo-reconnaissance sortie over Kaa Fjord. The Fireflies were met by intense flak and artificial smoke: the Germans did not take any chances. However, the raids had seriously depleted their ammunition stocks. Apart from seventy-five 38 cm and 510 150 cm calibre grenades fired, only some 60 per cent of flak ammunition stocks remained. In his post-raid report, Kapitän zur See Junge stated:

> The attack on 24.8.44 was undoubtedly the heaviest and most determined so far experienced. The English showed great skill and dexterity in flying. For the first time they dived with heavy bombs. During the dive-bombing, fighter planes attacked the land flak batteries which, in comparison with earlier attacks, suffered heavy losses. The fact that the armour-piercing bomb of more than 1,540 pounds [sic] did not explode must be considered an exceptional stroke of luck, as the effects of that explosion would have been immeasurable. Even incomplete smoke-screening upsets the correctness of the enemy's aim, and it has been decided from now to use smoke in wind strengths up to 9 metres per second, irrespective of possible gaps. It has also been ordered that the time of notice for smoke (at present 10 minutes) is to be reduced to 7 minutes.[22]

The British Flotilla remained in the area for a further five days, with another raid, Goodwood IV, being conducted on 29 August. As with previous raids, it was a failure. The sixty-seven aircraft consisting of twenty-six Barracudas, seventeen Corsairs, ten Fireflies, seven Hellcats and seven Seafires, found the *Tirpitz* completely covered in artificial smoke and failed to score any hits. However, there were several near misses. Six sailors suffered injuries due to bomb shrapnel. One Corsair and a Firefly were shot down with the crews being killed. The raid further depleted the stocks of flak ammunition with only about 40 per cent remaining. During the Operation *Goodwood* raids, about 52 tons of bombs had been dropped with eight aircraft, including their crews, being lost. *Tirpitz* had barely been scratched.

The Fleet Air Arm raids against the Beast during the summer of 1944 were largely unsuccessful. Forty FAA aircrews had lost their lives with seventeen aircraft being either shot down or lost in crashes. During the raids, the Germans had fired off huge amounts of flak. Going by the rate of fire, another two raids would have seen the *Tirpitz* run out of ammunition. Also, the flak guns were in need of maintenance while some barrels needed to be replaced. Incidentally, it is of some significance that the Luftwaffe had failed to intercept the FAA raids. *Tirpitz* was highly vulnerable to air attacks and there was little or no co-operation between the Kriegsmarine and Luftwaffe. It seemed as if the huge battleship was left to fend for herself.

Despite the damage, the Beast was alive and retained her ability to breathe fire. With the Fleet Air Arm option for sinking the Beast at a dead end, Churchill turned to the Commander of RAF Bomber Command, Air Chief Marshal Arthur Harris. Some years after the end of the war, the historian Dennis Richards recalled an interview with Harris during which he reiterated his conversation with Churchill:

> Churchill: 'Harris, I want you to sink the *Tirpitz*.'
> Harris: 'Why bother, Prime Minister? She's not doing any harm where she is.'
> Churchill: 'I want you to sink the *Tirpitz*.'
> 'So,' added Sir Arthur, 'I sent the boys out and they sank the *Tirpitz*.'

In his memoirs published in 1947, Harris elaborated further on the issue. According to Harris, the British Home Fleet was kept in readiness at Scapa Flow just in case *Tirpitz* would sail into the Atlantic. If *Tirpitz* was sunk, most of the Home Fleet would be able to leave the European theatre of war and reinforce Allied forces in the Pacific against the Japanese. Harris stated that Bomber Command would sink *Tirpitz* if it did not drain too many resources away from the main offensive against German targets on the Continent. Indeed, Harris stated that Bomber Command would sink the Beast in its 'spare time'. RAF Bomber Command, which had flown five unsuccessful raids against *Tirpitz* during the winter and spring of 1942, would now be ready to bring about the final demise of the battleship. It may be argued that at this time, *Tirpitz* did not represent any real danger to the Allies and the Royal Navy enjoyed a complete naval supremacy in the Atlantic. Apart from *Tirpitz*, the remaining Kriegsmarine heavy surface warships had all sought refuge in the confined waters of the Baltic Sea. However, sinking the Beast, which for such a long time had haunted the minds of Churchill and the Joint Planning Staff, would represent a considerable propaganda coup. Also, with *Tirpitz* gone, not much would remain of the once mighty fleet of Kriegsmarine surface warships. Sinking *Tirpitz* would quite possibly shorten the war.

CHAPTER THREE

Operation *Paravane*[1]

Friday 15 September 1944

Even before the final Fleet Air Arm strike, the Joint Planning Staff had been discussing alternative ways of finally slaying the Beast. Even though *Tirpitz* had not been fully repaired following the damage sustained during Operation *Tungsten*, it was still believed that the battleship represented a threat to the Allied convoys. Additionally, *Tirpitz* could, if the German High Command decided upon such a high-risk venture, breakout into the Atlantic in a similar fashion to her ill-fated sister *Bismarck*. In case of such an event occurring, however unlikely, no effort would be spared to hunt down and sink the *Tirpitz*. This meant that considerable numbers of warships and aircraft would have to be diverted from other duties on all fronts.

The raids from the spring until late summer had failed to conclusively damage the Beast beyond repair. Assembling a task force, including aircraft carriers and escort warships, meant draining resources needed elsewhere. With *Tirpitz* at anchor within the confined Alta Fjord, the Fleet Air Arm's strike aircraft could not attack with torpedoes. Had *Tirpitz* deployed to the Atlantic, it would have been a different matter. But, with the battleship securely anchored at Kaa Fjord and covered by anti-torpedo nets, flak units and artificial smoke generators, *Tirpitz* represented a difficult target. Additionally, poor weather had hindered the execution of some of the raids. It was finally realised that the single-engine Fairey Barracuda was not the right aircraft for the job. The Barracuda simply did not have enough speed to surprise the German defenders and had a fairly meagre bomb-carrying capability. However, it should be noted that out of 176 Barracuda sorties during six air raids, 174 reached the *Tirpitz*. Two Barracudas were shot down by flak with another three being lost in accidents. Although slow and unable to carry the necessary bomb load, the FAA Barracuda squadrons fared comparatively well during the raids against the well protected battleship. Thus, the opinion held by Vice-Admiral Sir Henry Moore on the Barracuda's lack of capabilities was confirmed. Aircraft with a higher bomb-carrying capability would be needed to inflict permanent damage to the Beast and brief consideration was given to modifying the twin-engined de Havilland Mosquito for carrier operations. The Mosquito B. Mk IX had a maximum speed of 397 mph at an altitude of 26,000 feet and could carry 5,000 lb of bombs, including one 4,000 lb Cookie high-explosive bomb.

In the end it was decided against using Mosquitos for this operation.[2] Although the Mosquito had proved itself as a versatile and capable warplane, both in the fighter-bomber, night fighter and reconnaissance roles, it had not operated from aircraft carriers even though it had been carrier-qualified earlier in the year. The major factor was that RAF Mosquito squadrons were heavily involved in tactical operations against German forces on the European mainland. As a result, General Eisenhower thought that removing one or more Mosquito squadrons from operations over France was 'unjustifiable'.

Planning begins

On 23 August, the Joint Planning Staff delivered a report concluding that the Beast was 'still capable of performing limited operations'. It was noted that it was possible to transfer the *Tirpitz* to Germany where she would be repaired and returned to full operational status or alternatively German High Command might consider trying to sink as many Allied ships as possible by sending the *Tirpitz* on a desperate last ditch voyage.

Instead of persisting with attacks by FAA strike aircraft, a recommendation for using RAF four-engine heavy bombers was put forwards once more.

The RAF four-engine bombers

Since 1942, *Tirpitz* had been moved to Kaa Fjord in northern Norway, far out of range for UK-based RAF bombers, but in the intervening two-and-a-half years the range and overall capability of the bombers had also increased considerably. In the summer of 1944, the RAF had three different four-engine bombers in service: the Short Stirling, Handley Page Halifax and Avro Lancaster. Additionally, some RAF squadrons, particularly in Italy and India, were operating the American-built Consolidated B-24 Liberator heavy bomber. The Stirling had been largely withdrawn from frontline service, instead being utilised as a glider tug and transport. The Halifax was the workhorse of the RAF with no less than twenty-one squadrons equipping Bomber Command in August 1944 with several more squadrons serving with Coastal Command, Transport Command, special duties and meteorological squadrons. In addition, Halifaxes served with a wide variety of second-line and training squadrons, including Operational Conversion Units. The newest Halifax bomber variant, the B. Mk VI, had entered production in early 1944. The Halifax B.VI was powered by four 1,675 hp Bristol Hercules 100 radial engines, having a range of 1,260 miles with a maximum bomb load of 13,000 lb. One major drawback of the Halifax—apart from its lack of range regarding the distance involved between the UK and northern Norway—was that its bomb bay could not carry the new Tallboy high-explosive bomb. As a result, the Halifax was never a serious contender for the planned *Tirpitz* raids.

The evolution of the Avro Lancaster

The third and final four-engined bomber in RAF service was the Avro Lancaster. Early in the war, the Lancaster had been developed from the unsuccessful twin-engine Avro

Manchester. Although the Manchester was considered an operational failure, this was mainly due to the 1,845 hp Rolls-Royce Vulture engines which, among other things, were underpowered. Simply put, the Manchester could not stay aloft on one engine. The heavy losses of Manchesters caused members of 207 Squadron to bitterly joke that future squadron reunions would be held in German Stalags. However, it was realised that the basic Manchester airframe was of sound construction. Various options to increase the lacklustre performance of the Manchester were investigated, including fitting more reliable and powerful engines such as the 2,100 hp Napier Sabre or 2,520 hp Bristol Centaurus. With the lack of engine power output being one major drawback, plans were put forward to modify the bomber to carry four Rolls-Royce Merlin engines—a solution which had first been proposed back in September 1939. The Merlin-powered variant was to be designated as the Manchester Mk B. III. A standard production Manchester was subsequently converted by fitting a redesigned wing of greater span that could accommodate four 1,145 hp Merlin X inline engines. The tailplane was also enlarged, becoming 33 feet in span. The two outer fins and rudders were also enlarged with the centre fin being disposed of. The end result of the conversion process was a four-engine bomber similar in appearance to the original Manchester albeit slightly larger. The name Manchester was dropped with the modified aeroplane renamed as the Avro Lancaster making its maiden flight on 9 January 1941. Flight testing and operational evaluation continued until late 1941 with the first production Lancaster delivered to 44 Squadron. During the following months, intensive operational training and familiarisation with the new bomber took place. As described earlier, *Tirpitz* could well have been the target for the first operational raid using Lancasters. On 25 January 1942, 44 Squadron was ordered to raid the German battleship that had only days before arrived in Norway, but plans were changed and the squadron did not participate in the first raid on 29 January. Operations with the new bomber did not begin until 3 March 1942 when mines were sown off Heligoland during a 'gardening' operation.

Lancaster participation in previous raids on the Beast

Three days after the initial Lancaster sortie into enemy territory, on 6 March 1942, 44 Squadron was ordered to stand by for a secret and highly dangerous operation. On 8 March, eight Lancasters were flown north from Waddington to Lossiemouth. The mission was to bomb *Tirpitz*. However, the raid was cancelled. Of the remaining 44 Squadron Lancasters, two took part in a bombing raid on 10 March against the industrial city of Essen. This attack marked the first time that Lancasters were used operationally for regular bombing. One solitary 44 Squadron Lancaster took part in the 30–31 March raid. However, *Tirpitz* was not destined to be the target as the Lancaster crew was ordered to make a diversionary raid against the Luftwaffe airbase at Værnes. Both 44 and 97 Squadron (the latter being the second RAF squadron to re-equip with the Lancaster) took part in the two final 1942 raids against *Tirpitz* on 27–28 and 28–29 April. One 97 Squadron Lancaster, L7572, was lost on the first of these raids and the crew of seven was killed.

RAF Lancaster operations

By the summer of 1944, the Lancaster was well and truly established as the mainstay of Bomber Command. No less than forty squadrons were operating Lancasters in the night bombing role with additional second-line squadrons, including Operational Conversion Units. To the British public, the Lancaster appeared to be the only RAF bomber serving in Bomber Command as seen in propaganda films and mentioned in countless newspaper articles. From its introduction into service in early 1942 until the end of the war, Lancasters dropped 608,612 tons of ordnance against Axis targets or two thirds of all bombs dropped by Bomber Command from early 1942 until 1945. Lancaster squadrons attacked numerous important targets, including Berlin, V1 sites and U-boat pens. Demand for Lancasters was so high that in addition to A. V. Roe, Armstrong Whitworth, Austin Motors, Metropolitan-Vickers and Vickers-Armstrong also built the bombers, and a Canadian production line was established. Between 1941 and 1946, 7,377 Lancasters were built. Out of these, about 3,300 were lost on operations and in accidents during the war.

Range issues

Air Chief Marshal Arthur Harris clearly indicated that Bomber Command was more than capable of sinking the *Tirpitz*. According to Harris, two squadrons with a total of twenty-four bombers could be made ready within ten days, which meant that any raid against the Beast could be conducted on 7 September at the earliest. Withdrawing two squadrons from regular operations would mean a slight and temporary decrease in Bomber Command's strength in the night-time raids against German cities and industrial areas as well as the daily support raids of the Allied invasion forces in France and the Low Countries. Therefore, *Tirpitz* was seen as a one-off target, a mere sideshow to the strategic bombing campaign against Nazi Germany.

However, the Joint Planning Staff deemed that the use of four-engine bombers was the only available option to finally sink *Tirpitz*. Air Vice-Marshal R. A. Cochrane, RAF, was given the task of planning such an attack. In his classic book *Dam Busters*, author Paul Brickhill gives the story that Cochrane decided to use the services of 617 Squadron to sink *Tirpitz* when he was taking a bath. Having decided that it would be possible to sink the Beast, Cochrane subsequently asked 'Bomber' Harris for permission to go ahead with the raid. Some of IX(B) and 617 Squadron's aircrews thought that Cochrane had made repeated requests to Harris that 5 Group would be able to finish off *Tirpitz*. The battleship was a high-priority target with the accompanying prestige if the mission was accomplished.

One major headache was that *Tirpitz* was anchored at Kaa Fjord, just out of reach for UK-based bombers. If the bombers were to take off from an airbase in Great Britain, they would not have enough fuel for the return flight. It is unclear if the idea of a one-way raid, similar to the one proposed in early 1942, was discussed. In theory the Lancasters could have landed in neutral Sweden after the bombing raid, but if this was ever discussed is not known and it remains unlikely. The average range of the Avro Lancaster was 1,730 miles with a six-ton bomb load. With a full bomb load, the Lancasters could carry 2,154 gallons of fuel with an additional 250 gallons of extra fuel in a fuselage tank. In order to provide definite proof that it was impossible to reach the Beast and make a return flight, three Lancasters, fully loaded with fuel and bombs, were dispatched on a long distance flight, equivalent to the distance of Scotland to Alten Fjord. Another three Lancasters flew the same distance with half a load of fuel and no bombs. This practical test showed beyond doubt that *Tirpitz* was indeed out of range. It was simply not possible to reach her from UK bases and this problem had to be resolved.

Russian deployment

One possibility was to bomb the Beast from temporary bases in Russia. With the approval from Soviet authorities, which was quickly forthcoming, RAF bombers were to be based at Yagodnik, a small airfield on an island in the River Dvina, some 20 km south of Archangel. Although primitive by RAF standards, the airfield at Yagodnik had been built on very sandy soil, which removed the risk of water logging for its sole grass runway. Yagodnik was also large enough to accommodate the forty or so Lancasters deemed necessary for the job. The greatest advantage of operating out of the Russian airfield was that the distance involved in reaching *Tirpitz* was reduced considerably. Support equipment, fuel and accommodation, including food and lodging, were to be made available to the RAF detachment by the Russians. Also, since 1942, the strength of the Luftwaffe had been seriously depleted, both in experienced pilots and aircraft. As a result, the risk of the Luftwaffe venturing an air raid against Yagodnik was not great. The Soviet air arm had been considerably strengthened with the fighter and ground-attack elements being substantially strengthened compared with 1942–1943 levels.

IX(B) Squadron

By late August, the Joint Planning Staff finalised its decision. Two of the RAF's premier heavy bomber squadrons, Nos IX(B) and 617, were assigned the job of sinking the *Tirpitz*. These squadrons were considered to be the cream of the crop within RAF Bomber Command. The background histories of IX(B) and 617 Squadrons could not have been more different, however. IX(B) Squadron had been formed on 8 December 1914 at St Omer, France, from the nucleus of the Royal Flying Corps Wireless Flight. Initially known as No. 9 (Wireless) Squadron, its main operational duty became army co-operation. Initially, BE 2c two-seater biplanes were used with RE 8s arriving in 1917. Both aeroplanes were slow and lumbering two-seat biplanes which could not match the German Albatros and Fokker fighters of the day. Early in the war, the losses of BE 2cs were so high that they were referred to as 'Fokker fodder' and as a result, losses in aircrews and aircraft were high. Upon formation of the Royal Air Force on 1 April 1918, IX Squadron was based at Proven, Belgium.

Following the end of the war, IX Squadron became part of the British Army on the Rhine, which served as a force of occupation of Germany. However, RAF cutbacks in the immediate post-war era meant that many squadrons were disbanded, IX Squadron being disbanded on 31 December 1919 at Castle Bromwich. In the event, the squadron was reformed at Upavon on 1 April 1924 as a heavy bomber squadron, its designation amended to IX(B) Squadron. The Vickers Vimy was the first type of bomber received. In early 1925, the Vimys were replaced by Vickers Virginias. The Virginia's remained in service with IX(B) Squadron until March 1936 when the first Handley Page Heyfords arrived. The Heyford 'express bomber'—named by Handley Page due to the high speed of the Heyford as well as the short amount of turnaround time needed between sorties—was of unique configuration. The fuselage of the biplane Heyford was attached to the underside of the upper wing, which gave its crew an unobstructed forward and upper view. During the 1938 Munich Crisis, IX(B) Squadron was put on readiness in case of war between Britain and Germany. The first monoplane bomber of IX(B) Squadron was the twin-engine Vickers Wellington that finally replaced the lumbering Heyfords in February 1939.

The first sortie following the outbreak of war for IX(B) Squadron took place on 4 September 1939 when Kriegsmarine warships off Brunsbüttel were hit by six Wellingtons and two bombers failed to return. By this time, IX(B) Squadron was based at Honington. The first Lancasters arrived during the summer of 1942 with the first raid with the new four-engine aircraft flown against Düsseldorf during the night of 10–11 September 1942. On 17 August 1943, IX(B) Squadron took part in a highly significant raid against Peenemünde on the German Baltic Sea coast. At Peenemünde, design and test work was conducted on the FZG-76 and Aggregat 4 secret weapons, better known as the V1 and V2 rockets respectively. By the summer of 1944, large numbers of both the V1 flying bomb and V2 rockets were fired against Britain from heavily defended sites along the French coast.

Between April 1943 and July 1945, IX(B) Squadron was based at Bardney in Lincolnshire. IX(B) Squadron was considered to be the premier bombing squadron of the RAF and its motto was *Per noctem volamus* ('Throughout the night we fly'). There was also a highly unofficial motto: 'There's always bloody something.'

617 Squadron

617 Squadron had been formed at Scampton on 24 March 1943 by re-designating C Flight of 106 Squadron. 617 Squadron was formed for one highly dangerous raid, codenamed Operation *Chastise*. Led by Sqn Ldr Guy Gibson—who had accumulated much operational experience as a night fighter and bomber pilot earlier in the war—was able to handpick crews for the forthcoming raid. The target for Operation *Chastise* was to destroy three large dams, Eder, Möhne and Sorpe, which provided the majority of the electrical power and water for the heavily industrialised Ruhr area. (The Ruhr area was known to the aircrews of Bomber Command as 'Happy Valley', a sarcastic comment on its large quantities of flak defences.)

Operation *Chastise*, executed during the night of 16–17 May 1943, saw the Eder and Möhne dams breached using the rotating mines developed by Barnes Wallis.³ The Sorpe dam was damaged as was a fourth dam, Schwelme, although neither was breached. As a result of the success of the highly dangerous raid, 617 Squadron subsequently earned the name 'Dambusters'. Its squadron motto was the aptly chosen *Aprés moi, le deluge* ('After me, the flood'). The casualty rate was high. Of the nineteen Lancasters that participated in the raid, eight were lost. Only days after the successful raid, Gibson was awarded with the Victoria Cross. On 28 May, The *London Gazette* wrote:

> This officer served as a night bomber pilot at the beginning of the war and quickly established a reputation as an outstanding operational pilot. In addition to taking the fullest possible share in all normal operations, he made single-handed attacks during his 'rest' nights on such highly defended objectives as the German battleship *Tirpitz*, then completing in Wilhelmshaven. … On conclusion of his third operational tour, Wing Commander Gibson pressed strongly to be allowed to remain on operations and he was selected to command a squadron then forming for special tasks. Under his inspiring leadership, this squadron has now executed one of the most devastating attacks of the war—the breaching of the Mohne and Eder dams. … Wing Commander Gibson has completed 170 sorties involving more than 600 hours' operational flying. Throughout his operational career, prolonged exceptionally at his own request, he has shown leadership, determination and valour of the highest order.

Guy Gibson would eventually lose his life in September 1944 when his Mosquito crashed in the Netherlands.

Much has been written about the success of Operation *Chastise*, but in its wake, 617 Squadron became the RAF's most highly publicised squadron. It became involved in specialised bombing operations such as a raid on Dortmund–Ems Canal on 15–16 September 1943 and Operation *Taxable*, a diversion sortie in anticipation of the Allied invasion of France on 6 June 1944. By this time, 617 Squadron was commanded by Wing Commander Leonard Cheshire. Undertaking his first operational sortie in June 1940, Cheshire went on to make four tours and flew more than 100 sorties. Having completed his third tour in October 1943, Cheshire relinquished his rank of Group Captain in order to qualify for a fourth tour. Having completed 100 sorties, Cheshire was taken off operations.

In July 1944, Cheshire was awarded the Victoria Cross. Although most of the recipients of the Victoria Cross were awarded for actions during a single sortie, Cheshire was awarded the medal for his 'courage and determination of an exceptional leader' (also, an April 1944 raid against Munich was singled out in the *London Gazette* on 4 September 1944). It was the Commander of 5 Group, Air Vice-Marshal Ralph Cochrane, who recommended Cheshire for the Victoria Cross. Cheshire was eventually replaced as Commander of 617 Squadron by James Brian 'Willie' Tait DSO and Bar, DFC, on 12 July 1944. Tait was a highly accomplished bomber pilot having previously served with 51, 35, 10 and 78 Squadrons and completed more than 100 operational sorties before joining 617 Squadron.

463 Squadron

Apart from the two heavy bomber squadrons, a single Lancaster detached from 463 Squadron would also fly to Russia. 463 Squadron (Royal Australian Air Force, RAAF) was formed at Waddington, Lincolnshire, on 25 November 1943 from C Flight of 467 Squadron. The squadron's motto was 'Press on regardless'.

Although a regular bomber squadron, the RAF Film Unit was attached to 463 Squadron. Two Lancasters, DV171 and LM587, had been modified to carry a film camera and operator. As no bombs would be carried, the fuel load could be increased to 2,954 gallons so that a return flight to the UK could be achieved. A film unit was essential to document the demise of the *Tirpitz* and the filming of the sinking would be definite proof that the seemingly indestructible warship had once and for all been destroyed. Apart from losing their greatest warship, Germany would also suffer a huge propaganda loss. Therefore, having a Lancaster of the RAF Film Unit accompany the raid was considered essential. Apart from the film camera, a reporter from the Press Association would also be on board and the resulting film would, it was hoped, show the final moments of *Tirpitz*. The sinking of *Tirpitz* would also mean the final nail in the coffin for the Kriegsmarine's surface warship operational activities. The remaining warships represented little threat to the Allies and these would be picked off one by one.

A new and heavier bomb

The 1,600 lb armour-piercing bomb carried by the FAA Barracudas had proved to be inadequate of penetrating the thick armour hull of the *Tirpitz*. It appeared as if these bombs were a mere nuisance to the Germans, not doing any serious damage at all to the Beast. As a result considerable effort went into developing a bomb that could penetrate the thick armour deck of the battleship. Mines had been attempted during the 1942 raids with less than resounding success. The answer lay with the Tallboy heavy bomb. Designed by the brilliant engineer and inventor Barnes Wallis, the Tallboy weighed 12,000 lb, 5,200 lb of which consisted of Torpex high explosive and was some 50 per cent more efficient than TNT. The four small fins, inclined by 5 degrees and fitted to the rear section of the aerodynamically-shaped Tallboy, would initiate a rotational movement around the bomb's vertical axis when dropped. The rotational movement would increase the possibility of the Tallboy to penetrate targets protected by armour or thick concrete. Built out of high-quality steel with a special hardened nosecone, the Tallboy could penetrate the ground or thick armour of a target before exploding. The detonation would then create an earthquake-like effect. In fact, the subsequent shockwave was more destructive than the initial blast. When dropped from an altitude of 18,000 feet, the Tallboy would strike the ground thirty-seven seconds later. When striking the target, the Tallboy had reached a velocity speed of 750 mph and was able to penetrate thick armour or concrete submarine pens. The only RAF bomber capable of carrying the Tallboy was the four-engine Avro Lancaster and in order to carry the heavy Tallboy, the internal bomb-bay bomb shackles had to be strengthened.

By the end of 1943, 325 Tallboy heavy bombs had been ordered by the Air Ministry. Out of these, 125 were to be produced under licence in the United States. The first of the highly secret bombs were delivered to 617 Squadron during early June 1944 and the squadron was not immediately informed about the arrival of the new bomb. After spotting a large flatbed truck with a huge load covered with tarpaulins on the tarmac at Woodhall Spa, Leonard Cheshire and Les Munro decided to investigate. When asked about the load, the driver stated that he was delivering new geysers to the kitchen. This seemed rather strange as the kitchen was not located near the tarmac and driving to the kitchen did not involve passing the runway. Loosening the tarpaulin somewhat, Cheshire discovered the geysers were huge bombs. Both Cheshire and Munro were taken aback by this discovery. Escorting the lorry to the bomb store, Cheshire and Munro discovered to their amazement that the place was brimming with Tallboy bombs. Scurrying back to the office, Cheshire called Cochrane saying he had 'just inspected the new kitchen geysers'. Cochrane drily replied that 617 Squadron would be using the new explosive devices on operations and this took place later the same month.

In all, 854 Tallboys were dropped in 1944–1945 against various targets, including submarine pens, V-weapon sites, bridges and shipping. If a Tallboy could not be released over the target, the crew was under strict orders to bring the valuable bomb back to base. As related later, this order was to thoroughly test the tenacity of the crews of IX(B) and 617 Squadrons.

During the final months of the war, an even larger high capacity bomb named Grand Slam was brought into use. Also designed by Barnes Wallis, the Grand Slam weighed 22,000 lb and was first used on operations in February 1945. When the war ended, forty Grand Slam bombs had been dropped against heavily protected and high value targets such as U-boat pens and railway tunnels.

The first time the Tallboy was used on operations was during the night of 8–9 June 1944 when the railway tunnel at Saumur in the Loire Valley was destroyed by 617 Squadron. The intention was to cut off the possibility of having the Germans send reinforcements against the Allied invasion force. The raid took place only a couple of days after Cheshire and Munro's accidental discovery of the bombs.

Although the Tallboy had not been specifically designed for use against surface warships, it was decided that using this type of bomb the RAF would stand a better chance of damaging the *Tirpitz*. Indeed, the forthcoming raid would be the first time that the Tallboy was to see use against a surface warship and would provide an excellent opportunity to test the Tallboy's efficiency against naval targets.

Hitting pinpoint targets from high altitude was a big problem. To eradicate this issue, a new bombsight had to be developed and the answer lay in the Stabilised Automatic Bombsight (SABS). Prior to dropping the bomb, the bomb aimer received information by the navigator regarding speed, altitude and wind deviation. The bomb aimer then instructed the pilot towards the target. The SABS might be referred to as a primitive bombing computer. In the event, the SABS bombsight was fitted to the Lancasters of 617 Squadron but the bombers of IX(B) Squadron retained the older but nevertheless efficient Mk XIV bombsight. When carrying the heavy Tallboy bombs to *Tirpitz*'s lair, it was obvious that the RAF bombers could not make a round trip flight from the UK. Having released the bombs over the target, the Lancasters would continue to Russia before refuelling and returning home.

'Johnnie Walker' aerial mines

The use of mines against the *Tirpitz* had not been ruled out. Apart from the Tallboy, the 500 lb JW ('Johnnie Walker') walking mine would also be carried by some Lancasters and were dropped by parachute. If it hit the water surrounding the Beast, the mine would sink to the bottom of the fjord before ascending towards the surface. It was hoped that the mine would then hit the under surfaces of the *Tirpitz* and the explosion would raise the hull out of the water with additional damage caused when the warship dropped back into the fjord. A dozen such mines could be carried in the bomb bay of the Lancaster. Despite the high hopes for the JW mines, the aircrews did not consider them to be an effective weapon. A pilot of 617 Squadron, Tony Iveson, later referred to using the mines against the *Tirpitz* as 'stupid'. Operation *Paravane*, however, would see the first operational use of the 'Johnnie Walker' mine. An interesting aspect of the 'Johnnie Walker' mine was that if it remained unexploded one hour after being dropped, it would self-destruct, thus depriving the Germans the opportunity of examining and evaluating a new British weapon. The lesson had been learned from the previous RAF use of mines against the *Tirpitz*.

Time running out

With winter fast approaching, the weather was deteriorating with fine, clear skies becoming less frequent. This meant that Operation *Paravane* would have to be initiated as soon as possible. Carrying out a bombing raid during the winter months meant no sunlight with natural daylight being reduced to between five and six hours—or less. Hitting a stationary target, which *Tirpitz* had become at dusk or night was, even with the SABS bombsight, far more difficult than during daylight. Also, the military situation on the Arctic Front was rapidly changing. On 4 September 1944, Finland had signed a peace treaty with the Soviet Union. As a result, German forces were ordered to withdraw from Finnish territory. By early October, Finnish and German forces had become engaged in a bloody and drawn-out conflict. With Germany on the retreat northwards into Norway, the frontline moved closer to the *Tirpitz*.

Operation *Paravane* goes ahead

Initial plans called for the Lancasters of IX(B) and 617 Squadrons to take off from RAF Lossiemouth, bomb the *Tirpitz* and continue to Archangel from where further raids could be mounted. Such shuttle missions had been flown before in 1943–1944 when USAAF B-17 Flying Fortress Bomb Groups based in Italy, after bombing German targets, had continued to temporary bases in the Ukraine. Such raids, codenamed Operation *Frantic*, would eventually be terminated during the summer of 1944.

In early September, the Air Ministry asked for a flight plan for Operation *Paravane*. With Lancaster bombers heading for the *Tirpitz*, the Russians offered to deploy strike aircraft to make diversionary attacks against Luftwaffe airfields. Flying such diversionary raids was cancelled at the request of the RAF as these would increase the risk of the Germans initiating the artificial smokescreen. If this happened, the *Tirpitz* would be entirely covered by smoke before British bombers had arrived over the target area.

The flight plan called for the RAF bombers to take off from Lossiemouth, pass north of the Shetlands and then continue to a point off Trondheim at 65 00N 06 00E. From there, they were to continue on an east-north-east heading to 65 60N 16 30E and then continue northwards to Kaa Fjord and to the *Tirpitz*. Following the raid, the Lancasters were to continue to Yagodnik where they were to land and refuel before returning to Britain. One problem was with the map on which the course was plotted. This map lacked national boundaries, thus making it very difficult to establish if they were flying over Norway or neutral Sweden.[4]

Preparations for the raid continued unabated. According to IX(B) Squadron's ORB, the first ten days of September was spent in 'practice bombing and wind-finding' exercises. On 9 and 10 September, practice bombing was conducted at Epperstone in Nottinghamshire and Wainfleet in Lincolnshire.

The plan to fly to Russia after bombing the *Tirpitz* was abandoned in the early hours of 11 September. Instead the sequence was switched around and the bombers would fly to Russia through Norwegian, Swedish and Finnish airspace. The RAF detachment to Yagodnik would then remain there until an air raid against the Beast could be mounted. After the conclusion of the raid, both IX(B) and 617 Squadrons would return straight to home. The weather forecast for the long ferry flight spoke of good and clear conditions, both over the North Sea and Russia. The Russian beam stations were said to be operational, which meant that navigation would be eased considerably. As a result, few problems were expected during the ferry flight to Yagodnik. A Mosquito reconnaissance aircraft had been dispatched to Yagodnik ahead of the Lancasters and was to provide accurate weather forecasts over northern Norway.

The plan to fly directly to Russia did not make much difference to the crews. Anticipation for the task ahead was high and morale among the aircrews was excellent with both squadrons having established an excellent record of bombing accuracy during earlier raids against high-value targets. *Tirpitz* would not, it was generally believed, pose any great problems. The take-off for IX(B) Squadron from Bardney was planned for around 17.00 GMT+1 on 11 September, which meant that the Lancasters would cross the North Sea and Norway, Sweden and Finland during the afternoon before arriving in Russia the following day.

Taking off for Russia

The eighteen Lancasters of IX(B) Squadron—twelve with Tallboys and six with 'Johnnie Walker' mines—took off from RAF Bardney in Lincolnshire between 16.59 and 17.26

hours along with the Film Unit Lancaster of 463 Squadron. The latter carried no bombs or mines, but in addition to the regular crew, Guy Byams of the BBC and W. E. West of the Press Association (both attached to the Film Production Unit) were aboard the bomber to document the demise of the Beast along with three cameramen: Fg Off. Eric Giersch, Fg Off. Loftus and Plt Off. Kimberley.

Shortly after take-off, the crew of one IX(B) Squadron Lancaster, piloted by Fg Off. Lake (coded WS-R), discovered to their horror that the Tallboy had come adrift from its mounts. There was no way to secure the heavy bomb and if the Tallboy exploded, the resulting detonation would blow both the Lancaster and its crew to smithereens. However, as an emergency measure, the Tallboy was released into the North Sea with the crew forced to return to Bardney. As events would unfold, this was not the only IX(B) Squadron aircrew that would find itself unable to participate in the forthcoming raid against the *Tirpitz*.

The first of twenty Lancasters of 617 Squadron to leave RAF Lossiemouth's runway at 18.56 hours was flown by Flt Lt Pryor. The final 617 Squadron bomber to take-off was flown by Flt Lt Levy (PB416) at 19.42 hours. The different take-off schedules for IX(B) and 617 Squadrons—from Bardney and Lossiemouth respectively—was due to an attempt for both squadrons to make simultaneous arrivals at Yagodnik.

Being about one ton overweight, the Lancasters struggled to get airborne. The flight across the North Sea was uneventful with radio silence being imposed. Although German defences had been alerted through radar, all of the aircraft made it safely across Norwegian airspace.

Apart from the Lancasters, two Liberator transports of 511 Squadron, based at RAF Lyneham in Wiltshire—carrying ground crew and spares, including a Merlin engine and large quantities of tinned food—were also part of the Operation *Paravane* force. The pair of Liberators was flown to Bardney on 7 September. The story of 511 Squadron's involvement in Operation *Paravane* has a couple of interesting twists. Not being told of their destination and with their ordinary job consisting of airmail deliveries to RAF stations across the Middle East and India, being ordered to take part in a secret operation would surely involve hotter climes. As a result, the Liberator crews, commanded by Flight Lieutenants Adams and Capsey, brought along their regular tropical kit. A message to send winter clothes was subsequently dispatched to Lyneham.

Over neutral and enemy territory

Few problems were expected during the flight across Sweden and the area was vast with little in the way of aerial defences. The Swedish aerial warning posts along the border with Norway subsequently reported that:

> …between 23.53 hours and 01.39 hours on 11–12 September, about 20 aircraft were noted in the Frostviken—Saxnäs area, some 20 aircraft at Överuman and some 30 aircraft in the Överuman—Saxnäs area. The course was mainly easterly. The aircraft were observed flying at altitudes between 2,000 and 5,000 metres.

The reports were, apart from single instances, based on the sound of engines and/or light emanating from the aircraft. Anti-aircraft artillery units at Boden and Luleå fired upon the Lancasters. The crew of Lancaster, LM713, reported that:

> We crossed Norway without mishap, but the Swedes decided to put on a little show for us. They fired shells off in all directions, some coming quite close.[5]

Nevertheless, the anti-aircraft fire was inaccurate with none of the British bombers being hit. The Lancasters left Swedish airspace between 00.43 and 02.19 hours in a wide area from Robertsfors in the south to Luleå in the north. A single Lancaster was heard passing over Karungi, even further north. With the aircraft flying close to the Arctic Circle, the magnetic compasses reportedly began to have a mind of their own. Instead, navigation was down to using a sextant to pinpoint the heading for Yagodnik.

With the lack of a blackout, the crews were able to observe lit-up villages that made navigation less of a problem. The Västerbotten and Norrbotten provinces, in the far north of Sweden through which airspace the British bombers passed, was 154,345 km² large—roughly about a third of the Swedish land area—or nearly twice as large as Scotland's land area of 78,775 km². The Flygvapnet—the Swedish Air Force—presence in the northern part of the country was meagre. The sole permanent unit in the area, Wing F 21 at Luleå-Kallax, had less than fifteen obsolete aircraft on strength, including two Hawker Harts, two Hawker Ospreys, one Beech 18R aerial ambulance as well as a number of training aircraft. The most modern aircraft available were three Northrop 8A-1s which arrived during the autumn of 1944, but fighter and bomber squadrons based in southern Sweden made regular deployments.

From October 1944, a squadron of Republic EP-106 fighters (designated J 9) was based at Kalixfors airfield near Kiruna. This was due to the increased number of refugees, both Norwegian and prisoners of war of various nationalities, making the arduous trek across the border from Norway. Additionally, with the Germans retreating from Finland and the Russian Army initiating an offensive against northern Norway, it was made necessary to keep track of the warring parties. For several years, the military situation in the Arctic had been fairly static; but this was to rapidly change.

Apart from the J 9s, a squadron of FFVS J 22 fighters would also be intermittently based at Kalixfors. A number of temporary airfields were also built to accommodate Flygvapnet aircraft, but these had no permanent units based at them. No radar coverage existed in this area until November 1944 when the first British-made ER IIIb radar was installed at Wing F 21. In fact, a chain of six radar stations would be installed in the north of Sweden in the following months and assisted by British technical instructors. Instead, a large number of observation posts were established which relayed information by telephone to a central air defence central. A small number of anti-aircraft guns were available, being mostly based in the cities and along the border with Finland. However, it would be fair to say that Swedish air defence in the area was, until late 1944, virtually non-existent.

Northern Finland was a different matter. Here, heavy and accurate flak was directed against the RAF bombers. One 617 Squadron Lancaster, NF920, had both of its ailerons damaged, a radio antenna was shot away and the fuselage was hit. The flak guns probably belonged to the German Army or Luftwaffe units. The tail gunner responded in kind, spraying a small building with machine-gun fire. Flg Off Gerald A. Witherick then spotted a sole occupant evacuating the building with some haste, his trousers down by the ankles.

Only the previous week on 4 September, Finland had signed a truce with the Soviet Union and war operations ceased at 07.00 hours. Great Britain, which had declared war on Finland on 6 December 1941, was also included in the truce as was the United States. Two weeks later, the truce was confirmed when an armistice was signed in Moscow. More than 200,000 German troops were still based in Finland. In northern Finland, the 20th Mountain Army remained and was supported by some 200 Luftwaffe aircraft, including fighters and Ju 87 Stuka dive bombers. According to the truce, remaining German forces in Finland were to be evicted from the country by 15 September. This deadline represented a logistical nightmare for the German High Command. Organising and completing the retreat of 200,000 troops and vehicles (including some 60,000 horses) within less than two weeks was almost impossible. The German General in command, Lothar Rendulic, fervently hoped that the Finns would reject the harsh and unrealistic Soviet terms. This was not to be.

With German forces still present in large numbers in northern Finland, Finnish forces began operations against the Germans in early October, slowly driving them northwards. Although most Germans had been pushed out of Finland by January 1945, it was not until 27 April—less than two weeks before the war ended—that the final German forces left Finnish soil.

Problems ahead

When the Lancasters crossed into Russian airspace, increasingly poor weather was encountered with a low cloud base reducing visibility to 1,500 feet. Reducing their altitude to as low as 100 feet, the Lancaster crews pressed ahead, the bombers hugging the ground. Only small-scale inadequate and inaccurate maps of the area were available to the RAF aircrews. With northern Finland and Russia being sparsely populated, the landscape beneath the bombers appeared to consist of seemingly endless forests occasionally broken up by rivers or lakes. There were few landmarks available to ease the job of the navigators. Further problems occurred when the wireless operators failed to contact ground control at Yagodnik. The RAF wireless operators dispatched Morse code messages in English using the Latin alphabet. The call sign was 8WP that was correctly translated from Russian into English as 8BP. However, even if the call sign was correct regarding numeric and alphabet translation, it was not the same for Morse code transmissions. This simple misunderstanding made communication considerably more difficult. The knowledge of Russian was limited among the RAF wireless operators while the Russians lacked a working understanding of English. As a result, the increasingly desperate Morse code messages sent from the Lancasters went unanswered. Quite possibly, the Russians could not make any sense out of what to them must have appeared as garbled, unintelligible transmissions. It is unclear if the Russian ground control at Yagodnik made any efforts to establish radio or telegraphic contact with the RAF bombers on different frequencies. The weather, and in particular the inoperable beam stations as well as the lack of radio or telegraphic contact, made the ferry flight far more difficult than it should have been. Out of the thirty-nine Lancasters that had set out from Scotland, only twenty-three arrived safely at Yagodnik. One IX(B) Squadron Lancaster had to abandon the flight early on and safely returned to Bardney. The remaining Lancasters had been forced to land where possible.

Forced landings

617 Squadron Lancaster NF920 that had been damaged by flak over Finland did arrive at Yagodnik, but could not be repaired in time for the raid. The dozen 'Johnnie Walker' mines carried by NF920 were subsequently removed and loaded onto another Lancaster, ME554, instead. One IX(B) Squadron Lancaster flown by Fg Off. Adams also arrived at Yagodnik in a damaged state. While approaching the coast of Norway, the outer starboard engine developed a coolant leak and Adams feathered the propeller. Although it would have been possible to return to Britain, Adams and his crew decided to press on towards Yagodnik. Due to the poor weather, Adams had to fly at 300 feet for two hours before making a safe landing. Releasing the Tallboy to reduce weight was never considered by Adams and his crew. The damaged Merlin engine of Adams' Lancaster was beyond local repair and had to be replaced. The damaged Merlin engine was removed and replaced with the spare engine carried in the cargo hold of one of the Liberators; however, there were no cranes or lifting gear available. Instead, the ground crews built a ramp and simple A-frame out of trees. Changing the heavy engines was arduous work. In spite of the valiant efforts by the ground crews, the Lancaster was not ready by 15 September and thus unable to take part in the raid. Adams and his crew received some consolation by being singled out in a report prepared after the raid that stated:

> It is most regrettable that (Lancaster coded WS-) 'W' (Fg Off. Adams) could not be made ready for the operation as this Captain and crew, in spite of great difficulties, made every effort to take part in the operation and it is considered that their effort is worthy of record here.

The other fifteen Lancasters were spread across a vast area, having come down in several different places. Five landed at Kegostrov, two near Vaskova, another two near the city of Onega, with the others landing at Chubalo-Navolsk, Belomorsk, Molotovsk and Talagi. Four IX(B) Squadron Lancasters, LL884, NF938, NF985 and PD211, were damaged beyond repair in forced landings as were two 617 Squadron bombers, EE131 and ME559. It may be considered a miracle that no one had been killed. Locating the Lancasters and aircrews was achieved with amazing speed with everyone accounted for within three hours. One of the Russian pathfinders quickly located one RAF crew and bomber, but then got lost when he was leading the fliers back to civilisation. They were not found until twenty-four hours later.

Running low on fuel, Fg Off. Camsell of IX(B) Squadron set down his four-engine bomber at Belomorsk. Although both starboard engines stopped during the landing run, Camsell managed to get the Lancaster down in one piece; however, Lancaster, PD211, was so badly damaged it could not be repaired. Another IX(B) Squadron Lancaster flown by Fg Off. Laws landed at a small temporary airfield at Vaskovo. With its undercarriage down, Laws' Lancaster skidded across the runway with the starboard undercarriage collapsed, causing damage to the right wing. A second Lancaster, arriving over the airfield moments later, then overshot the runway and got stuck in the thick mud.

The pair of Lancasters that had come down near Onega both managed to reach Yagodnik, albeit with problems. With Wing Commander Tait flown to the site in an ancient Polikarpov Po-2 biplane to keep track of the proceedings, preparations to fly to Yagodnik went quickly. Tait had been slightly worried when a Russian pilot prior to take-off experienced problems in starting the engine. The pilot then hit the engine of the Po-2 with a large hammer. After a couple of heavy and accurate blows, the M-11 radial engine eventually burst into life. Tait nevertheless went along to meet the crews to check damage sustained to the two Lancasters. It turned out that Iveson, flying Lancaster ME554, had enough fuel remaining to reach Yagodnik. (According to 617 Squadron's ORB, Iveson had been forced to release his dozen 'Johnnie Walker' mines in a lake as a safety precaution.)

The other Lancaster, LM492, and flown by Flt Lt Knilans, was an altogether different matter. Knilans was something of a rarity within the RAF being an American citizen. After being rejected by the USAAF following the Japanese attack on Pearl Harbor, Knilans eventually found his way to Britain via the Royal Canadian Air Force and had flown thirty sorties with 617 Squadron. With almost dry fuel tanks, Knilans managed to put the huge Lancaster down in one piece and both Iveson and Knilans' crews remained aboard their aircraft. Having survived the highly dangerous ferry flight, Knilans' crew found themselves taken into custody by a number of local Russians. Several Russian soldiers arrived later, some being dressed in German fatigues. Conversation was mostly limited to sign language as the Russians spoke little or no English with the RAF airmen's Russian vocabulary limited to a few words. The RAF airmen were huddled into jeeps and driven to a nearby town in the middle of nowhere. The British were lodged in an old derelict house with a guard placed outside. Fish with black bread and drink were supplied but the Russians forbade the airmen to leave the house. One of the gunners, Pierre 'Paddey' Blanchet, spotted a large glass of fluid. Thinking it to be water, Blanchet took several gulps swallowing the fluid. Unfortunately, it was not water, but vodka. As a result, Blanchet was unfit for duty for the next couple of hours. In order to provide light entertainment for the stranded British, a Russian woman lifted a soldier from the ground by using only one arm… Having spent an uncomfortable night at Onega, the crew was relieved to see a Soviet Douglas C-47 Skytrain—delivered under the Lend-Lease agreement—arrive loaded with fuel. With the Russians having refuelled the Lancaster, it was turned 180 degrees into the wind. Apparently, this was performed with the brakes being fully applied, requiring an inordinate amount of manpower. Revving the Merlin engines, Knilans initiated the take-off for nearby Yagodnik. Upon lifting off from the runway, Knilans ordered the flight engineer to retract the undercarriage. His order was misunderstood and the flight engineer instead raised the flaps. Rapidly losing altitude, the Lancaster literally scraped the tree tops. With a tall pine tree rising up in front of them, Knilans immediately kicked the rudder pedal with the tree lining up with the fuselage. Seconds later, the tree smashed into the nose, exploding the windscreen into a thousand shards and ripping off the bomb-bay doors. The SABS bombsight was destroyed and the howling wind entering the stricken Lancaster caused the navigator's maps to be blown out of the aircraft. Thankfully, Knilans managed to keep the bomber from stalling, eventually managing to gain enough speed to climb to a safer altitude. In order to protect his vision, Knilans had to keep one hand over his eyes and looked through the gaps of his fingers during the short flight to Yagodnik. To make the flight even more problematical, the right outer Merlin engine soon overheated, having to be turned off with the propeller feathered. After arriving safely at Yagodnik, it was discovered that lumps of trees had lodged in the radiator, much reducing its efficiency in cooling the engine. Remarkably, the tree branch that exploded the windscreen was later presented to Woodhall Spa and proudly mounted in the Officers' Mess. The caption underneath the almost 1-metre-long branch was 'Believe it or not.'[6]

The Film Unit Lancaster, flown by Flt Lt Buckham, was also unable to land at Yagodnik and came down at Kegostrov:

> We descended through cloud to Onega Bay, some 200 km past Murmansk, to find 8 or 10 other aircraft milling around, and ultimately led them around the coast, about 50 ft above the beach to Archangel where it was raining heavily. Yagodnik couldn't be found then, so as everyone was running low on fuel we landed, after 12 hrs flying, on Kergostov [sic] Island which was about the same size as a small 'Tiger' drome. Some incongruous sights met our eyes. There were Lancs with their noses pushed into buildings, some only their tails showing through walls or roofs and others on their bellies. Not all of us were there either; half the force was spread out over Russia. When the weather cleared we had the job of getting our big bombers airborne and flying 9 km down the Dvina River to Yag Ddnik [sic], which we did somehow by flying out between the buildings. We were there (at Yagodnik) for three days billeted on the 'Ivan Kalleyev' which was a bug ridden river steamer anchored off the island.[7]

The ORB for 463 Squadron states that:

> Nav. Skill in appalling weather conditions was responsible for greater percentage of a/c landing at YAGODNIK. Absolutely no facilities, as Beacon U/S, and Liberators landed after Main Force—hence no W/T or R/T. Area maps inaccurate. Pinpoints no value.

The other Lancasters which came down at Kegostrov were Fg Off. Harris of IX(B) Squadron (ME198) and Sqn Ldr Wyness of 617 Squadron (ME559). Following Wyness down through the clouds, Harris entered a holding pattern before putting the Lancaster down, eventually overrunning the runway before ending up in a potato field. The soft ground worked as a brake with the Lancaster ending up on its nose. The crew quickly evacuated the Lancaster with the bombardier, Plt Off. Parsons, being forced to make his way in complete darkness to the cockpit, eventually exiting the Lancaster through the pilot's overhead hatch. Parsons later reminisced that this was 'a terrifying experience.' With the RAF crew safe, the Russians then initiated an attempt of getting the Lancaster back on an even keel. This involved assembling large amounts of hay underneath the rear fuselage. After a large enough haystack had been produced, a number of Russians—both men and women—walked into the fuselage, weighing it down until it hit the haystack. Harris was able to fly the Lancaster to Yagodnik. Sqn Ldr Wyness was not as lucky as his Lancaster was substantially damaged when the undercarriage collapsed on landing. It was subsequently declared as Cat E and written off RAF charge. In the event, ME559 would be repaired as described later.[8]

Plt Off. Ross of 617 Squadron, flying in Lancaster EE131, landed on marshy ground near Molotovsk (now Severodvinsk). The hard landing caused the 12,000 lb Tallboy to break through the bomb-bay doors and skidded across and in front of the reeling Lancaster. Thankfully, the heavy bomb did not detonate. The shaken crew quickly climbed out of the badly damaged bomber after destroying the secret SABS bombsight.

Several Lancasters had been damaged with seven sustaining severe damage. In all, six Lancasters, four from IX(B) Squadron and two from 617 Squadron, had received such serious damage that they, after being thoroughly inspected by RAF mechanics, were written off. On 13 September, six Russian mechanics were flown to the site of Sqn Ldr Wyness' Lancaster by Tony Iveson. Their job was to remove any usable parts from the badly damaged bomber. It could have been far worse, however. None of the RAF aircrews had been killed and although the force of Lancasters had been reduced by 25 per cent, there were still a sizeable number of bombers available for the raid on the *Tirpitz*. From the initial chaos, an accurate overview of the situation was soon established.

The *War Chronicle of the Soviet Northern Arctic Fleet* stated that:

On 12 September, 38 Lancasters, two Liberators and one Mosquito aircraft arrived to attack *Tirpitz* at Alta Fjord. Due to poor weather, the aircraft landed between 06.07 and 08.21 hours at Yagodnik; 29 Lancasters, two Liberators, one Mosquito; at Belomorsk one Lancaster; at Kegostrov three Lancasters; at Onega one Lancaster; at Vaskovo one Lancaster; in the Motovsk area one Lancaster; at Tjubalo-Navolok one Lancaster and at Tagali one Lancaster. During the landing seven Lancasters were destroyed (unfit to fly).

Russian-British co-operation

Having arrived at Yagodnik, the VVS Commander at Yagodnik, Colonel Loginov, warmly welcomed the RAF crews with a speech that emphasised Russian-British co-operation against a common enemy: Nazi Germany. A large banner proclaiming 'Welcome to the Glorious Flyers of the Royal Air Force' had been raised at the airfield. Immediately after the RAF fliers had arrived, a welcoming lunch was arranged. The food and drink was highly appreciated by the aircrews after having been airborne for around twelve or so hours. Indeed, the Russians made every effort to make the RAF personnel feel welcome. Later on, movie showings (which, according to Arthur Ward, consisted of '…continuous war—terrific banging of guns and marching of men for two solid hours'.) and lectures on the co-operation and solidarity between the capitalistic Great Britain and communist Soviet Union against the common Nazi enemy were arranged. The war movies were not going down that well with the RAF personnel and after repeated requests, were replaced by cartoons. Apparently, the Russians did not fully understand the reasoning behind this request, but nevertheless withdrew the 'blood and guts' propaganda war movies.

A football match between the RAF crews and their Russian counterparts also took place. Apparently, the Russians did everything they could to ensure a solid victory against the RAF team. A professional football team is said to have been flown to Yagodnik for the match. The Russians won by four goals to none and their victory apparently worked wonders for Russian co-operation with the British. (Depending on the source, the score differs, but everyone agrees that the Russian team came out as winners.) A dance was also arranged where the British did their best to teach the Russians to Jitterbug.

Accommodation was a problem with the Russians expected about 250 RAF personnel. Instead, the number was 325, including aircrews and mechanics.

Daily excursions to the nearby town of Archangel were also arranged which usually included lunch, a visit to the local opera house and vast quantities of vodka. One RAF pilot apparently attempted to swim back to Yagodnik while two others were late for the boat transport back to the airfield. After the raid, the Russians sent a bill for 9,239 roubles as 'being expenses incurred by personnel at Archangel for entertainment of RAF and Russian personnel concerned in Operation *Paravane*'.[9]

Arthur Ward, a 617 Squadron wireless operator, later recalled that:

> Our 'quarters' were on a large paddle-steamer (the *Ivan Kalyev*), moored close by and as we made our way towards it, a silver band struck up a lively tune to welcome us. Right across the side of the boat was a large banner in red and white, 'Welcome to the glorious fliers of the Royal Air Force.' We were considerably shaken and walked up the gangway very self-consciously. The amusing thing was that as the various crews came in we were able to have a good laugh at their reaction when the band struck up for their special benefit.
>
> We were very hungry, of course, after ten or eleven hours in the air, and rather curious to see what kind of fare would be provided. Our first meal consisted of four slices of bread arranged on one plate—one had a piece of raw bacon, another jam, a third cheese, and the fourth spam. To wash down this queer mixture was a glass of sweet, hot tea without milk. A refreshing drink it was too! Next morning there were hardboiled eggs and raw bacon. One or two enterprising chaps went down to the galley and soon showed the cooks the British way—from then on it was OK.

It would appear, however, that the quality of food and drink decreased substantially during the deployment to Yagodnik. Being served good meals, as well as a seemingly unlimited supply of vodka, could well have been a propaganda manoeuvre. But when the RAF deployment was prolonged for a few days, food and drink returned to basic and ordinary levels. It would seem that the initial prolific supply of food and drink was a mere propaganda trick. Even the porcelain plates and fine cutlery mysteriously disappeared as the days went by.

Eastern adventures

The cramped and primitive accommodation had one major disadvantage: bed bugs. Such things had been expected by the accompanying RAF doctor who sprayed the small cabins as well as dusting the pillows with Keating's (an insect powder). However, a few of the RAF personnel were still affected:

> …several of the lads were covered in enormous red blotches, one chap's eyes were completely closed up and another looked as if he'd developed mumps in the night. What a voracious appetite these little red devils had![10]

The raid was delayed by poor weather with heavy rain and winds sweeping across Kaa Fjord. This turned out to be a blessing in disguise as the RAF bombers required both maintenance and refuelling. Due to the fact that only a couple of 1,500-litre fuel bowsers were available, refuelling the Lancasters took eighteen hours. The process of refuelling and engine changes as well as other necessary regular maintenance kept the ground crews busy. For three days it rained continuously, making it impossible to even consider flying. However, this meant that there was ample time to repair the damaged bombers. To ease boredom among those not involved in repairing and refuelling the bombers, Wing Commander Tait ordered a mass physical training. This was not particularly popular, but the Russians appeared to appreciate the British knack for keeping fit at all times. To provide a good example for his men, Tait also joined in the physical exercises.

Despite the valiant efforts in getting the Lancasters ready for the raid, many aircraft could not, for various reasons, take part. Out of the eighteen Lancasters from IX(B) Squadron that had set out from Bardney on 11 September, only ten were available for the raid on the Beast. 617 Squadron had lost two aircraft written off. This meant a significant reduction of the force that would strike the *Tirpitz*. In fact, only twenty-eight Lancasters, excluding the 463 Squadron Film Unit aircraft, were available.

Having endured forced landings, poor weather, maintenance issues, as well as Russian food and liberal quantities of vodka, bed bugs and war movies, the news of a break in the weather came as a relief to the RAF aircrews. In the early hours of 15 September, the Mosquito crew returned with excellent news: 'Weather clear above Kaa Fjord and up to 130 km to south-southwest.' During the pre-raid planning, it had been decided that the strike force would attack *Tirpitz* at the same time. The twenty-one Lancasters carrying Tallboys—LM715, W4964, PB289, LM448, LL914, LM548, LL845 and LL901 of IX(B) Squadron and EE146, LM489, ME434, PD233, PD238, DV405, NF923, DV391, LM482, ME561, PB415, DV246 and LM492 of 617 Squadron—called Force A would fly at an altitude of between 14,000 and 18,000 feet, attacking in four waves consisting of five aircraft each in line abreast. Each wave would occupy about 1,000 feet in height. The seven Lancasters carrying the 'Johnnie Walker' mines (NF925 and LM713 of IX(B) Squadron and ME554, ME562, LM483, PB416 and ME559 of 617 Squadron) made up Force B.

Approaching the Beast

During the morning of 15 September, the twenty-nine Lancasters took off from Yagodnik and headed west for Kaa Fjord and the *Tirpitz*. During the take-off, a Russian military orchestra played uplifting tunes. The first of the ten IX(B) Squadron Lancasters to take off was Fg Off. Stowell in NF925 who lifted off at 09.46 hours. (The timings for take-off, bomb runs and return to Yagodnik have been extracted from the respective squadron's ORB, except where noted.) The last one off the ground was Fg Off. Scott in LL901 at 10.12 hours. Unfortunately, the 617 Squadron ORB does not provide the time for take-off from Yagodnik for their eighteen Lancasters. Incidentally, the ORBs of both squadrons states 'Alten Fjord' as the target with no mention of Kaa Fjord. Kaa Fjord is a small inlet of the larger Alta (Alten) Fjord.

Over northern Finland, the strike force flew over a large airfield—presumably, this was Rovaniemi, the largest city in Finnish Lapland. Although the airfield was lit up with several aircraft parked on the ground, no Luftwaffe fighters attempted to intercept the Lancasters. As with the ferry flight to Yagodnik four days earlier, the bombers used Swedish airspace for part of the flight. They were first spotted some 3 km northeast of Pajala at 11.05 hours local Swedish time (GMT+1) and initial reports identified the aircraft as Soviet 'TB-7s' (Petlyakov Pe-8). The 'twenty-six to twenty-eight' bombers flew on a north-westerly course, later slightly changing to a more westerly course before heading northwards. A number of the Lancaster crews appeared to fly northwards soon after passing over the Finnish-Swedish border, heading straight for Kaa Fjord and *Tirpitz*. The altitude was between 1,000 and 3,000 metres. Half an hour later, between 11.26 and 11.35 hours local Swedish time (GMT+1), the Lancasters passed over the small city of Karesuando and into Norwegian airspace. Before they left Sweden, anti-aircraft guns fired upon a formation of nineteen Lancasters. Crossing the frontline at an altitude of 5,000 metres, the RAF bombers were observed over the small Norwegian town of Kautokeino. German soldiers manning the observation post immediately alerted the Luftwaffe air defence centre at Alta, stating that 'forty four-engine bombers' were flying westwards.

The first report on the impending raid reached *Tirpitz* at 12.46 hours. The Commander of the huge battleship, Kapitän zur See Wolf Junge—who had replaced Hans Meyer as *Tirpitz*'s Commander after Meyer had been injured during Operation *Tungsten*—did not feel threatened by an air attack. The British had attacked *Tirpitz* on numerous occasions with little to show for their efforts. Anti-aircraft guns, both aboard *Tirpitz* and on flak ships anchored close by and on shore, anti-torpedo nets and artificial smoke generators protected the battleship. Junge immediately ordered the latter into action and just over ten minutes later, *Tirpitz* was largely covered in smoke. Frantic preparations among the flak crews ensured that the RAF bombers would be warmly welcomed when they arrived over the *Tirpitz*.

The Raid

Less than ten minutes later, the first Lancasters arrived over Kaa Fjord where they discovered that the *Tirpitz* was largely covered by artificial smoke. As a result, bombs were dropped through the smokescreen where *Tirpitz* was assumed to be at anchor with German gunfire assisting the bomb aimers' job somewhat. Standing on the bridge of the Beast, Junge was unable to visually observe the approaching enemy aircraft. During the previous air attacks earlier in the year, British aircraft had attacked from low altitudes. This time, the bombers were flying high, making their presence known through the noise of their engines.

First to attack was Plt Off. Evans of IX(B) Squadron at 10.55 hours, closely followed by Wg Cdr Tait, Flt Lt Howard, Plt Off. Kell, Flt Lt Stout, Flt Lt Pryor (all of 617 Squadron) and Fg Off. Tweddle of IX(B) Squadron at 10.56 hours (12.56 hours DBST). Bombing from 15,000 feet, the bomb aimer clearly saw the stern of the *Tirpitz* through the SABS bombsight. The crew noted five Tallboys exploding in close proximity 'between the ship and boom'. Immediately following the release of the 12,000 lb Tallboy, the nose of the Lancaster rose sharply with the aircraft beginning to climb. The heavy bomb represented nearly 20 per cent of the Lancaster's all-up weight of 65,000 lb. Tait's bombardier, W. A. Daniels, directed Tait towards the *Tirpitz*. The Tallboy struck the water near the side of the battleship. Although a near miss, the bomb ripped open the hull of the Beast. Other bombs fell nearby.

With the initial Tallboys being dropped within twenty-two seconds, this meant that the first bomb would not have reached its target before the last one had left the bomb bay of the final Lancaster. Bombing from 17,400 feet Plt Off. Kell and his crew noted that the *Tirpitz* 'was in the gratiale (perhaps something to do with the bomb-aiming gear) on the commencement on the run up, but before the release, the vessel was obscured by the smokescreen. Impossible to assess result of bombing.' Fg Off. Howard in NF923 dropped the Tallboy at 12.56 hours from 16,000 feet. 'Run commenced on ship, which soon became obscured by smoke from screen. Bombed from ships guns. 5 bombs seen to explode in area of ship.'

Although the flak was intense, most of it was inaccurate. Only a few of the bombers, including ED763 of 617 Squadron flown by Flt Lt Grael, were damaged by flak. Flt Lt Knilans' Lancaster was also hit by flak that damaged a Merlin engine. Even with one damaged engine, Knilans continued to circle the *Tirpitz*. During the return flight to Yagodnik, the damaged Merlin had to be shut down and Knilans had to make the seventh three-engine landing following an operational sortie.

Not everything went according to plan, however. Several Tallboys failed to release with some returned to Yagodnik. Others did not release their Tallboys due to the large smokescreen covering the *Tirpitz*. Flt Lt Hamilton in PD233 experienced great difficulty in releasing the Tallboy. Hamilton made three consecutive runs against the battleship with the Tallboy remaining firmly in the bomb bay. Hamilton and his crew did not observe a direct hit although 'One big explosion seen about 20-30 yards to port of target.' At 14.15 hours DBST (more than one hour after the main attack), some two-and-a-half miles south of the target, the Tallboy finally dropped away from the Lancaster. Fg

Off. Gingles in LM489 did not drop the Tallboy as *Tirpitz* had been completely covered by smoke. Instead of dropping the bomb blindly—and risk missing the battleship—the valuable bomb was returned to Yagodnik.

Regarding the 'Johnnie Walker' mines carried by Force B, most were dropped less than ten minutes after the first Tallboys. Their success was, as expected by most concerned, limited to the point of uselessness. Flt Lt Iveson in ME554 carried a dozen 'Johnnie Walker' mines which were originally transported in NF920. As the latter Lancaster had been damaged by flak, the mines were loaded aboard Iveson's bomber. The mines were dropped at 13.04 hours from 10,800 feet, a considerably lower altitude than the Tallboys. No results were seen with 'Target completely covered by smokescreen'. Of the pair of IX(B) Squadron Lancasters that carried mines, Fg Off. Stowell (NF925), reported that 'Own bombs believed in correct area', while Fg Off. Macintosh (LM713) stated that some of the 'Johnnie Walker' mines fell '...in water and some on east side of fjord'.

With their primary mission to document the raid, Flt Lt Buckham of 463 Squadron carried no bombs and filmed the mission, its camera operated by Flt Lt John Loftus. Loftus was a Canadian who in 1937 had enrolled in the Royal Canadian Air Force (RCAF) as a photographer. According to 463 Squadron's ORB, Buckham arrived over the target at 12.55 hours, circling for five minutes while the Tallboys and 'Johnnie Walker' mines rained down on the battleship. Buckham later reported:

> Take-off went smoothly and all a/c set course behind the leader dead on Time. Mat. to Target was very accurate, but trip was hindered by battery of med. flak opening up approx. 69.30N/22.10E. First impression was that this battery warned Target of our approach, as the smokescreen was seen to be in operation for 5 Mins. before Target was reached. However, Target was ascertained visually to be on North side of Fjord from direction of our approach. This was confirmed by Leader. The bombing of the Leader and the following two a/c appeared to be very accurate, and an explosion followed some seconds later. This was backed up by black smoke which later was inclined to billow. The J.W. a/c then came in, but by this time smokescreen was very effective. The J.W. bombs viewed from pilot's seat fell in centre of smokescreen. We continued to circle, but no more explosions were seen. Flak from the defence positions, cruisers and destroyers was moderate but inaccurate. No a/c seen to be damaged.

Of the ten Lancasters of IX(B) Squadron that arrived over Kaa Fjord, two failed to deposit their Tallboys on the *Tirpitz*. The eight Tallboys that were dropped by IX(B) Squadron were released on target within twelve minutes from 10.55 to 11.07 hours. The first IX(B) Lancaster to drop its Tallboy on the *Tirpitz* at 10.55 hours was flown by Flt Lt Melrose. Flying Lancaster LM715, Wing Commander Bazin attacked the target from 15,000 feet at 11.04 hours. Bazin:

> ...identified by intense light flak from position of ship. Smokescreen started at 10.55 hours. On first run ship believed visible but made second run to make sure: smokescreen however prevented accurate observation, and no results of bombing seen.

Fg Off. Dunne, flying LM548, subsequently reported that 'Target not attacked as bomb hung up owing to technical failure. "Tallbot" [sic] returned to base from which sortie was made.' The Tallboy carried by Fg Off. Scott in LL901 did 'not release in spite of making four runs over target. It eventually fell through bomb doors.' In all, seventeen Tallboys were dropped on the *Tirpitz* with four of the huge bombs returned to Yagodnik. The bombardiers on two Lancasters had been unable to get a clear view of the Beast with the release mechanism on two other bombers failing to work.

Following the end of the raid, Junge noted that:

> Several powerful tremblings in the forecastle and in the immediate vicinity of the sides of the ship. The ship is still too poorly covered in smoke. This is clearly visible from altitude.

The Lancasters were forced to return to Yagodnik, uncertain if they had managed to deliver a decisive blow to the *Tirpitz*. Although a few of the crews had visually observed the battleship, many had been forced to bomb blindly through the smokescreen. Initially, the raid was considered to have been a disappointment. One positive aspect of the raid was that the German flak, although considerable, was largely inaccurate. Only one of the Lancasters, ED763, of 617 Squadron had been lightly damaged by flak and no Luftwaffe fighters had been spotted in the target area.

Upon their return to Yagodnik, the Russians apparently 'minced no words' over the failure of the RAF to sink the *Tirpitz*. One Norwegian source speaks of contempt by the Russians against the RAF aircrews that the Beast was still afloat. However, the Russians did consider the battleship to be a very difficult target to hit and even more so to damage or even sink. The *War Chronicle of the Soviet Northern Arctic Fleet* (classified until 1990) had the following to say about the raid:

> On 15 September, 28 Lancaster aircraft took off from Yagodnik in order to attack *Tirpitz* at Alten Fjord. Between 13.57 and 14.04 hours 16 6,370 lb [sic] bombs and 72 200 lb bombs were dropped from altitudes of 3,500 to 4,500 metres. During the approach, it turned out that the ship was covered by a smokescreen, which led to the bomb aiming having to be directed against the centre point of the smokescreen. According to the crews and (subsequent) aerial photographs, the bombs fell close to the ship, but no significant damage resulted. Four of the Lancaster aircraft were damaged by enemy flak.

Buckham's return to the UK

Immediately following the end of the raid, Flt Lt Buckham headed out for the open sea and dived down to sea level. Heading back to the UK, Buckham and his crew encountered appalling weather over the North Sea before landfall was made near Aberdeen. Shortly afterwards, Buckham landed at Lossiemouth at 22.55 hours with nearly dry fuel tanks and established a Bomber Command record in the process. They had remained airborne

Operation Paravane 15 September 1944

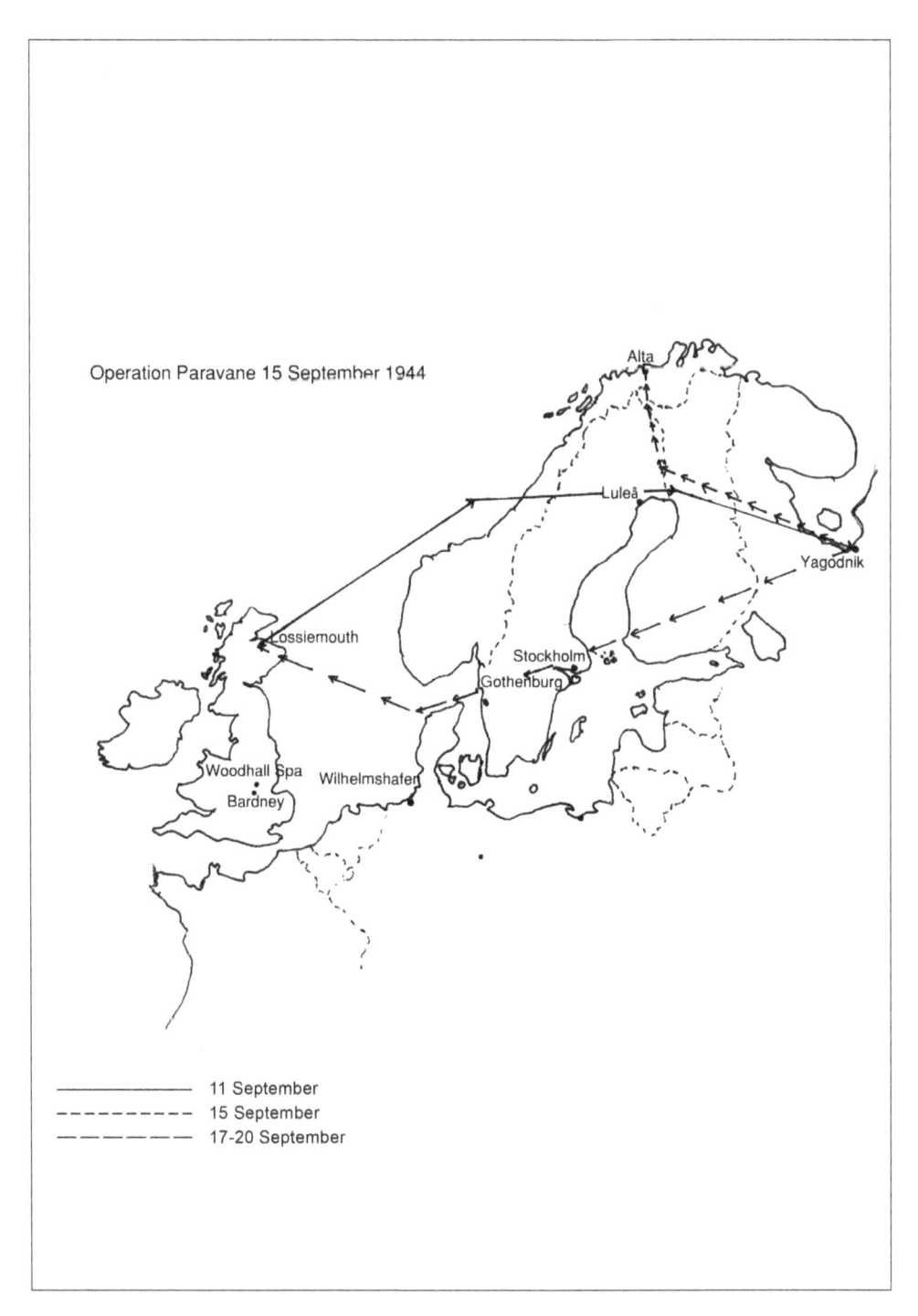

——————— 11 September
- - - - - - - - - 15 September
— — — — — 17-20 September

Operation *Paravane* ranks among the most risky operations flown by RAF Bomber Command during the Second World War. (*Anders Eriksson*)

for fifteen-and-a-half hours, making the flight the longest Lancaster operational sortie during the war. The reason for this was to analyse the movie shot during the raid as quickly as possible. Unfortunately, the film showed that even though the battleship had been seriously damaged, *Tirpitz* remained afloat.

Return flight of IX(B) and 617 Squadrons

Following the conclusion of the raid, the IX(B) and 617 Squadron Lancasters returned to Yagodnik where they flew to the UK between 16 and 20 September. There were too few Tallboys left to consider mounting a second raid from Yagodnik. Instead, IX(B) and 617 Squadrons returned to the UK as previously planned. Flying across Sweden, the first group of sixteen Lancasters passed north of Stockholm. Swedish air defence reported that between 21.05 and 01.11 hours (local Swedish time, GMT+1) on 17–18 September, 'about twenty foreign aircraft' crossed into Swedish airspace from the east and headed southwest. The bombers left after passing over Höganäs—Halmstad and Kungsbacka—Fjällbacka on the Swedish west coast. None of the bombers were visually observed with all reports being solely based on engine noise.

With no blackout, the landscape and cities made a lasting impression on the RAF crews. With the blackout still being the order of the day in Britain, observing lit-up roads and communities was extraordinary. With the Flygvapnet lacking night fighter capability altogether, no attempt was made to intercept the RAF bombers. As a result, the Swedish leg of the flight was the easiest one. The only drawback on this leg of the flight was occasional Swedish anti-aircraft fire. The Lancasters were fired upon over Stockholm, Gothenburg and other places. The flak was not particularly accurate, but it nevertheless made the RAF airmen feel rather uneasy. When a couple of flak bursts came too close for comfort, Knilans screamed over the intercom: 'Hell, I thought these guys were supposed to be neutral!'[11]

On the return flight to the UK on 17 September, tragedy struck when the Lancaster flown by Fg Off. Levy, PB416, crashed into mountains at Rukkedalen, Nesbyen, in south central Norway. The crash occurred at 02.15 hours (local Norwegian time GMT+1). The cause of the crash was put down to engine trouble, but this part of Norway has peaks 1,500 metres high. If the crew had been flying a mere 15 metres higher, they would probably have cleared the peak. The entire crew perished in the crash, including Fg Off. Frank Levy, Fg Off. Charles Lawrence Fox, FS Peter William Groom, FS George Muir McGuire, Plt Off. Allan Frank McNally, FS Eric Edward Stephen Peck and FS Daniel Gorowny Thomas. In addition, Fg Off. Denis Charles Shea and Fg Off. James Frazer Naylor were travelling as passengers and were also killed in the crash. Shea and Naylor were part of another crew whose Lancaster had been left behind in Russia. Curiously, the body of a tenth and unnamed individual was also recovered from the wreckage—the identity of this individual is still unknown. All ten were buried in a mass grave by the Germans. Following the end of the war, the bodies of the British airmen were exhumed and reburied at Nesbyen Cemetery with full military honours. A white wooden cross marked with ten black spots stands at the site of the crash and debris of the Lancaster can still be found in the area.[12] The fatal crash of PB416 was the only RAF service personnel losses during the three 1944 raids against *Tirpitz*. The crash is briefly mentioned in a Swedish military summary report of airspace incursions during September 1944: 'According to German information, during the night of 16/9–17/9, a British aeroplane of the Lancaster type crashed north of Oslo.' Through various materials recovered, the Germans were able to conclude that the bomber had been part of a special unit that on 15 September had attacked *Tirpitz* and breached Swedish airspace in the process.

The following night on 18–19 September, most of the remaining Lancasters left Yagodnik. Passing over Sweden at an altitude of between 1,000 and 3,000 metres, the RAF bombers were fired upon over Karlskoga (site of the world famous anti-aircraft manufacturer Bofors), Karlstad and north of Gothenburg. The final Lancaster to return to British shores was NF920 of 617 Squadron that had been repaired at Yagodnik after being hit by flak over Finland; it arrived in the UK five days after the raid on the *Tirpitz*. When Plt Off. Carey and his crew prepared for take-off, a Russian orchestra provided a musical backdrop. Climbing for altitude, one of the Lancaster crews fired a couple of red identification signals from a Very pistol as a goodwill gesture. Unfortunately, the cartridges landed in a heavily forested area and set it ablaze. The return flight back to the UK was uneventful, however, with Carey returning to Lossiemouth at 15.55 hours on 20 September. The final clearing up of the RAF detachment at Yagodnik took several days. It was not until 27 September when the two cargo Liberators of 511 Squadron returned to Bardney in Lincolnshire.

The next raid for IX(B) Squadron following the end of Operation *Paravane* was a night bombing raid against Munster on 23 September. Out of the twelve Lancasters committed, two failed to return. On the same night, 617 Squadron visited the Dortmund–Ems Canal as part of a force of 125 Lancasters.

Russian Acquisitions

Of the thousands of warplanes handed over to the Russians through the Lend-Lease agreement, only one RAF four-engine bomber (a Short Stirling) was officially delivered in 1945. Although the Russians made repeated requests for four-engine bombers, particularly American B-17 Flying Fortresses and B-24 Liberators, none were delivered. Supplying fighters and tactical light and medium bombers was one thing with heavy strategic bombers being a different matter altogether. Several B-17s and B-24s would eventually be incorporated into Russian service through unconventional methods. During the latter stages of the war, many USAAF heavy bombers made emergency landings in Russian-held territory following raids over Germany. Although the aircrews were allowed to return, several of their aircraft were not. Of the twenty-three Flying Fortresses that entered service with the Russians, many remained flyable until the late 1940s. One task for which they were used was to train Russian aircrews to fly and operate the Tupolev Tu-4, a reverse-engineered copy of the Boeing B-29 Superfortress. Three of the latter had been interned in Siberia after being damaged in raids against Japan and subsequently 'confiscated' by the Russians. With the war in Asia being considered as a separate conflict, any US aircraft that landed in Siberia following raids against Japan were interned. The crews were released with the aircraft being retained. The USSR did not declare war against Japan until 8 August 1945.

However, the Operation *Paravane* force had left behind six Lancasters in Russia, these being considered as beyond repair. The aircraft in question were subsequently written off RAF charge as Category E (non-combat) with various spares and classified gear being removed or destroyed by RAF personnel. The crashed Lancasters abandoned by the RAF were thoroughly inspected by Soviet engineering specialists of the White Sea Flotilla Naval Air Force with the aim being to possibly repair the bombers for further use. Incredibly, at least two Lancasters were repaired and subsequently entered service with the Soviet Naval air arm. According to a contemporary engineering report:

> The British dismantled or destroyed radars, certain elements of radio stations, bombsights and additional equipment on all aircraft. In addition, all aircraft were stripped of the most scarce units of power plants.

However, it was concluded that two or three Lancasters could be restored to airworthiness with the remaining cannibalised for spares. Having few long-range aircraft available, the Lancasters would be an excellent addition to the aircraft inventory of the White Sea Flotilla Naval Air Force. The Lancasters would not be used as bombers, but rather for long-range maritime reconnaissance and as cargo aircraft.

One IX(B) Squadron Lancaster, LL884, had come down at Chubalo-Navolok, Hope Island. Although having suffered extensive damage to the left wing with one engine destroyed, orders for the restoration of the Lancaster arrived on 7 November. The repairs were assigned to the 86th Aircraft Repair Shop at Yagodnik with the nose section repaired and armament removed. Spare parts came from another Lancaster, ME559, of 617 Squadron. The turrets of LL884 were removed with makeshift aluminium panels fitted in their place. A Perspex nose was also fitted. The basic RAF camouflage was retained with the roundels replaced by red stars and the tactical numeral 01 was painted on both sides of the fuselage. Following completion of repairs, the Lancaster was handed over to the 16th Air Transport Detachment (TRAO) commanded by I. I. Mazuruk. Lancaster, LL884, was presumably the first to enter Soviet service. Even though the Lancaster was formally attached to a transport unit, it was used until January 1945 for convoy escort duties and as a maritime reconnaissance aircraft searching for German submarines. It was usually flown by V. Sh. Yevdokimov (pilot) and V. Ya. Andreyev (navigator) and it is unclear if any success was achieved in locating submarines. One operational sortie took place on 24 January 1945 when the Lancaster was flown on an ice reconnaissance sortie from Guba Belezhua to Naryan-Mar.

Having successfully restored one Lancaster to airworthiness, efforts were then focused on two other aircraft: EE131 of IX(B) Squadron and NF985 of 617 Squadron. The former had sustained considerable damage in the forced landing at Molotovsk with the fuselage being damaged, the nose smashed and propellers bent. However, there is no evidence that this Lancaster was repaired by the Russians. The third aircraft, NF985, was located at Vaskovo with severe damage to the engines, right wing, flaps, tail section and forward fuselage. With further parts destroyed or removed by the British, it was subsequently determined that the bomber was repairable. As with the first Lancaster restored to airworthiness, similar modifications were made to NF985. It subsequently entered service with the 70 OTRAP (coded as '02') and flown by I. I. Dubenets. Lancaster, LL884, was still in service with the 16th TRAO in mid-1945 as was NF985. On 1 July 1945, Lancasters 884 and 985 were recorded as being in service with the 16th TRAO. The unit's main base was Yagodnik with Lancaster flights to Naryan-Mar and Vaenga being recorded.

In July, Lancaster 01 was flown to Moscow. A few weeks later, it was flown east to form part of the Soviet invasion force of Japan. Due to a lack of fuel, the Lancaster only reached Krasnoyarsk where it remained until the Japanese surrender. It was returned to Moscow and later to Yagodnik, still being operational in the spring of 1946. On two occasions, the Lancaster was subjected to small repairs. The 16th TRAO was then disbanded with its aircraft sent south to the 65th Special Purpose Air Regiment based at Izmailovo outside of Moscow. In the event, both Lancasters ended up with this unit. Lancaster, 01, was sent to the Aviation Engineering School at Riga for instructional purposes and its final fate remains unclear, but it is likely that it was scrapped. The fate of Lancaster, 02, is known, however. According to one source, pilot Dubenets overshot the runway during a landing at Izmailovo outside of Moscow, ending up in a potato field. Repairs to the Lancaster were 'inadvisable' and it may be assumed that the Lancaster was cut up and scrapped. However negligible, the two Lancasters had certainly contributed to the Soviet war effort.

Post-raid assessment

In all, seventeen Tallboys had been dropped against the *Tirpitz* with one direct hit and several near misses. One Tallboy had struck the battleship about 15 metres from the bow causing permanent and irreparable damage as detailed below. Seven Lancasters had carried 'Johnnie Walker' mines; however, the results from these were disappointing. It was believed that the *Tirpitz* did not suffer any damage from the mines and this belief turned out to be correct, and the 'Johnnie Walker' mine was never used on operations again.

Cochrane was furious that the battleship had not been sunk; it was frustrating having been so close to sinking the *Tirpitz* and then having to fail. During a post-raid discussion with Willie Tait, Cochrane stated that if the aircrews had had one more minute at their disposal, the battleship would surely have been sunk. It was simply a case of bad luck. However, Cochrane did not intend to let the *Tirpitz* slip through the net and Bomber Command would finish the job.

Almost immediately after the raid, a German report stated that the *Tirpitz* had not suffered any damage and yet again the pride of Kriegsmarine had managed to avoid the attention of the British bombers. Indeed, the *Tirpitz* was seemingly invincible having suffered numerous British air attacks; however, the truth could not be hidden for long.

Only four days later, the German High Command admitted that the battleship had been hit by a bomb that had caused some damage. On 25 September, Grossadmiral Dönitz reported:

> After successfully defending herself against many heavy air attacks, battleship *Tirpitz* has now sustained bomb hits but by holding out, her presence confounds the enemy's intelligence.[13]

Initial Allied reports on the effects of the raid were contradictory. There appeared to have been at least a couple of direct hits against the Beast with some evidence pointing to at least four Tallboys falling within the torpedo nets surrounding the battleship.

On 20 September, the RAF Mosquito based at Yagodnik took a number of photographs which seemingly showed a clear discolouring to the area around the front gun turrets and bow (this appeared to confirm Russian reports of substantial damage to the bow). It appeared that at least one bomb had indeed hit its target. However, the *Tirpitz* was still afloat and contradicted an over-enthusiastic report from the Norwegian Resistance claiming that the battleship had been sunk. Although it was clear to all concerned that the *Tirpitz* had not been sunk, she appeared to have been damaged, the extent of which was unknown to the British. Indeed, the raid had resulted in the *Tirpitz* being severely damaged. Even though only five sailors had been killed in the raid with another fifteen being injured, the damage to the battleship was indeed serious. Only one of the seventeen Tallboys had hit the Beast, slamming down on the port side of the bow and sliced through the armoured deck in front of the forward gun turret before detonating below the waterline. Apart from the detonation of the bomb, the subsequent shockwave had caused much damage. Other bombs had been near misses, which even then had caused substantial damage to the warship. A large area of the ship's armoured hull below the waterline had been torn away. This had resulted in between 1,500 and 2,000 tons of water entering the *Tirpitz* through a 50 metre crack in the starboard side of the hull with an area measuring 10 by 14 metres ripped open. In fact, the bow remained attached to the rest of the battleship through the armoured steel plating on one side only. The damage was not confined to the exterior. Internally, the battleship had suffered considerable damage to the engines and generators, putting the former completely out of action for eight days. The damage was so severe that there existed no possibility to perform the necessary repairs in Norway. Cranes, auxiliary vessels and manpower were sorely lacking. One possibility was to tow the battleship to a German port; however, with Allied air and naval supremacy, this would be a very risky undertaking. It was inevitable that the *Tirpitz* would be subjected to heavy air and naval attacks if she tried to return to Germany.

The *Tirpitz* was not the only ship hit during the raid. Anchored close to the battleship, the steamer *KHZ-57*, trawler *Kehrwieder* and Dutch barge *Nord 29* were all sunk by British bombs. One Tallboy had hit the beach, blowing a huge crater into the rocky ground. It was very much apparent that the type of bomb used on this raid was far more powerful than the 1,600 lb bombs dropped during earlier raids. This new bomb indicated trouble ahead. The crater caused by the Tallboy created a minor migration among the German sailors—it appeared that everybody wanted to see the crater and discuss the new British super bomb.

According to a contemporary German report, 'It was estimated that repairs, if they could be carried out without interruption, would take at least nine months. It was eventually decided at a conference on 23 September 1944 at which Dönitz and his naval staff were present that it was no longer possible to make the *Tirpitz* ready for sea and action again...' The report concluded that 'The attack has confirmed that the defence installations are not adequate enough to resist raids from heavy bombers flying at high altitude. The ship can no longer remain at Kaa Fjord.'[14]

Even though the RAF had evidently failed to sink the Beast, it was appreciated that the raid had been fraught with problems. On 30 September, the Commander-in-Chief of Home Fleet, Henry Moore, dispatched a signal to Air Commodore Hesketh:

I would like to convey to the crews concerned my appreciation of the great effort... (I) can appreciate the difficulties and hazards involved. I will be glad if you would pass this to the crews who took part in this operation which from the photographs taken show the damage that has been inflicted on the last major unit of the German Fleet.[15]

The flights over Sweden meant that the Swedish government lodged a formal complaint to the Foreign Office. On 5 October, the Foreign Office sent a brief note of apology:

...a detailed investigation regarding overflights, Yours 1144, confirmed that a number of British Aircraft being part of considerable forces dispatched on operations over Northern Germany and the Baltic [sic] did in fact cross Swedish territory in the course of their operations. The British Government hereby (wish to provide its) sincere regrets for these regrettable incidents.

No evidence that the Swedish Government had given their tacit approval to the flights has been found. However, with the Allies rolling back German forces on every front, the diplomatic squabbling over the RAF use of Swedish airspace prior and after a raid against the *Tirpitz* did not go beyond a formal protest.

From seagoing battleship to floating fortress

Even though the heavy artillery of *Tirpitz* was substantially intact, it was obvious that she was finished as a seagoing warship. On 23 September, Dönitz decided that the *Tirpitz* was not to be repaired. However, abandoning the mighty *Tirpitz* and consigning her to an ignominious fate as a decoy would most likely have had a negative effect on the morale and fighting spirit—the Kriegsmarine in particular—of the German forces in northern Norway. A new role for the battleship was soon found, however, and she was to be moored near Tromsø as part of the Lyngen defence line as a static floating battery.

With makeshift repairs completed, *Tirpitz* left Kaa Fjord for the last time on 15 October. Exactly one month after the RAF raid, six tugs towed *Tirpitz* out of Kaa Fjord along with a strong destroyer escort. The highest speed allowed was eight knots as it was feared that if the speed exceeded ten knots, the bow would separate from the battleship. In the event of this happening, *Tirpitz* would sink ignominiously. Tromsø was reached without incident with Junge commenting that:

> Despite the large-scale damage, it was still possible to manoeuvre the ship. Worries that she would be difficult to control turned out to be exaggerated. Tromsø was reached under (*Tirpitz*'s) own power.[16]

Arriving on 16 October, the powerful Brown-Boveri turbine engines were shut down for the final time. Official German documentation after this date states that the *Tirpitz* by now had a new role as a *Die Schwimmende Batterie* (Literally the 'Floating Battery'). Two Ar 196 spotter floatplanes remained aboard the *Tirpitz* and were eventually transferred to nearby Skattøra, a floatplane air station. The Ar 196s had flown in excess of 100 operational sorties and were among the hundreds of Luftwaffe aircraft surrendered in Norway following the end of the war.

Nevertheless, not knowing the true amount of damage the Allies still believed that the *Tirpitz* constituted a major threat. As a result, further raids against the battleship would have to be conducted and the Joint Planning Staff did not wish to leave the job half finished. Even if the battleship had received major damage during Operation *Paravane*, she remained afloat. If the Germans decided to devote many hours of manpower and material resources to repair *Tirpitz*, this work would, even with a conservative estimate, last for several months.

It was obvious to the Germans that the transfer of *Tirpitz* from Kaa Fjord would not go unnoticed. In fact, three days after reaching a small strait between the island of Håkøya and Lille Grindøya near Tromsø, seven Firefly fighter-bombers of 1771 Squadron made an armed reconnaissance sortie over *Tirpitz* and the surrounding areas. The small-scale raid was not intended to damage *Tirpitz*, but rather confirming her whereabouts and state of the battleship. Several other vessels, including three destroyers, one flak ship and a repair vessel, were anchored nearby. The repair ship indicated that repairs to the battleship were underway. Also, a Firefly crew stumbled upon one Heinkel He 115 floatplane and shot it down.

Following the debriefing of the Firefly crews, the commander of the aircraft carrier HMS *Implacable* requested permission from the Home Fleet to carry out an air strike against the Beast with Fairey Barracudas. Permission was not granted as the armour-piercing bombs carried by the Barracuda were not large enough to cause serious damage. Later the same day, the daily photo-reconnaissance Mosquito from 540 Squadron appeared over the battleship's new lair.

With *Tirpitz* safely anchored off Håkøya, the Kriegsmarine sailors were given a brief reprieve and 700 of the crew were moved ashore to other duties; however, the flak crews remained aboard. Also, a Luftwaffe fighter squadron was based at Bardufoss, located about 50 km from Tromsø. Further protection came from two flak ships, *Nymphe* and *Thetis*, former Norwegian vessels that had been pressed into service with the Kriegsmarine.

CHAPTER FOUR

Operation *Obviate*

Sunday 29 October 1944

Although the *Tirpitz* had been substantially damaged during Operation *Paravane*, it was decided to conduct yet another raid.

When the *Tirpitz* was moved to Tromsø, southwest of Alta Fjord, it became apparent that the battleship was for the first time since the summer of 1942 within the range of UK-based bombers. Ralph Cochrane, Air Vice-Marshal of 5 Group, thought it would be possible to reach the Beast from Scottish airbases. Churchill wrote to Admiral Cunningham of the Joint Planning Staff on 26 October stating that every effort to sink the battleship must be made, even if such attacks would result in almost inevitable losses of aircrews and bombers. Nevertheless, Tromsø was still at the extreme range limit of Lancasters. With the bomb bay being occupied by the Tallboy high-explosive bomb, no additional fuel tanks could be fitted. Instead, long and thin fuel tanks fitted to the Wellington bomber could be located inside the rear fuselage of the Lancaster. Additionally, a drop tank off a Mosquito could be fitted inside the fuselage, but eventually such drop tanks were not fitted. This put the fuel capacity at 2,406 gallons, which was just enough for the 2,250 mile round trip. Concerns about range saw a directive being issued regarding alternate landing sites. If the crews had less than 900 gallons of fuel remaining following the raid, they would not be able to return to Lossiemouth and were to continue to Russia. In the event, no Lancasters participating in Operation *Obviate* diverted to Russia, although one ended up in Sweden.

This overload of fuel made the Lancasters severely overweight. Efforts to reduce weight included the removal of the dorsal gun turret as well as some of the armour plating behind the pilot's seat. Ammunition for the two remaining gun turrets was also sharply reduced. Even with these alterations the loaded weight of the Lancaster at 32 tons was about 2 tons above the nominal maximum take-off weight. Given the mediocre result from using 'Johnnie Walker' mines during Operation *Paravane*, these would not be used. The Tallboy was the obvious weapon for striking the Beast.

More powerful Rolls-Royce Merlin 24 engines were requisitioned along with paddle-blade propellers which would increase lift. The Merlin 24 delivered 1,610 hp at 3,000 rpm, considerably more than the standard 1,280 hp Merlin XX. The acting engineering officer of 5 Group, Sqn Ldr 'Paddy' Finucane, managed to locate the requested numbers of Merlin 24 engines and propellers at various 5 Group stations, and within five days, organised their transport to Bardney and Woodhall Spa. The surplus Merlin XX or Packard Merlin 28s [the American-built Packard Merlin 28 powered the Lancaster B. Mk III] removed from the Lancasters were sent in exchange for the Merlin 24s. In all, about 120 Merlin 24 engines were fitted to the Lancasters of IX(B) and 617 Squadrons.

The distance involved between the Scottish airbases and Håkøya was some 2,250, miles, and it was estimated that the bombers would be airborne for about fourteen hours for the round trip.

The German radar installations in northern Norway had been thoroughly checked by 100 Group that specialised in electronic warfare and countermeasures. The subsequent analysis of the data provided by sorties flown by 100 Group showed that a gap in the radar coverage existed in the Horta Fjord area. As a result, it was decided to cross into Norway at Horta Fjord and then continue eastwards into Sweden where the Lancasters would assemble over the Suorva water power plant dam north of Porjus. Following this, the course would be set northwards for Tromsø and Håkøya where the Beast was waiting in its lair. Crossing into Sweden and flying north to attack the *Tirpitz* had some distinct advantages. As the Germans expected an Allied invasion of northern Norway, the coastline was liberally dotted with defence installations. However, the Germans had made little effort in establishing a line of defence along the border with Sweden. With part of the flight path crossing Swedish airspace, German flak and fighters would be avoided. Additionally, the range of mountains on the Norwegian-Swedish border made detection by German defences more difficult. Thus, breaching Swedish neutrality was a small price to pay for reducing the risk of the Lancasters being detected.

Tirpitz had been moored south of Håkøya, a small island some 4 km from Tromsø. Apart from having a formidable anti-aircraft defence aboard the *Tirpitz*, two flak ships were moored nearby. Several land-based flak batteries provided additional protection. The bottom of the fjord was dredged with considerable amounts of sand, gravel and stone being moved underneath the *Tirpitz* (this was to further strengthen the final anchorage of the battleship and reduce the risk of her capsizing and sinking). This work began in early November and had not been completed when the RAF initiated Operation *Catechism* on 12 November, something which would have fatal consequences for the battleship and her crew. The mighty *Tirpitz*, built for combat on the high seas, had now been reduced to a stationary although virtually impregnable and unsinkable floating fortress.

Very soon after *Tirpitz*'s arrival at Tromsø, the Norwegian SIS agent Egil Lindberg—who operated a radio transmitter codenamed Vidar—was able to forward information to Britain regarding her whereabouts and status. Lindberg had previously noted that the Germans had begun dredging mud and gravel off Tromsø; however, Lindberg failed to make any sense of this and disregarded this observation. But when seeing *Tirpitz* slowly but surely making its way towards Håkøya, the significance of the dredging immediately became apparent to Lindberg. Working at the meteorological office at Tromsø, Lindberg regularly sent meteorological and intelligence reports to the British. His radio transmitter was hidden away at the top floor of the local hospital. Suffering from a limp as well as a bent spine, Lindberg never aroused the suspicion of the Germans.[1]

Apart from Lindberg's reports, the code breakers at Bletchley Park had cracked the Kriegsmarine code, which meant that every encrypted radio and telegraphic transmission sent and received, could be read and analysed within hours. Despite of having access to the official Kriegsmarine correspondence, the Norwegian reports were of great value, functioning as a way of confirming or even expanding on the information provided through the former source. Additionally, if the Germans decided to change the encryption, the information sent by Lindberg would for the time being be the only source available to the British.

The small Norwegian population had to make way for 7,000 German sailors and soldiers. Families were evicted from their houses in order to find lodging for the Germans. As with the area around Kaa Fjord, Håkøya and Lille Grindøya were soon brimming with flak units and smoke generators. The huge battleship was to be defended against any future RAF air raids and the Germans were certain that the RAF would return. If so, they would be warmly welcomed by scores of anti-aircraft guns, radar and artificial smoke.

Scorched earth warfare

In order to put the military situation in Finnmark from the autumn of 1944 until the end of the war—and the subsequent changed role of *Tirpitz* in the German defence strategy—into a larger context, it is necessary to make a slight digression and briefly describe these events. During the autumn of 1944, preparations for the expected Russian offensive into northern Norway had begun in earnest. The German authorities, along with the small but intensely fanatical Norwegian Nazi Party—Nasjonal Samling (NS), intended to evacuate the population of the northern province of Finnmark, then destroying everything of value before retreating southwards. These plans were outlined in a document dated 13 October: 'In the whole of the Finnish-Norwegian area ... all buildings shall be destroyed during the retreat in order to deprive the possibility to gain a foothold during the winter.'

An attempt to get the 75,000-strong population in Finnmark to move voluntarily was made on 17 October by high-ranking members Jonas Lie and Johan Lippestad. Warnings of the red Bolshevik menace, rape, pillaging and godlessness did not persuade the resident Norwegians to leave their homes. As a result of the almost complete lack of success in getting the local population to move voluntarily, the German *Reichskommissar* in Norway, Josef Terboven, sent a plea to Hitler for assistance. On 28 October, a *Führerbefehl* (Führer's Decree) ordering a scorched earth warfare in northern Norway was sent to Terboven. The terse decree read:

> Due to the lack of willingness of the population in northern Norway of voluntary evacuation, Der Führer has concurred with the suggestion of the Reichs Kommissar and commanded that the entire Norwegian population east of Lyngen Fjord shall be forcibly evacuated and all houses be burned to the ground or destroyed. The

commander of northern Finland has the responsibility to see to that the Führerbefehl is carried out ruthlessly. Any compassion with the local population is uncalled for.²

The deadline for the evacuation was set for 20 November. Only about 25,000 Norwegians were forcibly evacuated with the remaining population seeking refuge in the vast wilderness, enduring much hardship while waiting for the Germans to leave Norway. In all, some 16,000 houses were destroyed as were 350 bridges while more than 300 ships were sunk until Russian troops had liberated Finnmark in February 1945.

Tirpitz was expected to function as the northern outpost of the Lyngen line of defence, bombarding the advancing Russian forces with her heavy artillery. This was a similar role to the few remaining Kriegsmarine surface warships in the Baltic Sea during the spring of 1945.

The long expected offensive began in late October with the border town of Kirkenes falling to the Russians on 25 October. The city had been the target of many Russian air raids with multiple buildings being damaged or destroyed. But upon entering Kirkenes, the Russian troops met complete devastation. Not one house had been left standing by the retreating Germans.³ At the time, the German forces in Finnmark consisted of 204,000 troops, many of them combat-hardened veterans. The Norwegian Government in exile, which was based in London, was following the development of the military situation in Finnmark as closely as possible. Here existed an opportunity to return to Norway, a Norway that had been liberated from German occupation. However, the Lyngen line of defence was where the Germans were to make a last stand. The northernmost part of the Lyngen line was at the small coastal town of Tromsø, which was located some 200 km west-south-west of Kaa Fjord. Here, the German forces would be able to dig in against the impending Russian assault. As a result, the battleship was to become a floating battery with her heavy artillery strengthening the static line of defence against the expected Russian military advance. *Tirpitz* would remain in Kriegsmarine service, albeit in a static role, with the command structure remaining intact and the battleship would still fly the flag of Nazi Germany. In the event, *Tirpitz* would not fire a single shot against Russian forces.

Following intense negotiations with both British and Soviet authorities, the Norwegian Government was allowed to send a small military mission as well as a few civil servants to Murmansk, which would initially operate under Russian command in the liberation of Finnmark. Sailing from Scapa Flow on 1 November aboard the aircraft carrier HMS *Nairana* and cruiser HMS *Berwick*, the Norwegians arrived at Murmansk six days later. On 10 November, they arrived at the small Norwegian border town Kirkenes. Meeting total devastation, it was obvious that the task ahead of rebuilding a civil society would be formidable indeed. The need to support the Norwegian mission from Great Britain was deemed very difficult due to the distances involved and the lack of space aboard merchant vessels. One neat solution was found when the Swedish Government gave permission to base a USAAF air transport unit in the north of the country that would deliver supplies to Finnmark by air. In all, ten USAAF Douglas C-47 Skytrains were flown to Sweden and arrived at Wing F 21 Luleå-Kallax on 30 December. An American request to also send a fighter squadron for escort duties was vetoed by the Swedes. This operation, codenamed Operation *Where and When*, delivered dismantled wooden houses, tents, food, medical supplies, power generators, various spares and almost everything in between.

Norwegian troops (diplomatically referred to as Police Forces) based in Sweden were also transported to northern Norway. These were part of the 13,000-strong force of Norwegian refugees who had received military training with the tacit approval of Swedish authorities. (A further 2,000 Norwegians were airlifted to Great Britain where they became part of Norwegian forces in exile and consisted of soldiers, sailors and aircrews.) The most serious incident during Operation *Where and When* occurred on 1 May 1945 when twenty-two Norwegian soldiers and nine others were injured during an explosion in a German minefield in Karasjok. A field hospital was requisitioned from Sweden and transported to Karasjok by air. Also, part of the aerial assistance consisted of Swedish Fiesler Fi 156 Storch liaison aircraft. When the first of these prepared to land at Karasjok, it was fired upon by Norwegian soldiers. Although clearly marked with large Red Cross insignia as well as Flygvapnet insignia, the Fi 156 Storch was of German design. Many had previously been used by the Luftwaffe over Finnmark, so it was only to be expected that any such aeroplane would be operated by German forces.

A new film Lancaster

As with the previous raid, a Lancaster of the RAF Film Unit was to take part. However, since Operation *Paravane*, both aircraft of the Film Unit, DV171 and LM587, had been lost on operations, the former on 24–25 September during a raid on Calais, with LM587 being lost two days later during a raid against Cap Gris Nez. As a result, a replacement Lancaster was converted into a cine-film camera aircraft and the aircraft chosen was PD329. The twin machine guns in the front gun turret were removed with a cine camera being fitted. To give the camera operator a wide angle as possible, the front fuselage was modified with one side panel being detachable in flight. Although this arrangement provided an excellent view, the camera operator had to carry a safety harness to prevent him falling out of the Lancaster. Work on converting PD329 was completed in double-quick time with both crew (once again led by Bruce Buckham) and aircraft ready for Operation *Obviate*.

Preparing for the raid

On 24 October, the forthcoming raid was codenamed Operation *Obviate*. According to the 5 Group Operational Order, B.432, *Tirpitz* had sustained some damage during the previous raid. The exact seriousness of this damage was unknown to Bomber Command as well as the intention of the Kriegsmarine High Command regarding the future use of *Tirpitz*. As a result, 'It appears likely that the Germans may attempt to get the battleship back to a base in Germany, where the necessary repairs and refit can be carried out.'[4]

On 25 October, the Admiralty received information on Operation *Obviate* along with a request for three destroyers to be located along the route. The destroyers were to, if necessary, perform search and rescue duties. Men, aircraft and material were transferred to Lossiemouth. Russian authorities were notified of the raid that was said to occur 'the first suitable day after 28 October'. In case of an emergency, the aircrews were briefed to continue to Vaenga. Once again, Wing Commander Tait would lead his men against the Beast.

On 28 October, twenty Lancasters of 617 Squadron took off from Woodhall Spa and headed for Lossiemouth. This number included one reserve aircraft flown by Flt Lt Dobson; however, Dobson and his crew were not needed. Dobson did nevertheless take part in the raid accompanying one of the other Lancasters as a passenger. The weather at Lossiemouth at dawn was fine with some clouds. It was perfect flying conditions although as usual during night take-offs with a reduced visibility. The atmosphere during the briefing was filled with expectation.

Take-off

In all, twenty Lancasters of IX(B) Squadron took part in the raid. Take-off occurred between 01.18 hours (Flt Lt Dunne, NF937) and 02.34 hours (Flt Lt Camsell, NF929). One of the Lancasters flown by Fg Off. Redfern (NG249) took off at 02.32 hours, but had to return to base when the port inner Merlin engine seized up over the North Sea and returned to Lossiemouth at 07.24. (The timings for take-off, bomb runs and return to Britain have been extracted from the respective squadron's ORB, except where noted.) Nineteen Lancasters of 617 Squadron took off from Lossiemouth. Each Lancaster carried one six-ton Tallboy bomb. At 01.14 hours, Carey and his crew took off from Lossiemouth. The take-off provided one hair-raising moment when Carey came too close to the control tower. If Carey had collided with the control tower, there would in all likelihood have been no survivors from the ensuing crash.

The Lancasters were flown across the North Sea singly at 1,500 feet, climbing higher just prior to crossing the Norwegian coast. The RAF bombers continued across Norway and headed for neutral Sweden. According to a Swedish military report dated 2 October, some '70 Allied bombers, American and/or British' passed into Swedish airspace between 07.00 and 07.20 hours (local Swedish time GMT+1) in several waves between Frostviken and Tärna.' The bombers were identified as either Bristol Blenheims [sic] or Consolidated B-24 Liberators.

The weather was excellent with the mountainous Swedish landscape sprawling below the RAF fliers. At 07.55 hours, the Suorva Dam was reached where 'about 50' Lancasters circled before heading north. The Lancasters of 617 Squadron took the lead slot with IX(B) in close tow. A number of Lancasters, including that of Wing Commander James Michael Bazin, arrived late over the rendezvous point. While passing over Abisko at 08.20 hours (local Swedish time GMT+1), Swedish flak opened fire on the RAF bombers. The flak was inaccurate with no hits being recorded. Eight minutes later, Torneträsk on the border with Norway was reached and the Lancasters, then split into several smaller formations, left Swedish airspace over the Kummavuopio border post at 08.35 hours (local Swedish time GMT+1). It was estimated that some fifty aircraft were involved and the bombers were flying at altitudes varying between 500 and 2,000 metres. The weather was reported as being mostly clear with a moderate north-easterly wind. Later on, Tony Iveson would recall that the weather was excellent with no clouds: this meant increased chances of finally sinking the Beast. However, the lack of cloud coverage also meant that their Luftwaffe opponents would be able to intercept the Lancasters more easily. With the Lancasters due to bomb from altitudes around 15,000 feet, the risk of being hit by flak was considered relatively minor. Luftwaffe fighters were another matter, though. Carrying heavy Tallboy bombs, the fuel-laden Lancasters would provide easy targets for the fast and nimble Fw 190 and Bf 109 fighters. Both the Fw 190A-8 and Bf 109G-6 had a maximum speed of over 400 mph at 18,000 feet. The performance and armament of the Luftwaffe fighters were far superior to that of the Lancasters. The Fw 190A-8 carried a basic armament of two 13 mm MG 131 machine guns and two 20 mm MG 151 cannons while the Bf 109G-6 had two MG 131 machine guns and one 30 mm MK 108 cannon. Only a few hits from the MK 108 cannon were needed to bring down a heavy bomber. To make matters worse, the dorsal gun turret had been removed to reduce weight, thus reducing the defensive capability of the Lancasters to six .303 machine guns. With no RAF fighters having the necessary range, the bombers would have to fly unescorted deep into enemy territory in daylight.

Having been airborne for seven hours, the Lancasters finally arrived over the target area just before 09.00 hours. The artificial smoke generators had not yet been installed; however, the predictable Arctic weather then came to the rescue of the Germans. Although weather conditions were generally quiet and calm, a large amount of mist drifted in over the fjord at 2,000 metres from the sea prior to the RAF bombers arriving over the target area. Having to bomb through the mist would make it far more difficult for the bombardiers to pinpoint the battleship. Just thirty seconds prior to the Lancasters initiating their bomb run, the mist came rolling across the battleship. The bomb aimers only managed to catch brief glimpses of the *Tirpitz* through the mist.

At the small town of Tromsø some 6 km away from Håkøya, the ground shook when the Tallboys exploded. It seemed as if an earthquake had hit the Norwegian town. The first IX(B) Lancaster to attack was flown by Wing Commander Bazin at 08.54 hours from 15,000 feet: 'The ship appeared to be beached at one end.—Wind at target westerly causing low stratus over fjord.' Fg Off. Adams dropped the Tallboy from an altitude of 15,200 feet. For some reason, Adams was the only one carrying an oxygen mask: 'All the crew except Captain were without oxygen and results of bombing could not therefore be accurately assessed.' Just after dropping the Tallboy at 08.58 hours, Fg Off. Jones in LM448 was slightly injured when a panel on his left side broke loose. In the event, the bomb aimer aboard the Lancaster temporarily replaced Jones, managing to fly the bomber across the North Sea with Jones performing a safe landing at Lossiemouth. Due to the mist, many of the crews experienced difficulties to visually observe the battleship. One of these was Flt Lt Melrose who attacked at 08.55 hours from an altitude of 14,200 feet:

Target was obscured by cloud at time of bombing. Moderate to intense heavy and light flak over target area. *Tirpitz* seen clearing on approach and did not appear to be in distress. Cloud obscured target at time of bombing, making it impossible to assess results.

Apart from Fg Off. Redfern who aborted early, two aircraft of IX(B) Squadron failed to attack the *Tirpitz*. Fg Off. Ardnell in NG252 made two runs against the *Tirpitz* at '08.56 and 08.38 hours' [*sic*], but with the battleship being completely covered by mist, decided not to drop the bomb that was returned to Lossiemouth. Also, Fg Off. Lake did not attack the Beast and returned to base with the valuable Tallboy. The film unit Lancaster, PD329, of 463 Squadron covered the raid. According to the Operational Record Book of 463 Squadron, the report stated that: 'Our final view of Target showed her to be still afloat and firing all her guns, including the "heavies". Owing to the low visual conditions, only 150 feet of film were shot. The resulting film, lasting mere seconds, did not conclusively show any direct hits to the *Tirpitz*. As a result, it was obvious that a third raid would be necessary. However, the Lancaster was damaged by flak in the starboard wing, the engine nacelles and starboard main undercarriage also being hit. As a result, the return flight was anything but 'uneventful' (as stated in 463 Squadron's ORB). The landing at Waddington was nevertheless successful and although the Lancaster was severely damaged, it was repaired and returned to service.

The raid

While approaching the Beast, 'Willie' Tait could clearly see the battleship. However, upon reaching the target area only minutes later, *Tirpitz* had been completely obscured by clouds. The clouds reached an altitude of 6,000 feet. The first of 617 Squadron's Lancasters to attack were flown by Sqn Ldr Iveson at 07.50 hours from 15,000 feet and Sqn Ldr Fawke at 07.51 hours from 13,400 feet. Fawke's bomb '…overshot—otherwise results unobserved'. One minute later, Flt Lt Knights attacked from 13,200 feet:

> Bomb seen to enter water and explode about 20 yards off starboard bow and ship rocked considerably. Made several circuits after bombing and saw thick brown smoke billowing from vicinity of midships.

According to 617 Squadron's ORB, one direct hit was scored on *Tirpitz*. Flt Lt Hamilton reported to have bombed at 08.00 hours from 16,000 feet: 'Own bomb believed direct hit on bows followed by big flash. Saw two bombs, followed by another, drop close to *Tirpitz*, believed to be near midships.' This was overly optimistic. Due to the persistent clouds, most crews reported that the results of the bombing were 'unobserved'. Indeed, many crews had to make repeated runs over *Tirpitz* in an attempt to catch a glimpse of the battleship through the clouds and smoke.

Three of 617 Squadron's Lancasters did not drop their Tallboys: Flt Lt Gumbley, Flt Lt Pryor and Fg Off. Leavitt. Gumbley made four consecutive runs over the *Tirpitz* with the battleship being completely covered by clouds each time. As a result, the Tallboy remained in the bomb bay of the Lancaster. He radioed Wing Commander Tait who gave his approval for Gumbley and his crew to abort and return to Lossiemouth. The exact cause as to why Leavitt failed to deliver the heavy bomb is unclear, but it is highly likely that the poor visibility may have been the reason. 617 Squadron's ORB only gives the brief and terse comment: '1 x Tallboy. Brought back to base. Did not bomb.'

The flak over the target area was 'light to moderate' with a number of Lancasters (including four from IX(B) Squadron) suffering slight damage. Hopes were high among the crews that at least some of their bombs had come down on or close to the *Tirpitz*. This turned out to be a futile hope. In the event, none of the Tallboys hit the *Tirpitz*. There were several near misses, however, with a bomb causing damage to a propeller shaft. One of 617 Squadron's Lancasters piloted by Plt Off. Kell remained over the target area for several more minutes. Failing to find a break in the clouds, Kell did not wish to waste the Tallboy in vain and due to lack of fuel as well as damage to the hydraulic systems, made a precautionary landing at Sumburgh in the Shetlands. Although ordered to drop the Tallboy into the sea, Kell did not oblige. Apparently, the ground staff and crews were reported as not being at all happy with having a Tallboy-laden Lancaster on the airfield. However, when Kell received a bar to his DFC in December 1944, the landing at Sumburgh with the Tallboy still in place was singled out as a remarkable achievement!

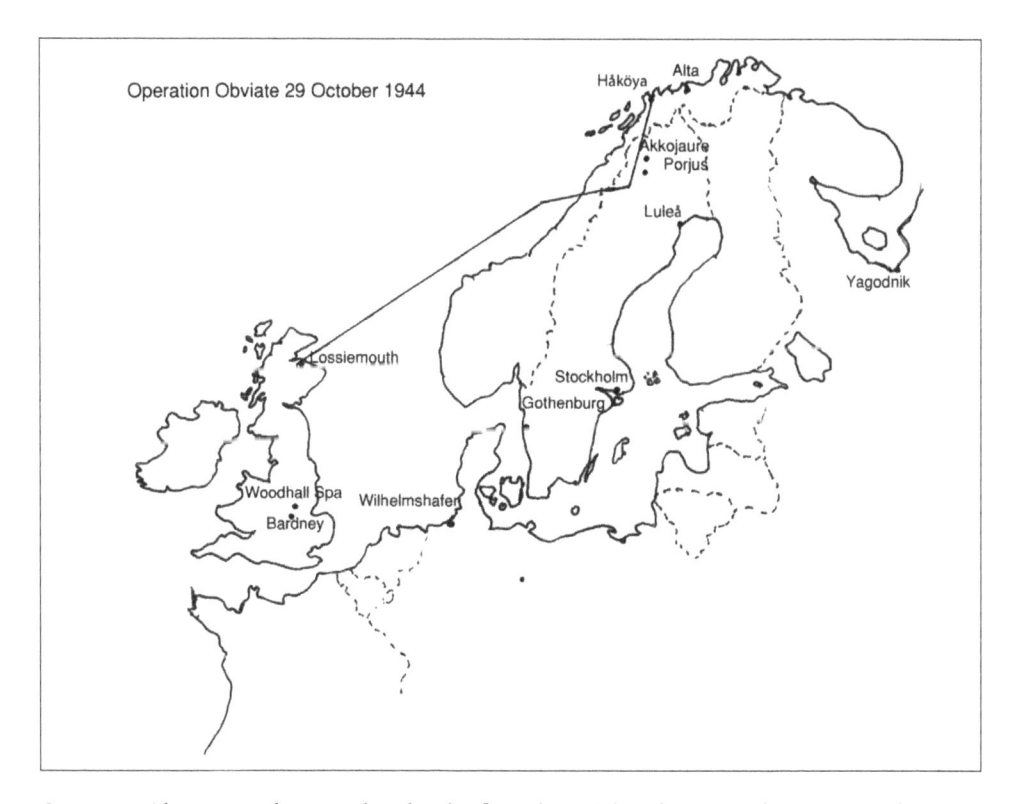

Operation *Obviate* was the second raid to be flown by IX(B) and 617 Squadrons against the Beast. (*Anders Eriksson*)

During the return flight, Flt Lt Buckham of 463 Squadron experienced a rather unsettling incident: 'About half way up the North Sea we heard a terrific crash, and in the morning light we could see the starboard leg hanging down, engine nacelles flapping in the breeze and a gaping hole in the wing. A shell had passed through the undercarriage and between No. 1 and No. 2 fuel tanks so we landed on one wheel.' The subsequent forced landing at RAF Waddington saw the Lancaster badly damaged. The flight had lasted fourteen hours and twenty minutes.

The Lancasters returned to Lossiemouth during the afternoon. Exhausted and weary from the long flight, the aircrews sensed that they had, once again, failed to deliver the final blow against the *Tirpitz*. However, it was obvious that the *Tirpitz* by now represented little or no threat to the British. Fg Off. Leavitt later put words to these feelings: 'I'm afraid they'll send us again, but I'm damned if I can see what damage the boat can do anymore.'[5]

The plight of NF920

The crew of NF920 had to make five attempts of dropping their Tallboy. On the first three attempts, clouds reduced vision of the target. On the fourth run, NF920 was hit by flak, probably causing the bomb bay doors to remain open. This was witnessed by Fg Off. Watts who later reminisced that he had seen pieces fall away from Carey's Lancaster. This was something that Watts 'had previously witnessed that was in Hollywood films'.[6] On the fifth and final run, *Tirpitz* was clearly visible. With only a few Lancasters remaining in the target area, the flak units were able to concentrate their fire against NF920. With the Tallboy spinning down towards the *Tirpitz*, the tail gunner aboard 'Easy Elsie' as NF920 had been named, Gerry Witherick, screamed over the intercom that the bomb had either hit the *Tirpitz* or in the immediate vicinity. However, additional hits from German flak caused further damage to the Lancaster, including the number four Merlin engine. The bomb-bay doors failed to close and fuel was streaming from a ruptured fuel tank in the wing. It would be a close call.

Even with the reduced speed caused by the open bomb-bay doors and starboard outer engine turned off due to flak damage, Carey and his crew set course for the Hebrides. Flying at an altitude of 300 metres, the Lancaster was hit by flak over Andøya Island at 09.25 hours. A further two fuel tanks were hit as was the port inner engine and radio, which was destroyed. By an incredibly good stroke of fortune, the wireless operator, FS Young, had felt the call of nature only moments before and was making his way back to the Elsan toilet. Had Young remained at his station, he would most likely have been killed. With the increased loss of fuel and two engines out of action, it was becoming clear to the crew that reaching Britain was out of the question. Attempting to reach Russia was one option, but that did not appeal to anyone aboard 'Easy Elsie'. The memories of the earlier deployment to Yagodnik did not encourage a return to Russia. One of the crew that was decidedly unhappy with the situation was the tail gunner, Gerry Witherick. Witherick was considered one of the lucky ones, always returning unscathed from sorties over enemy territory. On more than one occasion, Witherick had flown on sorties with a different crew to the previous one. Upon learning that they would not be able to return to Britain, Witherick angrily asked over the intercom about kind of silliness had brought this on. This was his 95th operational sortie and Witherick and the crew he was flying with always returned to base. According to Witherick, not returning to base would 'ruin his reputation'. This time, however, Witherick's usual luck had run its course.

Unscheduled return to Sweden

Checking the fuel gauge, it was obvious that their fuel was fast evaporating and it was estimated that some 770 gallons had been lost. Trying to reach an airfield in the Shetlands was out of the question and with the radio destroyed, the possibility of contacting a Royal Navy destroyer that had been stationed along the route was impossible. Ditching in the North Sea would mean an almost certain death. Witherick, whose brother was serving in the Royal Navy, caustically remarked that the navy was 'never at hand when you needed them' and that he would most certainly raise the issue the next time he met his brother.

Through the VHF radio, however, contact was established with Lancaster, LM492, flown by Flt Lt Pryor. Following a brief conversation, it was decided that Carey and his crew would try to reach Sweden. This was, in fact, the only option available to the crew of 'Easy Elsie'. Turning on a 140 degree heading, Carey climbed to 4,500 feet when the number two engine had to be shut down. At the same time, the crew dumped as much gear as possible overboard in order to save weight such as machine guns and ammunition belts. It is alleged that two machine guns fell into the huge Porjus-Suorva water electricity dam where they remain to this day.

By 11.05 hours (local Swedish time GMT+1), the Lancaster arrived over the Suorva Dam in Swedish Lapland. Spotting the small village of Porjus, Carey decided to force land. With the last removable items having been disposed of into the Stora Lulevattnet River, which supplied water to the Porjus-Suorva water power dam, the crew went to the back of the bomber to take up crash positions leaving Carey and Flight Engineer Les Franks up front. Carey extended the undercarriage and initiated the landing run. The spot chosen was the partly frozen Käinutjägge bog, some 7 km north-north-west of Porjus. The Lancaster bounced heavily, rolling some 180 metres before sinking through the frozen surface. The tail of the bomber rose as the front fuselage dug into the ground; after a few seconds, the tail fell back onto the ground. The pilot, Fg Off. Carey, had suffered an injured left knee when thrown against the large P4 compass, but otherwise the crew of 'Easy Elsie' was safe. Immediately after the Lancaster had come to an abrupt halt, the crew exited the bomber in double-quick time. Les Franks went missing for a while and the remainder of the crew began calling out for him, Franks eventually answering that he had landed head-down in the mud, but was unhurt. The tail gunner quipped: 'A bloody good job you did, else you might have got hurt.' The crew then helped Carey from his seat and attempted to set fire to the wrecked Lancaster. At first, they tried incendiaries; however, the bomber refused to burn. After soaking maps in petrol, setting them on fire and tossing them into the forward fuselage, the Lancaster finally caught fire. The fire soon petered out, although not before completely destroying the forward fuselage.

The crash had been observed by several of the local inhabitants as well as a small group of Swedish home guard troops. The airmen were given a meal with Franks curiously asking what it was. Witherick curtly responded, 'Shut up and eat.' A Swedish army officer then replied that the dish was cow's lung. Despite being very hungry after more than ten hours in the air, none of the crew was able to continue eating.

The day after their unscheduled arrival in Sweden, the crew of 'Easy Elsie' was taken by train to Stockholm and accompanied by a Swedish guard for interrogation and internment. During the train journey south, the British airmen were served a meal that included ice cream, a wartime rarity. Following their arrival in Stockholm, the crew was transferred to the Storvik internment camp. The stay at Storvik was brief, the airmen being put on another train for transportation to the Korsnäs internment camp outside Falun. On 11 November, Franks, McLennan, McKie, Young and Witherick were formally released. They arrived back in Stockholm soon afterwards and handed over to the British Embassy before being returned to the UK by the airline BOAC.

Due to his injured left knee cap, Carey did not accompany his colleagues, instead being transferred to a hospital in nearby Jokkmokk and was subsequently interrogated by Flygvapnet officers. During the interrogation, the Swedish military interrogators noted that the crew members were '…commendably quiet whenever military topics were discussed'. Carey explained their incursion into Swedish airspace had been due to a navigational error and that the signals fired off by the lead Lancaster were to assemble to bombers to turn back. This was, as noted by author Bill Sweetman, 'A decided case of economy with the truth.'[7]

Nevertheless, it was obvious that the target had been the *Tirpitz*. The fact that the RAF Lancasters had crossed into Swedish airspace was not brought up during the interrogation with the forced landing being explained as a navigational error. Following completion of the interrogation sessions, Carey arrived at the Korsnäs internment camp on 7 November. On 15 November, he was released and allowed to Stockholm. As with the rest of his crew, Carey was handed over to the British Embassy. Carey had to wait for air transport for several days and eventually returned to the UK on a BOAC airliner on 23 November. (According to Paul Brickhill's account in his book *Dam Busters*, Carey and 'Easy Elsie's crew were 'furious' that they had missed the final raid on *Tirpitz*.) In a 1964 telephone interview, Witherick described the arrival in Sweden.

> Well aware that we could not return to our base, we set course for Sweden, the nearest neutral nation. We began to remove everything loose, throwing machine guns, ammunition, etc., out of the aircraft in order to reduce weight. After about one hour, we noticed a large lake, completely surrounded by trees and a small village. We decided to take the chance and try to land. Our hydraulics had been shot away, which meant

that undercarriage, flaps and bomb-bay doors were down and open. This made landing a difficult and risky venture, particularly in a foreign, unknown piece of land. We got down in one piece, with our pilot, 2Lt Carey, suffering a broken knee and damage to his head, having struck the instrument panel.

Following the raid against *Tirpitz* and the arrival of the Lancaster at Porjus, the Swedish armed forces issued a statement to the media:

Some of the 4-engined aeroplanes that during Sunday morning flew over northern Sweden has, following close investigation, been found to have been of English [*sic*] nationality. One of the English 'planes made a forced landing northeast of Porjus. The crew and the 'plane has been taken into custody by military personnel.

After the war, none of 'Easy Elsie's crew had visited the site of their Lancaster's final resting place. However, this changed in 2002 when the navigator, Alex McKie, was given a trip to Sweden as an eightieth birthday present from his children. During his visit to Sweden in the summer of 2002, McKie was interviewed by aviation historian John Bryggman. McKie commented upon 'Easy Elsie's arrival:

We flew across the North Sea, then climbing over the Norwegian mountains. Naturally, we flew individually, so we did not see any of the other aeroplanes. According to the briefing, we were to meet up over Porjus. On the map, we could see that (Porjus) was a small village on the southern end of a large lake. As planned, we met at 11.30 hours. A few of the bombers were already present when we arrived. Then we set course for *Tirpitz*.

We were supposed to bomb from an altitude of 12,000 feet. If we bombed from a lower altitude, it was uncertain if our Tallboys would be able to penetrate the armour deck. We arrived from the south. As with the previous raid, the weather was not good. The battleship was partly covered by clouds. During our first pass, we could not see the target, so we turned around for another try. Then we were hit by flak with one of the engines being put out of action. In all, we made five passes before finally dropping our Tallboy. During the respective passes, the flak became more intense and accurate. The fuel tanks were damaged and we could see fuel streaming away. By this time, we only had two engines in working order.

During the briefing, we had received the radio frequency for a destroyer in readiness to pick up any downed aircrew from the North Sea. For two reasons, this was not possible for us. First of all, we had too little fuel remaining. Secondly, our radio had been destroyed by a flak hit. If the wireless operator had remained in his seat, he would have been killed. Instead, he had, with Carey's permission, moved to the rear of the Lancaster.

Things did not look particularly bright. We could not reach Britain and as we had no radio, we could not get in touch with the Royal Navy that we would ditch in the North Sea. Of course, putting down in Norway was out of the question. We decided to try to reach Sweden. But, would our dwindling fuel be enough to take us over the mountains in our shot-up bomber on just two engines?

The flight engineer worked with levers and pumps, trying to transfer as much fuel as possible to the undamaged fuel tanks. I calculated that we were going to reach Porjus. I chose Porjus due to the fact I knew where it was and that it was a populated area. And we managed to reach Porjus. We flew round the Porjusselet. Before this, we had thrown everything loose overboard so we could get across the mountains, apart from the four Browning machine guns in the rear turret. These might come in handy if we were attacked by German fighters. We now dispatched the Brownings into the lake, I don't know exactly where. Initially, we had planned to ditch into the lake outside Porjus, release the dinghy and row ashore.

While we were circling, our flight engineer was up front with the pilot. I was sitting by my small navigator's desk. Then Carey spotted a small field in the middle of a forested area. He concluded that it was just about large enough to make a normal approach and landing. With wheels and flaps lowered, Carey put the aeroplane down with a speed of about 120 knots. Unfortunately, the ground was too soft. Our wheels dug into the bog and (our bomber) quickly came to a halt. Luckily, we had taken up crash positions with our backs pressed against the rear main wing spar, which extends through the fuselage of the Lancaster. During the landing, our flight engineer assisted the pilot with adjusting the throttles and trim rudders. This was common practice during landings. When we landed, two things happened. The flight engineer was the first one to leave the Lancaster by flying through the windscreen. He had been unable to strap in as it was not possible to do so. The other thing was that the tail gunner's parachute came hurtling forwards. Normally, the parachute would have been fastened in the aeroplane. Luckily, no one was hit by the wayward parachute. The Lanc tipped up on its nose, but soon fell back on an even keel. We all sighed of relief.

The only one to sustain some injuries was Bill Carey. The straps broke away and he was thrust forward, breaking his knee cap against the compass. Extraordinarily enough, the flight engineer was uninjured, merely shaking his head before getting up on his feet. A tough bloke!

When we had all gotten out of the aeroplane, we decided to set fire to it. I destroyed all my maps and the radio gear. In order to set fire to a Lancaster, you were to use a torch. However, the torch did not work properly. Instead, we took an axe and punched a hole in one of the fuel tanks. We then put a match to the pouring fuel. Before this, we removed the dinghy as this should contain provisions, chocolates, juice, cigarettes, etc. But, when we pulled the rip cord, nothing happened. With the Lancaster burning, the dinghy suddenly opened with a huge bang. When we searched the inflated dinghy, we could not find any provisions. Apparently, someone in England had thought themselves to be in greater need of the provisions than we would be.

We were in the middle of the wilderness. Our pilot could not walk. We then deliberated about what next. I said: 'I—hopefully—know where we are. According to the map, we should walk to the east to get to a railway, which we then can follow south towards Porjus.' We decided that the wireless operator would accompany me. We then left, walking through the forest before reaching a large lake. We found a boathouse which we broke into, borrowing a rowing boat. After rowing across the lake, we reached the railway, which we then followed south.

When reaching the first house, we knocked on the door. An elderly lady opened, but when seeing us she screamed and immediately slammed the door shut. In fairness, we did not look our best considering what had happened in the last few hours. We had better luck at the next house. A friendly lady in her thirties let us in. She spoke very good English, telling us that she had seen us flying low over the village. She offered us coffee and then called her husband. After a while, the Swedish Army arrived, taking care of us.

I was brought to the police station for interrogation. An army officer wanted to know why we had dropped bombs in the lake and where was the rest of the crew. I explained that we had not dropped any bombs and showed on the map the location of the rest of the crew. A patrol was dispatched to recover them. I was also asked to provide my name, rank, etc.

The staff at the British Embassy thought it inappropriate that we would walk around in Stockholm wearing our flight suits. We were issued with coupons, both for restaurants and clothes stores. The first thing we did was to buy clothes, the cost for which was credited to the Embassy. Naturally, we bought the most expensive clothes available such as suits, shoes and ties. In fact, everything that we thought we needed.

While waiting for our flight back to Britain, we enjoyed the hospitality in Stockholm. When we walked into a restaurant, the guests rose and applauded. It was immediately apparent if any Germans were present as they did not participate in the celebrations. This was understandable. More often than not, our food and drink was free of charge!

About a year later, I was at the Mess when an officer I knew from before approached me. 'Mac,' he said. 'I've got good news and bad news. Which one do you want to hear first?' The bad one first, the good news should be alright. The bad news is that the Embassy has sent you a bill for £350 for the clothes you bought in Stockholm. The Embassy requests that you reimburse them and also tell them what happened with your navigator's watch. I told him that the watch most likely had been torn from my arm during the forced landing, an answer he accepted. But regarding the £350, I was on twenty-seven shillings a day and would never have been able to pay it back. However, my friend then said: 'If you buy me a large scotch, I'll lose the bill and you'll never hear any more about it!' I suppose I still owe £350 to the British Embassy in Stockholm, which with interest should be a considerable amount. (Note: the bill for £350 was excessive and it is possible that McKie might have recalled the sum incorrectly; however, it was a considerable amount of money.)

On 30 October, eighteen Lancasters of 617 Squadron returned to Woodhall Spa, including the spare aircraft flown by Flt Lt Dobson. The remaining two aircraft arrived back at Woodhall Spa the following day.

Post-raid assessment

The *Tirpitz* had not been sunk. According to the ORB of 617 Squadron:

> Unfortunately adverse weather was encountered over the target and although most of the bomb aimers were able to see the ship at the commencement of their bombing runs, cloud interfered with the runs or obscured the target at the time of release. Results were mainly unobserved, but three crews report a direct hit or very near miss off the stern of the battleship. Two or three others near misses were seen, one off the starboard bow and one believed midships. Three aircraft brought back their bombs to base as they were unable to make satisfactory bomb runs.

This was bad news. Despite the failure to sink the Beast, Air Vice-Marshal Cochrane sent this message: 'Congratulations on your splendid flight and perseverance. The luck won't always favour the *Tirpitz*. One day you'll get her.' During a visit to Woodhall Spa, Cochrane stated that Bomber Command would continue to send its bombers against *Tirpitz* 'again and again' until she had been finally sunk.[8] The Norwegian agent Egil Lindberg subsequently sent a message to the British: 'Give her another salvo.' A few Tallboys had fallen on solid ground with devastating effect and several Norwegian families built makeshift air raid shelters (the craters were still to be seen more than twenty years after the raid). With *Tirpitz* still afloat, it was quite obvious that further raids were to be expected.

As the Luftwaffe had not been able to intercept the RAF Lancasters, some thirty single-seat fighters were transferred to Bardufoss, some 50 km from Tromsø. This meant added protection for the battleship. Given enough pre-raid warning, the Luftwaffe fighter pilots would be able to decimate any bomber force daring to attack *Tirpitz*. The battleship had received some damage, however. According to a post-raid report, a near miss had caused some 800 tons of water to enter the hull. Further damage had been made to '…the port shaft and rudder and flooded almost 100 feet of the after end of the ship on the port side'.[9] This was, all things considered, not particularly serious damage. *Tirpitz* was still afloat and only three sailors had been killed during the raid. This was good news for the Germans—the battleship had been able to defend herself against the RAF bombers although failing to shoot down any of the Lancasters. Despite all the setbacks suffered by German forces on all fronts, the *Tirpitz* still fielded a huge array of heavy artillery. However, the cloudy conditions over Håkøya had made precision bombing extremely difficult. The failure of the raid meant that the *Tirpitz* got a reprieve. However, it was patently clear that the British would not stop before *Tirpitz* had been sunk.

CHAPTER FIVE

Operation *Catechism*

Sunday 12 November 1944

Even though the battleship had sustained heavy damage in the previous raids—particularly during Operation *Paravane* on 15 September, but also on 29 October—*Tirpitz* was still afloat. As a result, a third Lancaster raid, codenamed Operation *Catechism*, was planned to take place as soon as possible. In the event, this raid would deliver the final blow to the Beast.

One Whitehall official is said to have demanded a return to naval air strikes, reverting to using Barracudas armed with 2,000 lb armour-piercing bombs—presumably due to cost. This demand was quietly filed away.

Planning for a third RAF raid against the Beast began on 3 November. According to Operation Order B.439, the raid was to be codenamed Operation *Catechism*. Planning for the raid was identical as Operation *Obviate*. It was expected that the raid would be carried out two days later, using the same time slots and routes to and from the target area. For the second time in little over a week, IX(B) and 617 Squadrons prepared to take on the *Tirpitz*. In all, thirty-nine Lancasters, including twenty from IX(B) Squadron and nineteen from 617 Squadron, arrived in Scotland on 4 November. The third IX(B) and 617 Squadron raid was to be an all-out effort to finally sink the *Tirpitz*. Time was getting short, however. On 27 November, the sun would settle beneath the horizon (not rising above 12 degrees below the horizon north of the Arctic Circle) for the next couple of months, which meant that any daylight operations would be severely restricted due to the lack of sunlight. Conducting a night raid against the *Tirpitz* was, for obvious reasons, out of the question.

Daily Mosquito reconnaissance flights ensured that Bomber Command received up-to-date information on the weather in the area. Each day's weather information such as temperature, humidity and winds was assessed. It appeared that the raid could take place on 5 November. The crews of IX(B) and 617 Squadrons were placed in a state of readiness to make a third attempt at sinking the Beast. The crews of 617 Squadron took off from Woodhall Spa with nineteen Lancasters landing at Lossiemouth. However, during the evening, a gale warning over the target area was announced and the crews of IX(B) and 617 Squadrons had to return to their respective bases disappointed. The raid was postponed until further notice, but it was clear that *Tirpitz* had to be sunk within the next couple of weeks.

Activities at 617 Squadron were confined to regular flying training. On 8 November, the station commander's parade was held with all aircrew in attendance. Flying training resumed the following day with a 'gale and frost warning' being announced. In spite of this, preparations for the impending raid against the Beast began on 10 November.

The final days of the *Tirpitz*

Work on securing the battleship at her Håkøya berth began in earnest on 2 November. Several tons of rubble was dumped on the bottom of the fjord. The intention was to create a build-up on the bottom of the fjord to a level of two metres below the keel. When finished, it was hoped that this would stop the battleship from sinking completely in case of any further attacks occurring. However, this work had not been completed when RAF Lancasters arrived for the third time in less than two months. Only about 14,000 cubic feet of rubble had been moved below the keel of the *Tirpitz* by the time of the final raid. This was grossly inadequate for stopping the *Tirpitz* sinking to the bottom of the fjord.

On 4 November, only six days after Operation *Obviate*, Kapitän zur See Wolf Junge relinquished command of the *Tirpitz*. During his eight-month tenure as commander of Germany's last remaining battleship, Junge had never been able to inspire the crew the way his predecessor had done. In his place, Kapitän zur See Robert Weber arrived. During the next couple of days, the weather forecast did not show any chance of improvement. Strong winds and cloudy conditions still prevailed. During the evening of 11 November, the weather reconnaissance Mosquito reported foggy conditions over Alta Fjord. Despite the risk of bombing blind through the fog, Air Vice-Marshal Cochrane decided to press ahead for, what was hoped, the final raid on the Beast.

Life aboard the *Tirpitz* had to continue. Daily routines such as regular exercise and remaining on constant alert for British air raids kept the crew busy. As the days went by, the atmosphere aboard the battleship became even more tense. The Russian offensive into Finnmark was proceeding, albeit slowly. However, it was the risk of further RAF air raids that was the discussion point among the *Tirpitz* crew. The day before the raid, Tordis Ryeng was informed by her son Vidar that they were playing music aboard the battleship. With her grandmother in tow, Tordis walked towards the beach, listening intently to the music. Initially, the music consisted of pretty melodies which soon gave way to some 'horrible' shrill tunes. Tordis' grandmother turned to her daughter commenting that 'It sounds like a funeral march.' Her comment turned out to be prophetic.

On 11 November, nineteen Lancasters of 617 Squadron, including one spare aircraft flown by Flt Lt Gavin, took off from Woodhall Spa. The operation was finally given the go-ahead after a Mosquito weather reconnaissance aircraft reported an improvement in the weather. Conditions over the target area were said to be largely clear with some patches of cloud. Having experienced a 'butterfly feeling' in his stomach about the forthcoming raid, Fg Off. Leavitt later stated that the pre-raid briefing was very short and to the point. It was noted that the aircrews, most of which had already experienced two failed attempts to sink the *Tirpitz*, were 'determined but not optimistic'.[1]

Take-off

Walking to their bombers, the aircrews discovered that the mechanics were frantically attempting to remove thick layers of snow and ice on the Lancasters. This was a serious matter. The snow was removed from the wings and stabilisers by using brooms (with some of the aircrews assisting the mechanics) while the ice was hacked off. The ice would stretch the take-off weight even further as well as making it more difficult to control the overladen bombers. Winter had indeed arrived in Scotland which meant that apart from the iced-up aircraft, the runway was also covered in ice. Warming up the Merlin engines, the aircrews huddled at their respective crew stations. Take-off preparations complete, the first Lancaster weaved towards the runway.

At first, it seemed as if the Lancasters were far too heavy; however, take-off was accomplished without incident to everyone's relief. Out of the thirty-eight Lancasters, seven of IX(B) Squadron's Lancasters failed to take-off due to the icy conditions. Frustration ran high among the crews of these seven as they watched the other Lancasters struggle to get airborne, slowly climb for altitude and set course for the Beast. In the event, only thirteen of the twenty available IX(B) Squadron Lancasters would participate in Operation *Catechism*. All eighteen Lancasters of 617 Squadron led by Wing Commander Willie Tait managed to get airborne.

In all, thirty-one Lancasters of IX(B) and 617 Squadrons took part in the raid with a Lancaster of 463 Squadron equipped with film cameras accompanying the bombers in order to document the raid for damage assessment. As previously, it was fervently hoped that the film would show the final moments of the *Tirpitz*. In such a case, the resulting film would make history and be shown across the country at cinemas.

The flight across the North Sea was uneventful. Complete radio silence had been imposed with the aircrews occasionally spotting the outline of another Lancaster as the darkness of night turned into dawn. Most of the Lancasters made it across the North Sea singly with many of the crews not seeing another bomber until several hours into the flight. In order to avoid mid-air collisions, navigational lights were turned on until the aircraft arrived near the Norwegian coast.

The flight path to the target was identical to that on 29 October. Initially, the weather was good with clouds forming. Even though the visibility became worse, the Lancasters pressed on. At dawn, fog was forming over the North Sea and it dissipated slowly. Seconds turned into minutes which turned into hours. Beneath the RAF bombers was the sprawling black and icy water of the North Sea. The flight to the Norwegian coast went without a hitch with the Lancasters crossing into Norway at Hortafjord. Upon crossing into Norway, Fg Off. Leavitt later wrote: 'The terrain below was bleak, precipitous and barren, and at the same time magnificent… I have never felt so completely alone in my life.'[2]

Luftwaffe fighter opposition

One of the highest-scoring aces of Jagdgeschwader 5 (JG 5), and indeed the Luftwaffe, was the twenty-seven-year-old Heinrich Ehrler who had shot down 199 aircraft. An ardent Nazi, Ehrler was ordered during the autumn of 1944 to establish a new forward airfield at Elvebakken near Alta. While on his way there, Ehrler was instructed to pass through Bardufoss and inspect the pilots' capabilities as well as the condition of the airfield itself. Previously, it had been decided to split the fighter squadrons of JG 5 between Alta, Banak and Bardufoss. This meant that new lines of communication had to be established, pilots acclimatising themselves with new airfields and their surroundings while also maintaining their air combat and gunnery proficiency.

During the brief campaign of 1940, RAF fighters had been based at Bardufoss until 8 June when British forces evacuated the area ahead of the German advance. Bardufoss was taken over by the Luftwaffe, but mainly functioned as a transition stop for German aircraft and troops heading for the Eastern Front. Few Luftwaffe aircraft, and then mainly various liaison and transport aircraft, were permanently based at Bardufoss. However, during the summer and autumn of 1942, Bardufoss was a vitally important Luftwaffe airbase in the attacks against the PQ 17 and PQ 18 convoys. One interesting aspect of Bardufoss was that the runway was blocked to the north by mountains, which meant that fighter scrambles had to be made towards the south.

With Germans troops retreating from Finland and Russian forces advancing, northern Norway was becoming a battleground. JG 5 had previously had to make do with older variants of the Messerschmitt Bf 109. In late 1944, a batch of fifty-six new Messerschmitt Bf 109G-6s and twenty-two Focke-Wulf Fw 190A fighters were rushed to northern Norway to reinforce the depleted strength of JG 5. The Fw 190s were reportedly of two different subtypes.

On 9 November, Major Ehrler arrived at Bardufoss, finding few things to his liking and many things to improve upon. According to Ehrler:

The 'Focke-Wulf Fw 190 was completely unknown to most (of the pilots). None of the squadron leaders had flown it before. The young fliers that had just arrived as replacements for those who had been shot down had no frontline experience. They did not know anything about the weather or the particular conditions in the north. They had not received any formation flying training.

Ehrler immediately initiated a rushed training programme for the inexperienced pilots of JG 5 that were flying older variants of the Bf 109. Ehrler eventually decided to stay at Bardufoss until the early hours of 12 November when he and his aides continued to Alta. One of Ehrler's aides subsequently recalled that they had heard that the *Tirpitz* had been moved to Håkøya, but they did not know exactly where the battleship was anchored. Ehrler and his cadre of experienced pilots had, after all, merely been ordered to train the new pilots and reorganise JG 5 according to Luftwaffe headquarters' directives.

The artificial smoke generators which had been available at Kaa Fjord had not yet become operational at *Tirpitz*'s new lair. Instead, seven small fishing boats, each with a small smoke-producing generator, were put at the disposal for the defence of the battleship. It was thought doubtful if these would be sufficient as the waters around Håkøya were much wider than Kaa Fjord. The smoke would only be able to cover parts of the huge battleship.

At Lossiemouth, information was received that Luftwaffe single-engine fighters had arrived at Bardufoss. This was troubling news indeed. Heavily overweight with only two gunners in the front and tail turrets, the Lancasters would stand little chance if intercepted by the Luftwaffe. Instead of sinking Germany's final battleship, the risk of having IX(B) and 617 Squadrons decimated, or even annihilated, by Luftwaffe fighters was now a distinct risk.

Closing in for the Kill

The rendezvous point was, again, Lake Akkojaure in the Swedish Torne marshes, some 100 miles to the south east of Tromsø. At the Suorva hydroelectric dam, the local policeman, Mauritz Eriksson, and his aid were shovelling snow and scraping ice off a boat. Suddenly the heavy roar of Merlin engines shattered the silence and three Lancasters were soon spotted, entering a low level holding pattern over the Suorva Dam. Many more Lancasters followed. At first, Eriksson thought that the Suorva Dam was the target, but then a clerk came running out of a building, screaming, 'Hey lads, it's time for *Tirpitz*!' The location of the *Tirpitz* was well known in Sweden with Norwegian refugees having told of the previous attempts to sink the battleship. Eriksson later wrote that he watched the RAF bombers through a pair of binoculars and was able to clearly see the faces of several crew members. One of the tail gunners even waved at Eriksson. Just across the border, the Norwegian Milorg agent, Sigurd Senje, was forwarding homing signals to the RAF bombers.

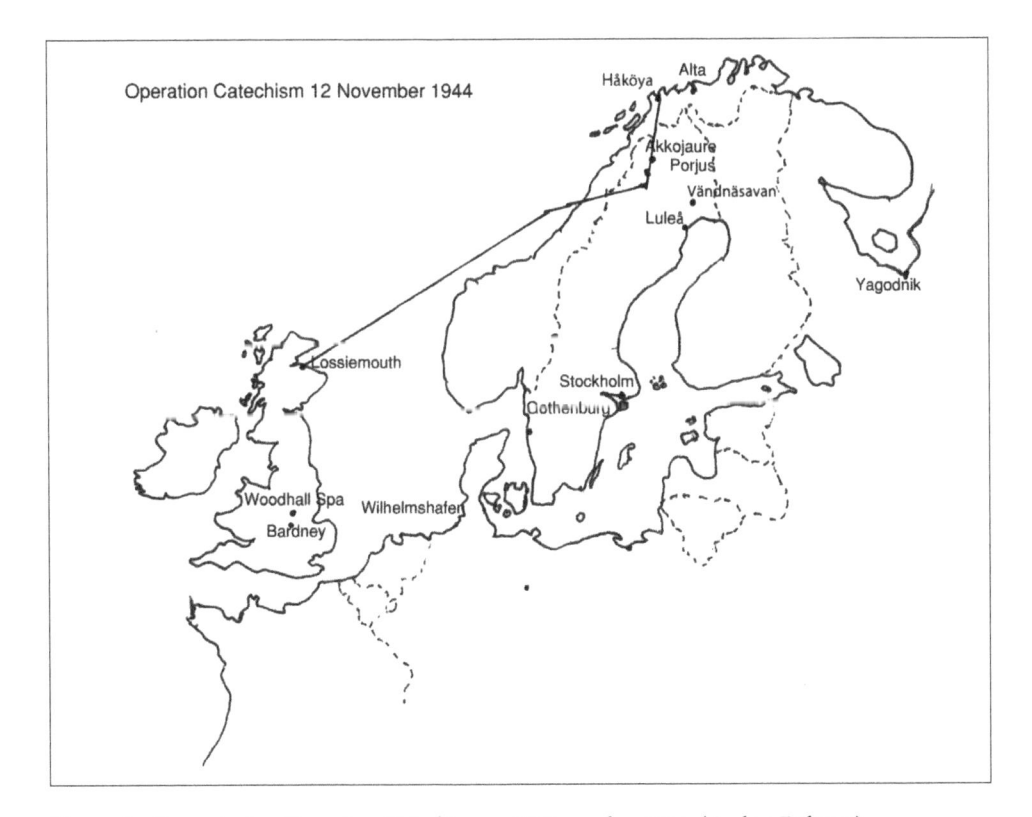

The routes flown during Operation *Catechism* on 12 November 1944. (*Anders Eriksson*)

When Tait arrived over the target area, he spotted the *Tirpitz* at anchor some 18 miles away. Freddie Watts, flying behind Tait's Lancaster, later recalled saying to his bomb aimer: 'My God, Mac. Today, we'll finish them.' Neither smokescreen nor Luftwaffe fighters could be seen. The Lancasters had been spotted, however, with inaccurate bursts of heavy shells and flak exploding beneath the bombers. In his book *Dam Busters*, Paul Brickhill wrote that the immobile battleship resembled a small spider or a black beetle surrounded by snow-covered mountains. This was the third raid against *Tirpitz* in less than two months and there was an overall feeling that this raid would have to succeed. The Beast simply had to be sunk.

The first indication to the Germans of the impending raid occurred at around 08.30 when it was reported that a formation of Lancasters had been sighted near Bodø. Robert Weber, the artillery officer aboard *Tirpitz*, did not know what to make of this report. It could be that the British bombers were heading for Soviet territory as had happened in mid-September. If so, a raid would almost certainly be forthcoming within the next couple of days from the east. Nevertheless, Weber demanded more information: 'I want to know on which course they are heading.' At the Luftwaffe airfield at Bardufoss, the fighters of Jagdgeschwader 5 remained on the ground.

Having joined the formation, the Lancasters soon left the Torne Marsh area. Heading north-west, the bombers climbed to 14,000 feet in order to clear the mountains in the Swedish–Norwegian border area. Another report of the approaching bombers was sent on 07.39 hours. Some twenty minutes later, a Luftwaffe fighter pilot at Bardufoss, Leutnant Beniers, received a report that three Lancasters had been spotted over Mosjøen. The bombers were flying on an easterly course. This report, along with one on a single Lancaster in the vicinity of Bodø also heading east, was deemed to be unconnected with each other. The distance between Mosjøen and Bodø was simply too great. One possibility was that the British bombers were on their way to Russia as had evidently been the case on 11 September. Another four Lancasters flew high over Mosjøen at 08.25 hours. More reports of Lancasters over northern Norway arrived; however, as incredible as it may seem, few of these reports of a possible impending air raid against *Tirpitz* reached the fighter pilots at Bardufoss.

At 08.15 hours, the report of the three Lancasters that had been observed over Mosjøen fifteen minutes earlier finally reached the *Tirpitz*. A few minutes later, yet another report of enemy bombers reached the battleship. As the minutes passed by, the suspicion grew that another bombing raid against the battleship was about to happen. However, no precise information regarding the course of the bombers, as well as their exact number, was received. A further report at 08.50 hours, stating that seven single-engine aircraft were heading in a north-easterly direction some 50 km from the *Tirpitz*, was received from an army observation post. One minute later, *Tirpitz*'s air raid sirens wailed and this was followed by the air raid sirens at Tromsø. (The exact time when the air raid warnings began to sound appears to be open to debate.) Subsequently, the report about the single-engine aircraft was found to probably be in error. Additionally, the reports on the Lancaster bombers are put into question.

At 08.58 hours, Kapitän zur See Weber informed the crew of the *Tirpitz* as to the reason for sounding the air raid sirens. A couple of minutes later, a formation of twenty

Grossadmiral Alfred von Tirpitz. (*via Even Blomkvist/Alta Tirpitz Museum*)

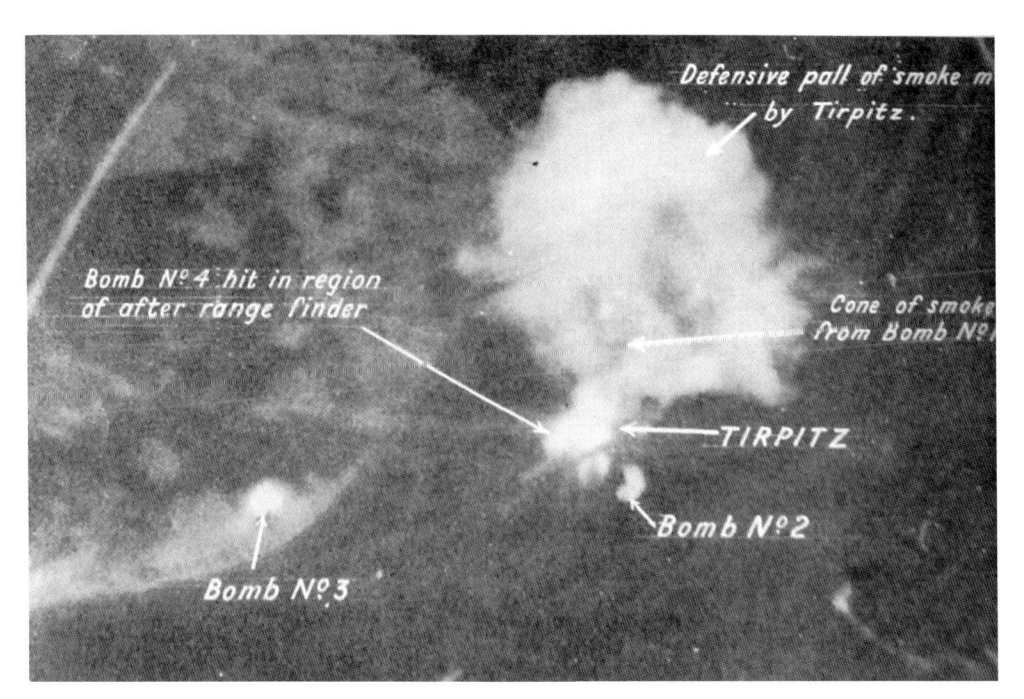

Tirpitz as seen prior to keeling over on 12 November 1944. (*via Even Blomkvist/Midt-Tromsö Museum*)

Tirpitz seen during sea trials in the Baltic Sea, summer of 1941. (*via Even Blomkvist/Midt-Tromsö Museum*)

On 5 May 1941, Hitler made a brief visit to *Tirpitz* at Gotenhafen. (*via Even Blomkvist/Midt-Tromsö Museum*)

A series of photos showing the last moments of *Tirpitz*. (*RAF Museum*)

A previously unpublished photo showing a Lancaster, two Liberators of No. 511 Squadron, a DH 98 Mosquito, and a Polikarpov Po-2 at Yagodnik during Operation *Paravane*. (*via Carl-Fredrik Geust*)

Diese Lüge kostete Millionen deutscher Soldaten und Offiziere, die Hitler und seiner Propaganda Glauben schenkten, das Leben.

DEUTSCHE MATROSEN!

Diejenigen von Euch, die immer noch dem Betrüger Hitler und seiner Lügenpropaganda Glauben schenken und die verbrecherischen Befehle Hitlers sowie seiner Admirale und Offiziere blind ausführen, weihen sich selbst dem Untergang.

Wer am Leben bleiben will,

soll gegen Hitler und seine Klique kämpfen.

Schliesst Euch denjenigen deutschen Matrosen und Offizieren an, die den Kampf gegen Hitler und seine Klique für sofortige Beendigung des Krieges begonnen haben!

Über Bord mit den Helfershelfern Hitlers, die den Krieg verlängern!

One of a large batch of British propaganda leaflets dropped over Sweden in late 1944. The leaflet urges Kriegsmarine sailors to throw supporters of Hitler overboard. (*via author*)

Lancaster, NF920, of No. 617 Squadron seen shortly after the forced landing at Porjus, Sweden, on 29 October 1944. While the forward and centre fuselage has burned out, the rest of the aircraft is relatively intact. The propellers and Merlin engines were removed in the mid-1940s. (*via Bengt Hermansson/Forced Landing Collection*)

Flying Officer Daniel William Carey photographed in 1944. (*via Porjus Archival Committee*)

Lancaster, LM448, of IX(B) Squadron seen shortly after belly landing at Vännäsberget, Sweden, on 12 November 1944. (*via Bengt Hermansson/Forced Landing Collection*)

Swedish Air Force officers by the tail section of Lancaster, LM448. (*via Bengt Hermansson/ Forced Landing Collection*)

HØVDING SKIPSOPPHUGGING
SANDNESSJØEN
Telegramadresse: ,,Tirpitzmetall'' - Telefon 407

OSLOKONTOR
Telegramadresse: ,,Tirpitzmetall'' - Telefon 46 39 63 - Postboks 5160 Oslo NV

An advertisement for the Einar Høvding Skippsupphugging company that bought the hulk of *Tirpitz* after the war. Scrapping lasted from 1947 until 1957. (*via Lars Gyllenhaal*)

The first issue of the tabloid *Expressen* (dated 16 November 1944) put the crew of LM448 on the front page. The headline states '6 of Tirpitz Killers Here'. (*via author*)

The tail section of 'Easy Elsie' as she appeared in the summer of 2001. (*Pär Erixon*)

The name 'Easy Elsie' was still clearly visible after nearly sixty years after the crash. (*Pär Erixon*)

Navigator Alex McKie made an emotional visit to 'Easy Elsie' in August 2002. (*John Bryggman*)

Above left: The site of *Tirpitz*'s final resting place as seen in 2012. (*Mats Johansson*)

Above right: During his 2002 visit to Sweden, Alex McKie also made a brief visit to the cell where he had spent an uncomfortable night in 1944. This time, the accommodation was somewhat more luxurious. (*John Bryggman*)

This shell was fired during Operation *Paravane* on 29 October 1944. It turned out to be a dud and was not found until the autumn of 1967. It was subsequently recovered, properly defused, and turned into an exhibit. (*Mats Johansson*)

The much foughtover *Tirpitz* bulkhead as it looked when mounted at IX(B) Squadron's Officers' Mess at RAF Bruggen in 1989. (*via Chris Henderson*)

Tirpitz was launched on 1 April 1939, exactly five months prior to the outbreak of war. (*via author*)

A page from the IX(B) Squadron's ORB detailing the final raid on *Tirpitz* on 12 November 1944. (*National Archives*)

A page from the 617 Squadron's ORB covering Operation *Paravane* on 15 September 1944. (*National Archives, Kew*).

The Firefly two-seat fighter-bomber made its operational debut during the raids on *Tirpitz* during the summer of 1944. (*Arlanda Civil Aircraft Collection*)

Four Arado Ar 196A spotter floatplanes were usually carried aboard *Tirpitz*. (*Arlanda Civil Aircraft Collection*)

A few Tallboy heavy bombs have been preserved, including this one at Brooklands. (*Jan Forsgren*)

A Barracuda seen immediately after returning to HMS *Victorious*. Note that the lower engine cowling has separated from the aircraft. (*IWM*)

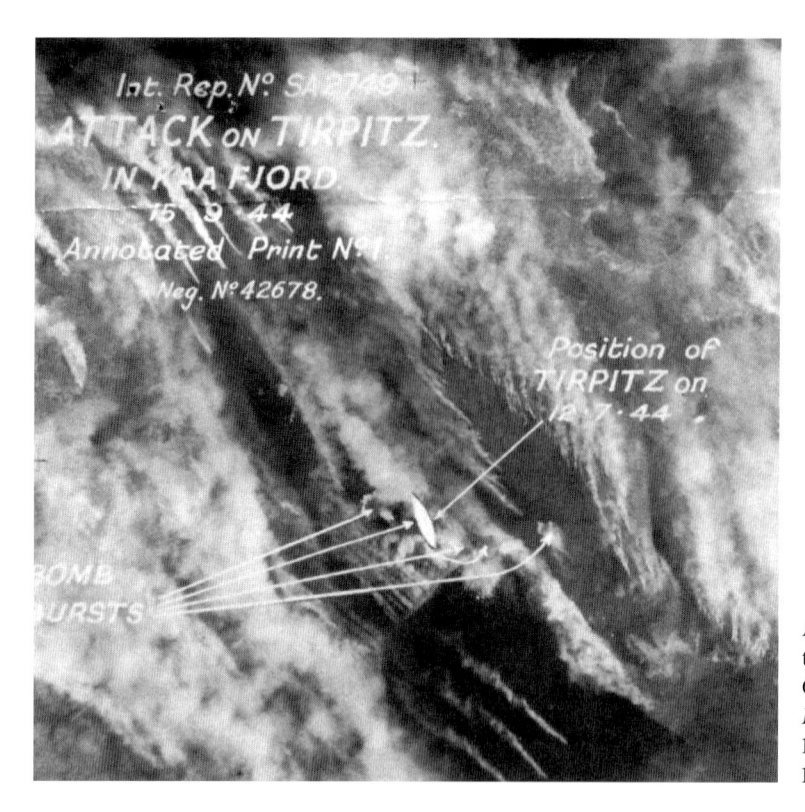

A photo taken during Operation *Paravane* on 15 September 1944. (*IWM*)

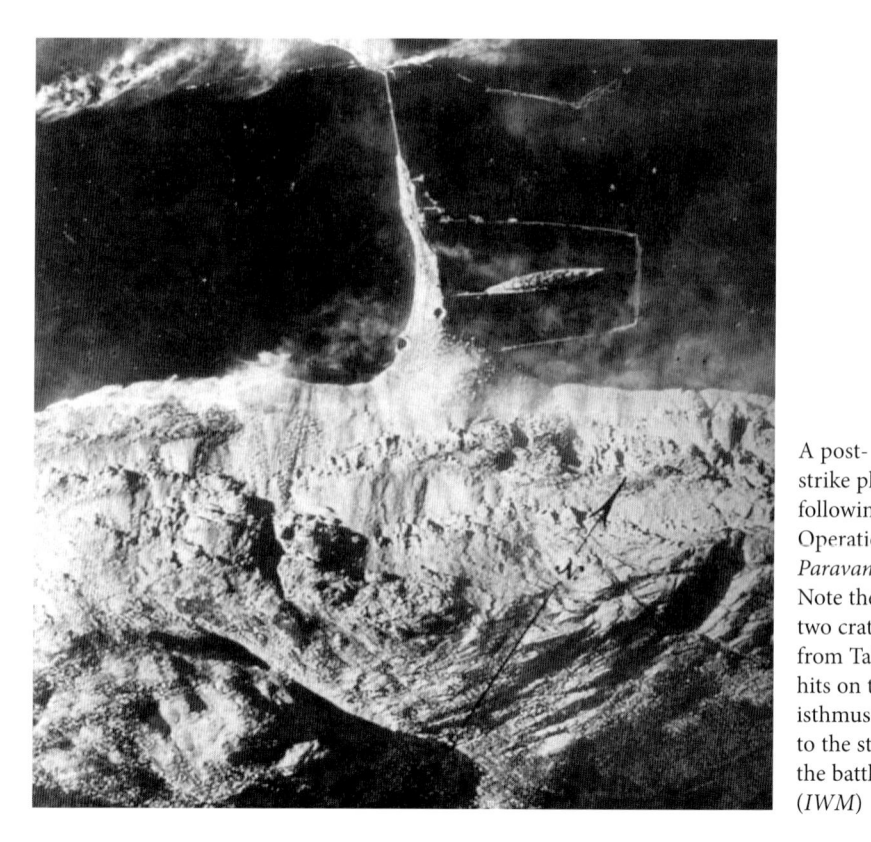

A post-strike photo following Operation *Paravane*. Note the two craters from Tallboy hits on the isthmus close to the stern of the battleship. (*IWM*)

On 22 March 1945, the last RAF sortie against *Tirpitz* took place. The photo was taken by a Mosquito of 541 Squadron. (*IWM*)

A view of the front section of Lancaster LM448. (*via Bengt Hermansson/Forced Landing Collection*)

On 5 May 1941, Hitler made a brief visit to *Tirpitz* at Gotenhafen. (*Even Blomkvist/Tirpitz Museum, Alta*)

A 1944 reconnaissance photo of the Beast. Note the large amounts of oil in the water surrounding the battleship. (*IWM*)

to twenty-five aircraft were spotted about 120 km south of Tromsø. The (unidentified) aircraft were heading in a north-easterly direction for the *Tirpitz*. This was serious news. The formation was continually observed with the bombers becoming visible from the battleship at a distance of 15 km.[3] In many accounts of the final raid against the *Tirpitz*, it has been stated that the RAF Lancasters flew directly across the Luftwaffe airfield at Bardufoss prior to reaching the target area. This appears to be without foundation as the bombers, having joined the formation over Lake Akkojaure in northern Sweden, flew on a north-north-easterly heading when crossing into Norwegian airspace. This put the Lancasters some 50 km east of Bardufoss. Having arrived at this point at 09.14 hours (local Swedish time GMT+1), they turned to the north-west, following the shores of Bals Fjord towards the Beast. Immediately, this was followed by an air raid warning at Bardufoss with the *Tirpitz* dispatching a request for fighter protection. This was too late, however, with the Lancasters being mere minutes away from the battleship. The requests from the *Tirpitz* became more insistent. The reply from Bardufoss was initially negative as it was not possible to scramble any fighters. The Luftwaffe headquarters at Moen stated that several fighters had indeed been scrambled, but that the enemy was nowhere to be seen.

Arriving from the south, the Lancasters of IX(B) and 617 Squadrons flew in a loose formation at an altitude of between 11,500 and 14,500 feet. The Beast lay straight ahead of the bombers, anchored some 120 metres from Håkøya. Only a few minutes passed from the moment the RAF aircrews spotted the battleship to the initial bombing run. The huge 38 cm guns of the *Tirpitz* were the first to open fire on the high flying Lancasters at 09.36 with the medium and light flak soon following suit. The bombers were then just over 12 km from the *Tirpitz*. Although the flak was intense, it was also inaccurate. Almost immediately after the guns aboard the *Tirpitz* had begun to fire, a cheer went up among the gunners as one of the bombers appeared to have been hit. This turned out to be in error, but it briefly raised the fighting spirit among *Tirpitz*'s crew.

Leading the formation was Willie Tait in Lancaster EE146. Arriving over the target area at 13,000 feet, Tait dropped the Tallboy at 08.41 hours. (The timings provided below are given in the 617 Squadron ORB when the respective crew dropped their Tallboy against the Beast are according to GMT, while the ORB of IX(B) Squadron states GMT+1.) According to 617 Squadron's ORB, 'We did not see our bomb burst, but the initial bombing was concentrated on the vessel. When we arrived there was steam coming from the funnel.' It would appear that Tait's Tallboy did not hit *Tirpitz*; however, other Tallboys certainly did hit the doomed battleship. Flying at 12,850 feet, Fg Off. Kell later reported: 'We bombed (at 08.43 hours) along the length of the ship turning to starboard and running in on the bows. Our bomb which registered a hit or a very near miss fell in the centre of the smoke coming up from just in front of the superstructure. We saw at least one direct hit which was followed by a big column of reddish brown smoke.' The last of the 617 Squadron's Lancasters to drop its Tallboy was flown by Flt Lt Anning. Flying at 16,000 feet, Anning bombed at 08.44 hours, three minutes after the initial Tallboy had been dropped. 'Ship was covered by smoke and our bomb fell in the centre of the smoke concentration. There was a big explosion on the ship at 08.51.'

One Norwegian eyewitness to the raid was Gunvor Wibe:

Living in a small cabin at Håkøya, Gunvor Wibe heard the first explosions and felt the floor shaking when the Tallboy hit the beach near to the cabin. The windows shattered with shards of glass flying through the air. Further explosions followed, while she huddled on the floor, her two children grappling at her skirt. Then everything grew quiet. She rose, telling the children to be quiet, and walked slowly towards the window facing the shore. A large cloud of smoke was rising out on the fjord, with the overturned hull of the once mighty battleship in the centre of the smoke. Despite the great distance, she heard screams from sailors swimming in the water as well as a number of men sitting on the hull. A curious feeling of terror and relief came over her. People were dying, but she and her children would be safe. *Tirpitz* was gone and the British would not return.[4]

Luftwaffe scrambles

At 09.18 hours GMT+1, Ehrler ordered the operational readiness of JG 5 to be stepped up one level. Radio reports from the battleship spoke only of 'noise from aircraft', but five minutes later, Ehrler finally gave the order to scramble. Just after taking off in his Bf 109G, Ehrler's radio packed up, making it impossible for him to contact the other pilots. In fact, Ehrler was initially the only one to get off the ground as a group of Junkers Ju 88 twin-engine bombers arrived over Bardufoss. (Other sources speak of a single Ju 88 or even one lumbering Ju 52/3M transport.) Being low on fuel, the Ju 88s had to land before the Bf 109 and Fw 190s fighters could take off. The Ju 88s landed singly and taxied to a parking spot before turning off their engines. It was not until 09.30 hours GMT+1 that the second Luftwaffe fighter, flown by Leutnant Werner Gayko, was able to take off. Gayko's scramble was delayed as he had to assist another pilot who experienced trouble in getting his engine started. Circling the airfield at an altitude of 2,000 metres, Ehrler could see the fighters of JG 5 with their propellers spinning, but none had managed to get airborne.

Gayko was followed by another five fighters, including Heinz Orlowski (flying Fw 190A-3), Franz Dörr and Oberleutnant Schulze; however, the Luftwaffe fighter pilots failed to spot the Lancasters. One of the fighter pilots, Hauptmann Dörr, claimed to have shot down an unidentified aircraft 20 km northeast of Bardufoss. (The identity of this aircraft is still unresolved, but it is thought to have been a Soviet photo-reconnaissance Spitfire.) Having failed to spot the reported formation of Lancasters, Gayko returned to Bardufoss at 10.38 GMT+1. Gayko subsequently submitted a report on his flight:

On the morning of 12 November, I was sitting in the Officer's lodging when I was alerted by the air raid siren. I saw a few four-engine bombers above the airfield flying in loose formation at an altitude between 1,000 and 2,000 metres. Together with Hauptmann Dörr, I immediately ran towards the runway. Dörr then turned over his car to me, so that I could reach the squadron's hardstand more quickly. He then proceeded by foot to the Fighter Ground Control Centre. The squadron, consisting of about 18 aircraft, included one Focke-Wulf, which engine refused to start. I then assisted the pilot in getting the engine to start. I took-off at 09.30 hours, some ten minutes after the rest of the squadron.

During the climb, I noted anti-aircraft fire and changed course towards the flak bursts. A couple of minutes later, the flak bursts disappeared. When I reached Tromsø, I saw a huge ship that had keeled over. There was no sign of the enemy or of my squadron. I then changed altitude, but could not see anything of note. My radio did not work and I then made a fruitless sweep before setting course for Bardufoss. In my opinion, the failure to catch the British was due to the late scramble. The squadron needed, due to the unusual topographical conditions at Bardufoss, nine minutes to get airborne.

Shortly before landing, I came upon a four-engine (bomber) that I attacked twice. I was only able to get off a few rounds before my machine guns jammed. Suddenly, a Messerschmitt appeared, but it did not join the air combat. Shortly before the Swedish border, I broke off the pursuit. I landed back at Bardufoss at 10.38 hours.[5]

Ehrler continued his lonely hunt for the British intruders, climbing to an altitude of 6,000 metres just northeast of Tromsø. He failed to spot any Lancasters and turned northwest towards Arnøya. Still failing in his attempts to find the RAF bombers, Ehrler turned again, this time to the west and then to the south-east before heading for Alta. Turning east, Ehrler spotted a large pall of smoke to his left as well as black patches of smoke from German flak. Ehrler had finally found the *Tirpitz*. Having operated between 5,000 and 6,000 metres, Ehrler had flown higher than the Lancasters. Quite exactly why the Luftwaffe ace had failed to spot the bombers is unclear, but it may be that the dark green and brown camouflage made the Lancasters blend in with the ground. Ehrler failed to catch up with the bombers, but he saw one Lancaster heading south (presumably, this was Coster's aircraft that ended up in Sweden). However, Ehrler and the Luftwaffe had failed to protect the battleship.[6]

The force of Lancasters arrived over the target in clear weather at 09.41 hours GMT+1. Wing Commander Tait dropped his Tallboy at 08.41 hours GMT from 13,000 feet. Tait: 'We did not see our bomb burst, but the initial bombing was concentrated on the vessel. When we arrived there was steam coming from the funnel.' (Tait eventually became known as '*Tirpitz* Tait' within 617 Squadron.)

Even though the Germans had not received any direct warning of the impending raid, the anti-aircraft artillery guns of the *Tirpitz* and surrounding flak vessels as well as the land-based guns soon began to fire. The artificial smokescreens also began to belch out in an attempt of hiding the Beast from the bombers; however, it was too late. Two Tallboys hit the battleship with several others striking the water close to the vessel. Of the eighteen Lancasters from 617 Squadron, nine dropped their Tallboys within one-and-a-half minutes, scoring two direct hits and three near-misses within 30 metres from the ship. The remaining nine 617 Squadron Lancasters all dropped their bombs within the following two minutes from an altitude of between 12,500 and 16,000 feet. Flt Lt Knights later reported:

> Bombing by 617 Squadron was concentrated and accurate.' Knights also stated that '…4 of 9 Squadron's bombs (using Mk 14 bombsight) fell app. 200 yds, 500 yds, ¾ mile, 1 mile (from *Tirpitz*).

The last 617 Squadron Lancaster to attack was flown by Flt Lt Sayers. The Tallboy was released at 08.45 hours GMT from 14,200 feet:

> We followed our bomb down nearly to the ship when it was lost in the smoke. It was either a hit on the bows or a very near miss.

In all, the attack lasted eight minutes and the weather had finally changed sides. With the *Tirpitz* being clearly visible, none of the RAF bombers was forced to make repeated runs as had been the case with the previous raids. Wing Commander Tait had scored a direct hit on the Beast; however, with so many Tallboys being released within such a short time frame, which crew released the bombs that hit *Tirpitz*, and which that were near misses was impossible to deduce. However, the damage sustained by the Tallboys caused the Beast to send up a huge cloud of steam after which the German guns fell silent. After the first Tallboy had hit the *Tirpitz*, damage control crews initiated a desperate attempt to counteract the increasing list of the battleship. This was done by flooding some of the watertight bulkheads; this was ineffective with *Tirpitz* listing at some 30 or 40 degrees four minutes into the raid. This was too much—had the *Tirpitz* been operational at sea, it might have been a different matter. Now, however, the once mighty battleship was a sitting duck for the RAF bombers.

With the listing gradually increasing, Kapitän zur See Weber ordered the evacuation of the lower decks. This had not been completed when the Caesar gun turret blew up, spinning up through the air like a small metal toy. It was believed that the ammunition storage compartment exploded. The reason for this was unclear, but a Tallboy had struck the battleship near the Caesar gun turret only moments before. *Tirpitz* continued to list slowly and began to turn over. At 09.52 hours GMT+1, eleven minutes after the first bomb had struck, the battleship settled at a listing of 135 degrees.

Very soon after dropping his Tallboy, the turn-and-bank indicator aboard Wing Commander Tait's Lancaster packed up; this made keeping the Lancaster in horizontal flight more difficult. To make things worse, the radio antenna iced up, which caused the radio to quit. With no chance of communicating with other Lancasters or Lossiemouth, Tait nevertheless continued flying on a south-westerly course. When they arrived over Lossiemouth, it was teeming with rain. Instead of chancing a landing on the rain-soaked grass runway, Tait instead landed at the small Coastal Command airfield at Dallachay. One of the ground crew innocently asked Tait if they had made a regular training flight. Being extremely tired and fatigued from more than twelve hours of constant flying, Tait quietly replied that they had. Soon afterwards, Tait spoke with the commanding officer of a FAA torpedo bomber squadron. According to the FAA pilot, if the RAF had failed to sink the Beast, the job would have been transferred to his squadron and this would not have been a job 'to his liking'.

IX(B) Squadron

Only thirteen Lancasters of IX(B) Squadron managed to take-off. The first of IX(B) Squadron's pilots to attack was Sqn Ldr Williams with the bomb being dropped at 09.45 hours GMT+1 from 16,000 feet. Williams observed:

> ...very near miss on starboard side aft seen just before bombing and about three other bombs seen to burst close to the ship. One hit believed as a column of smoke enveloped the ship and its guns stopped firing.

The remaining IX(B) Squadron Lancasters bombed the *Tirpitz* within the next four minutes. Fg Off. Tweddle of IX(B) Squadron, flying Lancaster LM220, was one of the first to drop the Tallboy at 09.45 hours GMT+1 from 14,800 feet. Making one bomb run, Tweddle saw one Tallboy hit the '...fjord side of ship'. Only one flak gun was observed to continue firing. '...we were still over the area when we saw *Tirpitz* start to roll over. I knew before we got back to Lossiemouth—when we were shown pictures taken later by a Spitfire—that the *Tirpitz* had been sunk.'[7]

They returned to RAF Waddington after remaining airborne for fourteen hours. However, two of IX(B) Squadron's Lancasters, flown by Flt Lt Camsell and Fg Off. Redfern, arrived over the rendezvous point. Camsell was seventeen minutes late with 'Only one aircraft identified as a Lancaster seen in the distance.' With radio silence being imposed, Camsell could not make contact with the other bombers. Redfern and his crew did not spot any of the other Lancasters. As a result, neither bombed the *Tirpitz*, instead bringing back their Tallboys to Lossiemouth.

463 Squadron

Flight Lieutenant Bruce Buckham, flying the film Lancaster of 463 Squadron, observed first-hand the last moments of the *Tirpitz*:

> We flew over it, around it, all about it and still it sat there with dignity under a huge mushroom of smoke which plumed up a few thousand feet in the air. There were fires and more explosions on board, a huge gaping hole existed on the port side where a section had been blown out.
>
> We had now been flying close around *Tirpitz* for 30 minutes or so and decided to call it a day so we headed out towards the mouth of the Fjord. Just then the rear gunner, Eric Gierch, called out 'I think she is turning over.' I turned back to port to have a look and

sure enough she was, so back we went again. This time we flew in at 50 feet and watched with baited breath as *Tirpitz* heeled over to port, ever so slowly and gracefully.

We could see German sailors swimming, diving, jumping, and by the time she was over to 85 deg and subsiding slowly into the water of Tromso Fjord, there must have been the best part of 60 men on her side as we skimmed over for the last pass. That was the final glimpse we had as we flew out of the Fjord and over the North Sea.[8]

Luftwaffe failure

A message from the Luftwaffe at Bardufoss to the *Tirpitz* claimed that RAF fighters were circling over the airfield. This was totally untrue, but contributed to the chaos and confusion during the raid. In the event, no Luftwaffe fighters intercepted the heavily-laden Lancasters. If any Luftwaffe fighters had been present, it is highly likely that several of the Lancasters would have been shot down. In fact, both IX(B) and 617 Squadrons would have risked total annihilation if intercepted. If the raid had failed, the *Tirpitz* would probably have survived until the end of the war. A chaotic situation with poor communications between the Kriegsmarine and Luftwaffe spelled the end for the mighty battleship. Bernhard Schmitz later recalled:

> We knew well in advance we were to be attacked and we requested the presence of the fighters. The request was granted and the take-off was reported to us. When 28 Lancasters came into sight from the south we enquired as to the whereabouts of our fighters only to discover that they had flown to our old berth at Kaa Fjord and they now did not have enough petrol to return to us and engage the Lancasters.[9]

Tirpitz was listing at a 40 degree angle to port, eventually capsizing turning 140 degrees. The manoeuvre lasted eleven gruelling minutes and the Beast had finally been slain, the raid being no more than four minutes. One of the *Tirpitz*'s crew members, Adalbert Brünner, was ashore during the raid. He later recalled that:

> Everything went so fast … with the detonations of the British bombs drowning out all other noises, including the hellish sound of our anti-aircraft artillery. … Suddenly, there was silence—no guns, no explosions.

The screams from the trapped sailors reached Brünner and other Germans on the shore. The thick smoke slowly drifted away from the battleship and Brünner:

> …could not believe his eyes. *Tirpitz* was gone. The hull was sticking out of the water like some huge whale. That was all that was left.'[10]

Three Tallboys had hit the *Tirpitz*, the first, dropped by Willie Tait, striking amidships to the port of the funnel. The other two Tallboys that struck the battleship sliced through

Håköya 1944

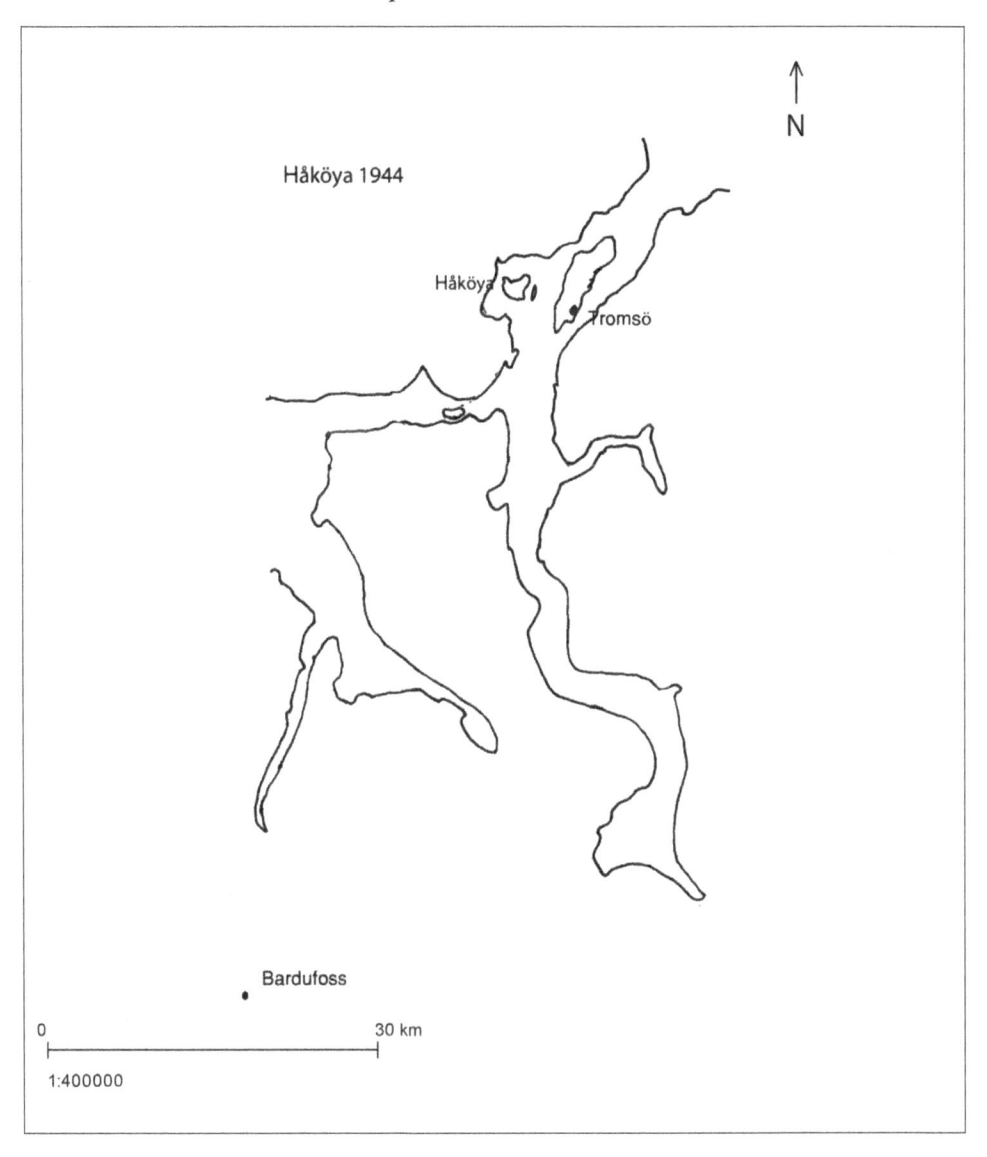

[Map showing Håköya, Tromsö, and Bardufoss, scale 1:400000, 30 km scale bar]

In October 1944, *Tirpitz* was moved to Tromsö where it was intended that she would function as the northern lock of the Lyngen Defence Line. In reality, the battleship had been damaged beyond repair by the RAF during Operation *Paravane*. (*Anders Eriksson*)

the armoured deck to the port of the Anton and Caesar main gun turrets respectively. There were several near misses with some causing additional damage to the port side of the hull. Ten minutes after the final Tallboy had been dropped, a huge explosion lifted the Caesar main gun turret clear from its mounts. In all likelihood, the explosion was caused when an ammunition storage bay blew up.

The wireless operator aboard Willie Tait's Lancaster, Arthur Ward, later wrote about what occurred immediately after the conclusion of the raid:

Every one of our bombs went down on the first run and immediately the *Tirpitz* was obscured from sight by a pall of smoke which made observation difficult. Danny was certain he'd got a good bomb and Willie agreed that the run in was as near perfect as could be. 9 Squadron came in as we were turning off and struck another very accurate blow. We circled round just out of range of the flak to assess the damage. The large mushroom of smoke made this difficult although we felt certain that she'd been badly hurt because even at that height (14,000 feet) flames could be seen.

Willie came though on the intercom and gave me a fairly long message to radio back to Group who were anxiously awaiting news. This message was to the effect that one direct hit was probable but results were difficult to assess accurately owing to heavy smoke. This was picked up immediately at Lossiemouth. Some 1,400 miles distant and passed on to Group Headquarters. Meanwhile, the weather was deteriorating and when we reached the Shetlands it was impossible to obtain an accurate pin-point owing to cloud and rain. I took a number of bearings for the navigator which gave him some idea where we were. A diversion message was coming through on the radio but I found great difficulty in picking it up owing to our aerials being iced up and the fact that we were in cloud. I got some very accurate bearings and we came over the airfield at about 500 feet in a rain storm. Tait turned off to the eastward where it looked slightly clearer and in a few minutes we made a perfect touch-down at Dallachay, a small Coastal Command station.[11]

Out of the Tallboys that had been dropped by the Lancasters during the three raids, four had struck the *Tirpitz*, one during Operation *Paravane* on 15 September and three during the final raid on 12 November. Of the other bombs, no less than thirteen had hit the nearby island of Håkøya during Operation *Obviate* and *Catechism*, only a couple of hundred metres from where the *Tirpitz* had been moored. Amazingly, six of these bombs had come down along the beach in an almost straight line.

Rescued from an armoured coffin

The German sailors made desperate attempts to save their comrades trapped inside the hull of *Tirpitz*. Two hours after the raid, 596 sailors had been rescued from the battleship. (This would indicate that between 1,500 and 1,700 sailors were on the active roster and aboard ship during the attack.) Some of the crew had a lucky escape. A few did not even get their feet wet when the battleship capsized, managing to cling to the hull. Others were blasted overboard by the shock waves of the Tallboys. Oil and burning fuel on the water surface initially made it impossible for rescue vessels to reach the stricken battleship or for sailors to swim ashore. Cries of 'Hilfe!' and 'Mutter!' echoed around the fjord as sailors died in the blazing water. One of those who died was Kapitän zur See Weber who had taken command of the *Tirpitz* on 4 November. Weber was the second commanding officer of the *Tirpitz* to become a casualty within six months.

For those trapped inside the *Tirpitz*'s armoured hull, time was fast running out. In desperation, German rescue teams scoured the countryside, searching for acetylene torches. However, the Norwegians made sure that all such equipment was hidden away. As a result, only one acetylene torch was available to the German rescue teams. It is not known how many German sailors that died aboard the *Tirpitz*, but most estimates state that between 940 and 1,204 were killed. The intense efforts to rescue sailors who had been trapped inside lasted for several days until every chance of rescue had evaporated. The trapped sailors were subject to exposure to fume and smoke inhalation as well as a rapidly decreasing oxygen supply. In all, eighty-seven people were rescued by cutting open parts of the hull. (Some published sources state, in error, that the Germans were unable to rescue any of the trapped sailors.) One of the trapped Kriegsmarine sailors was Alfred Zuba who later recalled his experiences immediately following the raid:

Now things hit us. The ship jumps up; vroom; a further two hits; everything flies about on the ship. The ship rocks as if it is being shaken by gigantic fists. The resonant sound of the hits is like cloud in the room. Now the ship begins to list, slowly and relentlessly. In horror I stare at the gauge. It is now showing 18 degrees. You have to hang on if you don't want to fall over. I hear voices and confused shouts on the telephone. Then it goes dead. More flak and the means of communication lines were dead—no answer. Our lifeline is dead. First Lt Mettegang is about to go the emergency telephone and stumbles, falling down the steeply sloping deck; pulls himself up and is now standing by the telephone, snatches the receiver to his ear, calls to the bridge and asks if we can get off. Everything has packed up working, no more electric power.

The force that keeps everything going has been clobbered. Since he has to shout to make himself understood, we can hear everything clearly, and 30 men are waiting for the answer. It can perhaps give them light, daylight and life, or it can keep them prisoners in the dark on the lowest deck of the ship in the space into which the water can already be breaking in the next moment. He repeats the order, 'Don't get out.' We have all heard that and we know what that means. So we stand there in groups and wait for our fate, enclosed in an iron space.

Above us it booms and thunders. Suddenly, new terrific hits, new gigantic shakings, stronger movement to its side and then an officer gives the order, 'Get out.' I took the head-set off, I keep the gasmask. I rush to the emergency exit—15 to 20 men are standing in front of it, each one wants to get up on the deck, wanting to escape death, and yet only one at a time can make their way through the narrow shaft. So we stand there and wait with the floor burning under our feet.

Now I climb up on deck, clambering along the pitch-dark narrow hold and reach the gun deck where something fearful awaits us. We cannot cross the smooth surface of the lino-covered deck which is now on an incline of 45 degrees. Some comrades try to go, slip down, slide out and roll down the sloping surface and desperately try to get up again. The others with trembling hands hold tight onto anything they can get hold of and struggle so far; they can get no further because they cannot reach the next hold. I am about to throw myself to the ground and to pull myself up that way but I slip back every time with each attempt.

The shaft that could rescue me is six metres above me. I desperately try to get up again, make two metres and then slip back again. The water breaks in, gurgling black and oily, and it comes up to my chest. Death takes hold of me with iron arms. Good God, I cannot die here! 'Help comrades, a life belt,' but no one could help me. I battle with my hands; more and more water comes streaming in, holds me tight and does not let me go. New hits boom through the ship. At last I find a hand-hold and pull myself up. A comrade stretches out his hand to me so that I can reach a ventilator. The ship is turning over more and more. It must now be at an angle of 90 degrees because now I am hanging on to a pipe that beforehand was standing vertical, holding tight with both hands. Three metres below me the water is whirling round. How long can I stand this? The cramped hands can hardly hold my body which has become heavier because of the wet clothes. I can literally feel the strength draining out of my fingers. A few more minutes then it will be over, I think, and I will become quiet and calm.

Then I manage to step on to a ventilator. I can release my hands. Someone shouted into the emergency exit. I am separated from him by two metres but I have to jump over. Beneath these two metres death is lurking. If I don't do it my body will splash into the water and then my life will be extinguished. My knees tremble; I have lost my cap long since. First of all I want to gather up a little strength, then pull my exhausted body together and jump over. Done it!

Behind me comes another chap, Hegendorf. I clamber back into the emergency exit. When Hegendorf tries this he is already in the water. He is about to give up the struggle. 'Leave me, I just want to die.' My answer is 'Don't talk nonsense.' I pull him quickly through the gap. My goodness is the fellow heavy! Then we close it and that way stop the water coming in. We climb further through the Mess with a number of comrades with whom we look for a way out of our prison. Volsing is there too. He sets off with a few people and searches. I stay with the others and pass on to them what he is saying, His voice now comes from far below somewhere in the dark. Now we hear them they answer, but they have not found anything. In the meantime we calm ourselves. None of us wants to show the others what he fears. Hegendorf panics. 'We will all die. I want to see my parents again.' I forbid him to talk like that. I quieten him down. No panic among the people—that would be the worst thing that could happen. When Volsing comes back, he starts lamenting. 'If you don't stop your lamenting I will shoot you down.' Now Hegendorf becomes calmer. Volsing takes me to one side and softly says to me, 'It is pointless, we will not get out.' We looked everywhere but loudly he says we will find a way out yet. I do not want to give up the struggle.

I seek further and at last manage to get into another part of the ship but the only thing I find is one of those lamps which unfortunately gives up working later, and I also find dry clothes to put on. Now we see about some food. All we find are a few stale loaves and some coffee. While we are searching we go into the A Deck radio room where I see several figures lying. First of all I thought they were dead or wounded, they turned out to be radio operators of whom only one is wounded. Because of the danger of the water breaking in, we take them over to where we are. We sit down and rest our heads in our hands and stare in front of us. I take out a few items of clothing in order to change my wet things—a white pair of trousers, over these trousers of green material, a blue shirt of some mechanic, and finally a sweater, which is the 'trademark' of a mechanic. The comedy of my situation becomes evident. Gallows humour flickers. Someone throws me a sailor's hat. Unfortunately, it is much too small. Suddenly someone says it is his birthday today. Everyone congratulates him on his birthday, yet many of us will be thinking 'Let us hope your birthday is not your death day as well.' Do life and death have to be so close to each other?

We have three bottles of cognac, a large box of cigarettes and one with sweets and also a tin of coffee. The birthday boy is allowed first to take a big swig and then it is the turn of the others. The sharp stuff runs invigoratingly down the throat. Now everyone gets a sweet and a few coffee beans. Everything has to be shared out fairly because no one knows how long we will have to stay here. The morale is good. Then someone utters the question that has occupied everyone—whether those outside will try to rescue us. The Master Radio Operator, an admirable fellow, says, 'Of course—it does take time for them to be here with the gear. Pay attention. Our boat has a beam of 36 metres, the water is 17 metres deep, so if our ship goes over, there is always going to be a bit sticking out of the water.'

To prove it I drop something to show where up is and where down is, because no one any longer has their bearing in the ship. Suddenly there is knocking from somewhere—bang, bang, bang. We answer with a fire extinguisher—bang, bang, bang. Now the bang is quite soft and weak, then it is very light indeed—bang, bang, bang. Always three bangs. It is a frightening sound through the space. Will we get out of here? What will my mother do if she has to be informed of the news of my death? A year and three days ago her eldest son fell on the Eastern Front and now me! What will Ruth say? When I saw her again before I went to the front, she was glad I was on a big ship because she thought less could happen to me.

Someone says, 'If I get out of here, I will get married at once.' Now they all start saying what they intend to do if they get off. They perhaps do not feel the drips falling from the deck, which was earlier the floor. Only the radio operator keeps asking, 'Is the water rising? Shall we get out (of) here? He is told to shut up. We have taken Hegendorf into a dark corner where no one can hear his frightened questions and his lamenting. From somewhere we have heard voices; now we join in a chorus, 'Where are you?' Quiet. We cannot understand the answer. Our shouts resound long and stretched out. We keep on roaring out the sentence in short phrases. Was that an answer, also in chorus?

We cannot understand the answer. Now each of us shouts with tense senses. 'Switch Room 3' we can understand with difficulty. We bellow (that) we are in the forward Mess. We do not know if our comrades have understood us. Gradually we become hoarse. Our shouts become weaker. Now we only beat out three short, three long, three short taps (SOS). All sorts of stories about trapped liners and people buried alive come to mind. One has too much time and thoughts go round and round in one's mind.

All at once there is a joyful shout and screaming in our ears. Someone thinks he has heard the words. 'Here we are' and 'deeper' and yet it all goes quiet again. After a period of time the same man thinks he heard the noise of cutting apparatus but it can only be the water coming in under high pressure.

The senior man takes the fire extinguisher and wants to break down the wall to the next compartment. He works like one possessed. When he has broken through the metal there is actually the wall or ship's side of steel which defies all blows however violent they are. Now I too hear the noise we have mentioned, the hissing that stops and starts. It can come from cutting apparatus. I still cannot believe it and again there is hissing, crackling and banging. The man who has been watching the water rising says that it is rising slowly.

There! We have all heard it, there is the hissing of cutting apparatus. Something, an iron blade, falls to the floor. And yet the water is hissing and rising. We shout, 'Hurry up, the water is getting higher. We need help!' A watery grave approaches with deathly slowness. The hissing comes nearer. The water rises higher. Our room is still dry.

We can see the water rising through the hatch, it will fill our space. The hissing carries on approaching and stops and starts again. Perhaps they are already cutting our wall. We shall give a knocking sound on the side of the wall which is most favourable for the cutting. No one can imagine these minutes, this uncertainty. Will we be rescued or will we be suffocated and drowned? And so we listen to the hissing. One type of hissing means rescue, the other is death or perish.

It strikes me as almost symbolic, a contest with death. A man at the hatch says the water is rising and he tells me it is rising very quickly. The senior man with the fire extinguisher carries on working. Now the noise is already quite near. Someone puts his hand on the steel wall. It is quite warm. 'Hurry!' we shout. We are happy, like small boys. There the steel blade is cutting red on one point. It is melting; sparks come out into our room. We can hardly contain ourselves for joy. We do not know where to go in the narrow cramped room. For us, these red sparks come pungent fumes. I put on my gasmask which I have still got with me and yet I almost don't get any air because it is so stale. And then I hold my wet clothes in front of my face and creep into some corner. My eyes are watering and my mouth is gasping for air. Now there is a hole that has been cut into this prison. I give a man my wet clothes and he smothers the flames which are already leaping up the walls. Tensely we stare at the narrow gap which is slowly becoming bigger. We stare at it, drinking in every centimetre of its growth.

Suddenly the hissing stops. We hear voices moving away. There is deathly silence around us. What is this then? Are we going to be deserted with rescue so close to our eyes? Will the ship sink further? Why have they not carried on cutting? We shout, screaming and banging. There is no answer, only the echo of our desperate shouting sounds from the walls. The water rises, hissing and crackling! It can't be possible! Are we now to become further victims of the water? The water carries on rising. We crouch where we are and wait. Time is running out drop by drop into the sea of eternity as the drops of water on the wall unite themselves with this mirror of black, gleaming water. There it lies and eats slowly at the walls, and we can do nothing but wait. Then they are back at last. The sparks start again. No one can imagine our feelings as we greet these red sparks.

The gap grows, takes on the form of a rectangle. Now only a small bit then it will fall out. There it is already thumping on the floor and there is no end to the shouts of 'Hooray' and there are two people in the rectangular hole and they speak to us.

They came towards me as if they had come from another world. We can hardly grasp it—rescue is at hand, and so we ask, 'Can we get out of here?' 'Yes, of course. We can come in there from out here,' comes the reply and now everyone is happy. We climb through the hole. It is so cramped with the men outside pulling us out and we have to push from inside to get a man out.

The passage behind the hole is only 40 cm wide and then we climb out the space onto a ladder and again through a narrow hole and now through a rectangle we see the sky. It is now evening. The stars are sparkling. I will never forget that moment. Now, just through this hole and there I am, standing free and saved and sucking better air into my lungs. Yet, where I am is the bottom of the ship across which I am led by a soldier. I cannot believe my eyes. Our ship has turned 180 degrees. The soldier tells me why our rescuers have gone away. They were taken away because they had lost consciousness through lack of oxygen. We present to the men a box of cigarettes which we found in the ship.

Now I go over the ship's bottom of the *Tirpitz*. I smoke a cigarette. Me, a non-smoker! After a few hours' rest and we have everything we need, enquiries begin. 'Where is this chap? Where is that chap?' Slowly tension is reduced. In answer to my enquiry about Mettegang, I learned that he is trapped with 50 men. The next day I am told that all suffocated. The rescue team were also to speak to them through a ventilator. However, despite desperate efforts it was not possible to get through to them and an influx of gas took them across into the great army.[12]

The sinking of the *Tirpitz* was a disaster for the German forces in Finnmark. Russian forces advanced into Finnmark, occupying large parts of the area for some months after the end of the war; however, the local Norwegian population had few complaints about the Russian presence, instead considering them as their liberators from German occupation.

The number of German sailors who lost their lives when the *Tirpitz* was sunk could have been far greater. Following the transfer to Tromsø and Alta Fjord, about 700 of the crew had been transferred to duties ashore such as manning shore-based flak units as well as other auxiliary duties. With the *Tirpitz* having been converted as a floating fortress, there existed no need to keep a full crew aboard. Instead, a skeleton crew manning guns, rangefinders and radar remained.

The following day on 13 November, a Norwegian family met a number of sailors from the *Tirpitz* on leave at Tromsø. Due to the mountains and inhospitable terrain, it was impossible to see the battleship at her berth from the city of Tromsø. Upon being told that the *Tirpitz* had been sunk, the Kriegsmarine sailors merely laughed and shook their heads at the crazy Norwegian. Although the Norwegian population at Tromsø and the remainder of Finnmark were undoubtedly happy that the mighty *Tirpitz* had been sunk, showing too much emotion in this matter inevitably brought trouble. The Gestapo subsequently arrested several local Norwegians for openly celebrating the sinking of the Beast. Some Norwegians, however, thought that the way the Kriegsmarine sailors had perished was a terrible way to die.

Return flight

The return flight to the UK was largely uneventful. Several of the Lancasters were, due to a lack of fuel, forced to divert to various airfields. In fact, only six Lancasters made it back to Lossiemouth: Fg Off. Sanders (at 15.14 hours; note: all timings are GMT), Fg Off. Lee (15.30 hours), Flt Lt Gumbley (15.37 hours), Flt Lt Marshall (15.50 hours), Plt Off. Watts (16.07 hours) and Flt Lt Sayers (16.20 hours). Of the others, four landed at Milltown: Fg Off. Ross (15.29 hours), Fg Off. Castagnola (15.46 hours), Flt Lt Anning (15.58 hours) and Fg Off. Gingles (16.02 hours). Also three Lancasters landed at Fraserburgh—Sqn Ldr Iveson (15.28 hours), Fg Off. Leavitt (15.58 hours) and Flt Lt Dobson (16.59 hours)—and two at Peterhead: Flt Lt Knights (15.39 hours) and Plt Off. Kell (16.14 hours). The three remaining crews landed at Scatsca: Fg Off. Flatman (14.47 hours, thus being the first of the 617 Squadron crews to return to British soil); and Fg Off. Joplin (14.59 hours) at Sumburgh. Meanwhile, Wing Commander Tait, as related earlier, landed at Dallachay.[13]

There was a feeling of both joy and relief among the aircrews. The mighty *Tirpitz* had been sunk and was a case of third time lucky. The ORB of 617 Squadron made a brief recap of the raid stating:

> On the 11 November, the Squadron was called upon to make yet another attack on the *Tirpitz*. Weather conditions promised to be favourable and eighteen aircraft took off for advanced Base at Lossiemouth. The Force took off for the operation on the 12th and for the first time found good weather over the Target. Flak opposition was severe but after the first few bombs had dropped the ship's defences appeared to have been silenced. There were at least two direct hits and several near misses and the vessel was soon covered by a dense cloud of smoke which hampered later bombing. The ship was seen to be on fire just aft of the funnel and the last aircraft to leave the area reported that she had a heavy list to port. Job done.

Later the same day, the regular photo-reconnaissance Mosquito arrived over Tromsø and Håkøya. The Mosquito crew was able to confirm that the struggle to sink the *Tirpitz*, the most feared warship of the Kriegsmarine, was finally over. The battleship had capsized and had turned over at almost 180 degrees. The German effort of rescuing the crew of the *Tirpitz* was on going with many smaller vessels seen around the hulk. The Norwegian secret agent Egil Lindberg also confirmed that the *Tirpitz* had been sunk.

Nearly three years had passed since the *Tirpitz* had first arrived in Norway. During that time, attempts had been made by the RAF, FAA and midget submarines to sink her. In fact, more than 700 RAF and FAA aircraft, excluding another 400 various support aircraft and thousands of airmen and other personnel, had been involved in the raids against the *Tirpitz*. The battle was over: *Tirpitz*, the lonely Queen of the North, was no more.[14]

Celebration day

On 13 November, ten Lancasters were flown south to Woodhall Spa with the remainder following the next day. Upon their return, the crews of 617 Squadron were warmly welcomed by the ground staff as well as the border regiment band (unfortunately, those crews that had been forced to land at other airfields missed these initial celebrations). The Secretary of State for Air, Sir Archibald Sinclair, visited Woodhall Spa. After lunching at the officers' mess, Sinclair addressed the crew members at the briefing room. Also the same day, Wing Commander Tait flew to London to be interviewed by the BBC on the successful raid. Upon his return the following day, all of the 617 Squadron crews were granted a forty-eight-hour leave.

It was time to celebrate. The mighty *Tirpitz* had been finally sunk. The war in Europe, however, would continue for several months and the next sortie for 617 Squadron would not occur until 8 December.

The importance of sinking the *Tirpitz* was reflected in a poem written by John Pryor DFC:

Among those fields rich with corn
Clear on a cool summer's morn
The clustered hangers of Woodhall stand
Green walled in the trees of bomber land
Around about them airfield sweep
Lancs in dispersal fruited deep
As fair as the garden of the Lord
In the eyes of that squadron board
Twenty Lancs with petrol stowed
Twenty Lancs with a Tallboy load
All ready in the morning sun
But the noon day saw not one
Higher rose six one seven's men
Bowed with their early teens plus ten
Taking up that late summer's task
What of us all Bomber Harris did ask
Down the track came the marauding throng
Willie *Tirpitz* Tait leading along
Under that slouched hat far to the right
Tirpitz the target met his sight
On went the dusty blue ranks so fast
Down went the bombs—up went the blast
Shoot if you must this young grey head
But spare your country's navy he said
To humbler nature within them stirred
To life at that squadron's deed and word
Who touches a hair of one Norwegian head
Dies like a dog—fly on he said[15]

The loss of the *Tirpitz* brought repercussions for several Luftwaffe officers. Having lost the last battleship of the Kriegsmarine as well as nearly 1,000 sailors meant that a scapegoat had to be found. However, it is a fact that the apparent lack of communication between the Kriegsmarine and Luftwaffe was a contributing factor to the loss of the battleship. The long-standing rivalry between the Kriegsmarine and Luftwaffe meant that only on rare occasions was common ground found and, as a result, co-operation remained elusive. With several previous British attempts of sinking the *Tirpitz*, it is quite remarkable that the protection of the battleship did not feature more prominently in the German High Command war planning.

The sinking of the *Tirpitz* brought many congratulations from Britain's Allies. United States President Roosevelt sent a brief telegram to Churchill that read:

> The death of *Tirpitz* is great news. We must help the Germans by never letting them build anything like it again, thus putting the German Treasury on its feet.

Josef Stalin said:

> The news that British aeroplanes have sunk the *Tirpitz* has greatly delighted us. The British airmen may legitimately pride themselves on this deed.

The Royal Navy, which earlier in 1944 had made numerous attempts to sink the *Tirpitz*, sent the following telegram (dated 13 November):

> The Naval Staff wish to convey their most hearty congratulations to your Squadrons for the truly magnificent and successful attack on the *Tirpitz* and for their persistence in continuing the offensive in spite of previous bad luck. *Tirpitz* is now no more and the threat she constituted to Northern convoys has ceased. Further, the moral effect of her loss will prove a headache to both Germany and Japan. The best of luck for the future from us all.

However, one high-ranking officer of the Royal Navy questioned if the *Tirpitz* really had been sunk. After all, large sections of the hull were visible above the waterline. But even if the battleship remained visible, she had been damaged beyond repair and attempts at raising the stricken battleship and repairs were far beyond the means available to the Germans. *Tirpitz*, the Beast and the Lonely Queen of the North had most definitely been taken out of the war by the Lancaster crews of IX(B) and 617 Squadrons. The question about whether the Beast was sunk by the Royal Navy or the RAF was hotly contested several years after the end of the war. The historian John Sweetman states that one civil servant 'a generation later' after the sinking of the *Tirpitz* noted that several 'acid memos' were passed between the Royal Navy and the RAF.[16] Crown Prince Olav of Norway sent a telegram (dated 22 November) to the Commander of 5 Group:

> Please accept and convey to all concerned within the R.A.F. my heartiest congratulations on the daring and outstanding operation resulting in the sinking of the German battleship *Tirpitz*.

Being well aware of the great effect which the sinking of this German 'fortress' will have on the naval warfare in all waters, it is with a particular delight that we Norwegians hail the achievement of this deed, thus reducing the German defence of the Norwegian coastline considerably, and also removing a permanent menace to the convoys to Russia and northern Norway.

Allow me, therefore, on behalf of the Norwegian forces to convey to you and your men, our heartiest thanks and admiration.

The sinking of the *Tirpitz* was a news event of global proportions. The battleship that for several years had been a potent symbol of the power and might of Nazi Germany on the seas had finally been sunk.

Another Lancaster arrives in Sweden

Even though the German flak had been largely ineffectual, Lancaster LM448 of IX(B) Squadron, had been hit. Accurate anti-aircraft fire had hit No. 4 engine that had to be turned off. LM448 had seen use in both previous attempts to sink the *Tirpitz* and then flown by Flt Lt Jones. Originally built as a Lancaster Mk III by Avro at Yeadon as part of a batch of 350 aircraft, LM448 was originally delivered to 467 Squadron on 28 January 1944. Soon after delivery, the Lancaster was converted from Mk III status to Mk I status, which involved replacing the Packard-built (US) Merlin engines with Rolls-Royce Merlins. On 16 July 1944, LM448 was transferred to IX(B) Squadron.

With the third engine also losing power, the pilot, Fg Off. David Coster, saw no other option than to try to reach Sweden. As with NF920 two weeks before, Russia was not seriously considered as an option by the crew of LM448. Heading south from the blazing hulk of the *Tirpitz*, two Luftwaffe fighters were spotted. The German pilots attempted to intercept Coster's damaged Lancaster, but eventually broke off just before the bomber reached Swedish airspace. Flying low on an eastwardly course the crew followed the Kalix River. At the same time, attempts of establishing radio contact with Swedish military forces were made. This proved successful with Flygvapnet personnel at a small temporary airfield at Naisjärv hearing the distress call and replied in broken English, providing co-ordinates for the airfield. Hurried and frantic preparations at Naisjärv were made to bring the Lancaster down safely, and several small fires were lit along the runway. Having passed near Naisjärv, Coster made a 180 degree turn. However, the No. 3 engine stopped working completely, making an immediate forced landing inevitable. Circling low over Innerträsket bog at around 12.00 hours, the crew dispatched a hatch to check the firmness of the ground; the hatch promptly sank into the ground, thus ruling out Innerträsket as a suitable place for a forced landing. Finally, a narrow field named Ormänget was chosen. The Lancaster roared at very low altitude over a couple of houses at the nearby village of Vännäsberget in Överkalix parish with Coster setting down the Lancaster in a belly landing shortly after noon. The final flight of LM448 ended in a huge cloud of grass and earth as the stricken bomber glided for over one kilometre before screeching to a halt. None of the crew, including Jim Pinning, Cliff

Black (navigator), Jim Boag (bomb aimer), Harry East (flight engineer) and Taffy Jones, was injured. Having exited the aircraft in double-quick time, the crew burned some documents while local Swedes ran towards them. One of the Swedes was Karl-Gunnar Bygren who later reminisced about the unscheduled arrival of the huge RAF bomber:

> I saw the Lancaster arrive and land. There was a bit of a drama among the women as the aircraft flew very low towards the houses. But it landed away from the house, skidding as it went before coming to a halt near the farms owned by Blomstedt and Hjärpe. The first one to arrive was Yngve Hjärpe who watched the RAF crew standing near the fuselage, burning maps. Apparently, they were uncertain where they had come down. … Having learned some English at school, Yngve was able to inform them that they had indeed arrived in Sweden. The crew began to cheer and hug each other.
>
> After a while, all of the people at Vännäsberget were present at the site of the forced landing. About 15 minutes later, the commander of the local home guard (who worked as a schoolteacher) arrived with another member of the home guard, named Blomstedt. Armed with a single Mauser rifle, Blomstedt and the schoolteacher/home guard commander yelled 'Hands up!' to the crew of the bomber. However, Blomstedt then casually mentioned that his rifle was not loaded. Despite this, the RAF crew politely—and smilingly—raised their arms into the air.

The crew was then brought to a school at Hedensbyn and served a meal. Regular army troops then arrived who secured the crash site before escorting the crew to Ekfors barracks. The local population stated that an unidentified object had been thrown from the bomber. A brief search was made by the home guard, but the object was not found (presumably, this object was the hatch). Two army captains, Bergholm and Colliander, then entered the Lancaster for a thorough search. A number of items were recovered, including six bags containing bills, maps and compasses, thirty assorted maps, the navigator's and wireless operator's logs, a revolver with seven rounds, three life jackets and one pair of asbestos gloves.

Interrogation

Coster, but apparently none of the other crew members, was subsequently interrogated on 13 November by Major Andsberg of Flygvapnet. During the interrogation, Coster stated that his squadron had taken off from a base in Scotland to attack targets in northern Norway. He did not deny that the target had indeed been the *Tirpitz*. Coster had participated in the raid and dropped his bombs on the target. Following the raid, the intention had been to return to 'England'. But due to damage to one of the engines, it was quickly realised that this would not be possible. A pair of Luftwaffe fighters had been observed, but with Coster heading directly against the sunlight, the German pilots had not been able to intercept the Lancaster. Due to the weather becoming worse, Coster had initiated a forced landing somewhat earlier than had been intended. Coster admitted that during the final minutes of the flight, he and his crew had no idea of where they were. This was mostly due to the fact that the ground was covered with snow, thus making it more difficult to pick out any known landmarks.

Coster also provided some interesting comments regarding the war and Allied co-operation:

> Coster was not an admirer of the Americans and most of the representatives of other Allied nations. A certain disenchantment with the higher pay rate of the Americans was vaguely hinted at. Regarding the Germans, C. considered that they were excellent soldiers, while the Japanese were referred to as 'rats'. C. stated that he had received twenty-four months of training before ending up in a front unit.

Following interrogation, the RAF airmen were sent by train to Korsnäs, Falun, for internment. Interestingly, Fg Off. Coster and his crew made the front page on the first issue (16 November) of the tabloid *Expressen* that proclaimed them as 'Slayers of the Beast'. The news that the *Tirpitz* had been sunk was big news in neutral Sweden.

A guard was placed at the site with a temporary fence being erected around the Lancaster. Neither military personnel nor civilians were allowed to go inside the fence or take photographs of the RAF bomber without permission. The Lancaster was then thoroughly examined by personnel from Flygvapnet and the Royal Air Board (KFF). The under surface of the fuselage was reported to be deformed, propeller blades bent and with shrapnel damage to one of the wing fuel tanks. The fuel gauge stated that some 2,700 litres of fuel remained; however, it was discovered than only about 800 litres of fuel remained in the tanks. It was obvious that the Lancaster would not fly again. The individual aircraft record card for LM448 shows that the bomber was declared 'CAT E Missing' on 12 November 1944, being formally struck off RAF charge four days later. The recovery and disposal of the Lancaster provided the Swedish military authorities with a couple of headaches. Due to the soft ground, the wreck could not be recovered immediately. The nearest railway station, Morjärv, was 30 km away. If the wreck was dismantled and transported to Morjärv, this would severely affect the building of road blocks along the border with Finland.

At the time, Finnish forces were engaged in a bitter war against German forces, which were retreating northwards, burning every village they passed and slaughtering cattle. As a result, tens of thousands of Finnish citizens sought refuge in Sweden. There existed a fear that German troops would—by accident or intent—attack Swedish territory.

With the arrival of the first snow and with the ground freezing the dismantled wreck of the Lancaster was removed by sled and lorry. The British Air Attaché decided that the Lancaster was to be sold as scrap with a few parts stored by Flygvapnet on behalf of the RAF. This was a fate common with most RAF aircraft that had for various reasons arrived in Sweden. The remains of the Lancaster was reportedly obtained by an unnamed vocational school and used for instructional purposes; one of the Merlin engines is said to have ended up with a vocational school at Piteå. It is likely that the main wreckage was scrapped and smelted down. Nothing now remains of LM448 apart from faded photographs and the memories of a few elderly people who witnessed the Lancaster's arrival.

In 1984, Jim Pinning visited Vännäsberget. It was an emotional return to the site of the crash forty years earlier. Unfortunately, further details on Pinning's visit to Sweden are missing.

CHAPTER SIX

Aftermath

The final RAF sortie against the *Tirpitz* took place on 22 March 1945, more than four months after she had been sunk. On this day, Sqn Ldr Dodd and Plt Off. Hill of 540 Squadron, flying a Mosquito, made a final photo-reconnaissance sortie. The overturned hulk of the once mighty *Tirpitz* was still present at Alta Fjord and resembled a beached whale more than a battleship. Apart from the *Tirpitz*, the fjord and surrounding waters only contained a few small German ships.

Following the end of the desperate efforts of rescuing trapped sailors, the Germans subsequently went to work with removing parts of the *Tirpitz*. The huge propellers as well as some other items were removed. The bronze propellers could be smelted down and the metal reused for the German war industry; however, none of the heavy equipment necessary to cut up the *Tirpitz* was available in Norway. Germany was losing the war and all necessary resources were channelled into fighting the Allied advance. At the end of the war, the overturned hulk of the *Tirpitz* still remained at her final resting place off Håkøya.

Few major Kriegsmarine surface warships remained afloat after the sinking of the *Tirpitz* with none actively taking part in the fighting on the Western Front. The pocket battleship *Gneisenau* had been decommissioned on 1 July 1942 with her gun turrets being used to strengthen the coastal defence of Norway (six guns) and the Netherlands (three guns). The hull of the *Gneisenau* remained at Gotenhafen (now Gdynia, Poland) and was used as a floating storage facility and an air-raid shelter. The Russian Army was by this time steadily advancing towards Germany and on 27 March 1945, *Gneisenau* was sunk at the harbour entrance as a blockade ship in a vain attempt to stop the Russians from entering the city from the sea.

The pocket battleship *Lützow*—which had previously been named *Deutschland*—sustained extensive damage in a 617 Squadron bombing raid on 16 April 1945. The warship settled on the bottom with her heavy guns continuing to fire at the Russian Army. This did not last long, however, with the *Lützow* being scuttled by her own crew on 4 May 1945, although some sources state that she sank two days after the raid.

The *Admiral Hipper* had been decommissioned in 1943, awaiting repairs. Although these had been initiated, they were never completed. On 3 May 1945, RAF bombers severely damaged the ship during a raid on Kiel and the crew subsequently scuttled the warship to prevent its capture by the British.

The heavy cruiser *Prinz Eugen* was surrendered to the Allies in May 1945. The warship was handed over to the US Navy, eventually being expended as a target during atomic bomb trials in December 1946 at the Bikini Atoll during Operation *Crossroads*.

Grossadmiral Karl Dönitz became the last leader of the Third Reich on 30 April 1945 after Hitler's suicide. Dönitz wanted to continue fighting on the Eastern Front and sought a separate peace agreement with Britain and the States, but Allied supremacy on all fronts saw Germany's unconditional surrender on 8 May. Dönitz was arrested on 23 May and tried at Nuremberg. Sentenced to ten years imprisonment, Dönitz was released in 1956 and died in 1980.

Luftwaffe scapegoat

On 17 December 1944, Major Heinrich Ehrler, along with six other Luftwaffe officers, was court-martialled for his failure to protect the *Tirpitz* from British bombers in Oslo. Ehrler was considered as a suitable scapegoat for the loss of Germany's last battleship and more than 1,000 of her crew. The court found some difficulty in finding a good case against Ehrler as he was an ace with over 199 enemy aircraft to his record. Cowardice in facing the enemy was out of the question; however, the court found that, according to a decree from Reichsmarshal Hermann Göring, a Luftwaffe officer must always be present at a command post and ready for immediate action. Three other charges were also raised:

1) That Ehrler had delayed the scramble of the fighters from 09.18 hours when the first report of the RAF bombers was received at Bardufoss to 09.23 hours.
2) The Ehrler deliberately had left his squadron by taking off alone.
3) That Ehrler had lied about his radio being unserviceable with it being impossible to lead his squadron to attack the British bombers.

The ace was subsequently found guilty and sentenced to three years in prison as well as loss of rank. Sentencing Ehrler to death was not an option as this would have created a furore among Luftwaffe ranks. In the event, Ehrler only had to spend one month behind bars, most of it at Akershus Fortress in Oslo. With Allied heavy bombers hitting the cities of Germany on a daily basis, having a high-scoring fighter ace confined to jail was not a good idea. Ehrler's sentence was reduced in a Führer decree, dated 1 March, to three months of house arrest. He also retained his rank of major. With his political beliefs unshaken by the verdict, prison sentence and time in jail, Ehrler eventually returned to service, being assigned to fly the revolutionary Messerschmitt Me 262 jet fighter. On 27 February 1945, Ehrler joined the fighter unit JG 7 based near Berlin and died when his jet crashed on 4 April 1945 during a USAAF bombing raid. Allegedly, Ehrler lost his life when he tried to ram one of the American bombers. He had shot down 208 Allied aircraft.

IX(B) Squadron post-*Tirpitz* operations

Following the sinking of the Beast, the aircrews of both IX and 617 Squadrons received their fair share of glory. They had sunk the battleship *Tirpitz* that since 1942 had taken on near-mythical status as an unsinkable floating fortress and a naval symbol of Nazi Germany. However, the war had not yet been won and more operations would follow.

During a daring daylight raid against the Dortmund–Ems Dam on 1 January 1945, a flak shell hit the fuselage of a IX(B) Squadron Lancaster. With complete disregard to his own safety, the wireless operator, FS George Thompson, managed to pull the dorsal turret gunner free from the flames, putting out the fire that had engulfed the gunner's clothes with his own hands. Thompson then made his way to the rear of the bomber, pulling free the tail turret gunner. Being severely injured, Thompson managed to reach the cockpit in order to inform the pilot of the situation and due to his excessive burns, the pilot initially did not recognise him. A forced landing was made forty minutes later with Thompson and one of the gunners later succumbing to their wounds. On 20 February, George Thompson was posthumously awarded the Victoria Cross.

The final sortie of the war occurred on 25 April when IX(B) Squadron in conjunction with 617 Squadron bombed Hitler's Berghof home at Berchtesgaden in southern Germany. It was thought that the Nazi dictator would attempt to reach Berchtesgaden from Berlin, then beleaguered by Russian forces, in order to organise and lead the defence of Germany; however, Hitler remained and died in Berlin.

Out of the seventeen IX(B) Squadron Lancasters, eleven hit the primary target with one aircraft bombing a bridge near Berchtesgaden; five bombers aborted the raid. The final sortie of the war on 6 May involved five Lancasters that returned to the UK with prisoners of war.

During the war, IX(B) Squadron had flown a total of 5,828 sorties, including 561 bombing raids, nineteen mine-laying raids and eight leaflet raids. In all, sixty-six Wellingtons and 111 Lancasters were lost with an additional twenty-two Lancasters being lost in accidents.

Following the end of hostilities in Europe, it was planned to deploy a number of RAF squadrons to the Pacific to bomb Japan. This operation was codenamed *Tiger Force* that would consist of several squadrons from 5 and 6 Groups, and both IX(B) and 617 Squadrons became part of 551 Wing. It was intended that operations using the Tallboy and Grand Slam heavy bombs would continue against Japanese targets. Both the Lancaster and its successor, the Avro Lincoln, would have been used. Training flights involving endurance and bomb practice began during the early summer; however, *Tiger Force* was cancelled following the Japanese surrender on 15 August 1945. It is likely that *Tiger Force* would have operated out of Okinawa or the Marianas—the distances involved in operations against Japan would have been a serious issue for *Tiger Force*, being far greater than during raids against targets on mainland Europe. The similarities between the three raids by IX(B) and 617 Squadrons against the *Tirpitz* and the projected raids against Japan were obvious. Huge distances were involved, much of it over water.

Specific and high-value targets such as industrial complexes and shipping were other similarities.

The immediate post-war years saw drastic reductions of RAF strength but IX(B) and 617 Squadrons remained in first-line operational service. Even though IX(B) and 617 Squadrons did not reach the Pacific theatre of operations before the end of the war as part of *Tiger Force*, both squadrons were deployed to Salbani, India, on 1 January 1946.

After the end of the war, IX(B) Squadron re-equipped with Avro Lincolns and in May 1952, IX(B) Squadron (based at Binbrook since 19 April 1946) was one of the first to receive the English Electric Canberra B. Mk 2 jet bomber. In June 1955, a more modern variant, the Canberra B. Mk 6, began to arrive. In early 1956, IX(B) Squadron visited Nigeria, which also coincided with a royal visit made by Queen Elizabeth II and the Duke of Edinburgh. The Canberras of IX(B) Squadron made ceremonial flypasts over Lagos as well as the regional capital cities.

From 7 April 1956 until June of that year, eight Canberras were deployed to Malaya. Many RAF squadrons flew operationally during Operation *Firedog*—the war against communist rebels that would last between 1948 and 1959—and IX(B) Squadron was no exception. Forty-one sorties were flown with sixty-eight tonnes of bombs being dropped. One hair-raising incident occurred when Flt Lt Stonham's Canberra suffered a double-engine flameout at 47,000 feet over the Andaman Sea. Stonham managed to relight one of the Avon jet engines, eventually making it back to Fort Butterworth some 500 miles away.

Along with several other Canberra squadrons, IX(B) Squadron also flew several operational sorties during the brief Suez War, known as Operation *Musketeer*, in October–November 1956. IX(B) Squadron was based at RNAS Hal Far, Malta, for the duration the conflict and the squadron disbanded in July 1961. IX(B) Squadron was soon reformed at Coningsby in Lincolnshire on 1 February 1962 with Avro Vulcan B.2s and the first aircraft arrived two months later. Subsequent bases included Cottesmore and Akrotiri in Cyprus. While based in Cyprus, IX(B) Squadron was part of the Near East Bomber Wing. In January 1975, IX(B) Squadron returned to the UK and took up residence at RAF Waddington, Lincolnshire. Disbanding on 29 April 1982, IX(B) Squadron was to reform two months later on 1 June with the Panavia Tornado GR.1; later on, IX(B) Squadron received the upgraded Tornado GR.4. The squadron remains operational and is currently based at RAF Marham in Norfolk.

617 Squadron post-*Tirpitz* operations

On 8 December 1944, 617 Squadron resumed operations, attacking the Urft Dam. American forces were preparing to cross the Ruhr River and it was feared that the Germans would unleash the water against the Americans who had advanced to only 5 km from the dam. Due to the dam being covered in low clouds, the nineteen Lancasters had to return to the UK with their Tallboys. A second attempt at breaching the Urft Dam was made three days later. The dam was hit, albeit not completely breached, with

4 metres of the top section being smashed. The Germans subsequently managed to save the dam by reducing the water level.

On 28 December, Wing Commander Tait relinquished command of 617 Squadron to Group Captain J. E. Fauquier RCAF. Prior to leaving the squadron, Tait received a third bar to his DSO—this was at the time a completely unique occurrence in the RAF.

On 14 March 1945, the 22,000 lb Grand Slam bomb was dropped in anger for the first time. The target was the Bielefeld viaduct in Germany which was destroyed. The viaduct had been the intended target both on 9 and 13 March, but these raids had to be scrubbed due to poor weather.

In order to carry the heavy Grand Slam, the bomb bay of the Lancaster had to be converted by cutting out parts of the bomb bay doors and fuselage. The resulting Lancaster was designated as the B. Mk I Special.

On 13 April 1945, 617 Squadron returned to ship busting with the target being the *Lützow* and *Prinz Eugen* off Swinemünde in the Baltic Sea. Due to the target area being completely covered by clouds, the raid had to be aborted, although not before a few Lancasters had been damaged by heavy and accurate flak. A second attempt two days later was also foiled by poor weather; however, on 16 April, the *Lützow* was severely damaged and permanently taken out of the war. It was a poignant end to the pocket battleship that had initially been named *Deutschland*. Nazi Germany would soon surrender unconditionally to Allied forces.

As with IX(B) Squadron, 617 Squadron was involved in the 25 April raid against Hitler's headquarters at Berchtesgaden. Eight Lancasters bombed the nearby Eagle's Nest with three others dropping their bombs over secondary targets. By this time, Fauquier had been ordered to cease operational flying with Squadron Leader Brookes due to lead this historic raid. Fauquier was quite frustrated by being grounded at this point of the war. During the pre-raid briefing, Fauquier bluntly said:

> I'd like to have this target in my log book, Brookes. In fact, I would like to have this target tattooed on my arse, but you have got to lead it.[1]

Between May 1943 and April 1945, 617 Squadron flew ninety-five sorties and lost 187 aircrew and thirty-two Lancasters. No less than 153 awards, including two Victoria Crosses, sixty-eight DFCs and twenty-three DSOs were awarded to the squadron.

Following the end of the war, 617 Squadron participated in Operation *Exodus*: the return of prisoners of war from the Continent. Following this, flights were made to several of the squadron's targets with the ground staff riding along as passengers. This was done to show what had been achieved during these daring raids. After all, the ground staff—including mechanics, weathermen and the WAAF—were part and parcel of the war effort. The wreck of the *Tirpitz* was not visited due to the long distance involved.

During the autumn, Operation *Dodge* saw prisoners of war being returned from Italy. Several 'sight-seeing' flights to Berlin were also made. In January 1946, 617 Squadron, along with IX(B) Squadron, was dispatched to Digri in India. After returning to the UK, 617 Squadron was sent on a high-profile visit to Canada and the United States.

In the same year, 617 Squadron also relinquished the venerable Avro Lancaster for its successor, the Avro Lincoln II. In 1952, the first jet bombers arrived in the shape of the English Electric Canberra. On 15 September 1955, 617 Squadron was officially disbanded. It was reformed three years later at Scampton, becoming the third RAF squadron to operate the Avro Vulcan. In 1962, a new weapon was introduced to 617 Squadron, the Blue Steel stand-off missile, which was withdrawn from RAF use in 1971. Shortly before the squadron was yet again disbanded in December 1981, a Vulcan was flown over the Lady Bower reservoir and Derwent Dam. This was an old stomping ground for 617 Squadron as this was where training for Operation *Chastise* took place. On 1 January 1983, 617 Squadron was reformed at RAF Marham with the Tornado strike fighter.

617 Squadron is still operational with the Tornado GR.4. The squadron has operated in Afghanistan, supporting British troops in Operation *Herrick*. The squadron disbanded in April 2014 as part of a reduction of RAF operational strength; however, 617 Squadron is set to reform in 2016 as the first RAF squadron to receive the highly capable and very expensive Lockheed Martin F-35B Lightning II fighter. The Lightning II will be operated jointly by the RAF and the Fleet Air Arm so that 617 Squadron pilots will fly its fighters off the decks of the new Queen Elizabeth-class aircraft carriers.

RAF post-war visits to the *Tirpitz*

John Loftus, who had shot the historic images of the *Tirpitz*'s last moments on 12 November 1944, was shot down in February 1945. Becoming a prisoner of war, Loftus was liberated when the war ended in May and was ultimately awarded with the DFC in December 1945. Interestingly, although attending a brief aerial gunnery course, Loftus was not allowed to wear aircrew wings. In spite of this, Loftus completed twenty-two operational sorties. In post-war RCAF service, Loftus proudly carried the DFC without wings, an unusual state of things.

Soon after the war ended, the Armaments Officer of Bomber Command, Air Commodore Bilney, visited the *Tirpitz* to observe first-hand the damage sustained by Tallboy heavy bombs. Four months later, Wing Commander Tait arrived in a Short Sunderland flying boat. The huge battleship resembled an enormous whale which had unsuccessfully attempted to reach the shore. From the hulk, a 'ghastly smell' rose from the corpses of the hundreds of Kriegsmarine sailors trapped inside what had become their armoured coffin.

Interest in the *Tirpitz* remained strong in the immediate post-war era, and the BBC transmitted an early television programme on 20 November 1949, five years after the sinking of the battleship. Here, the existence and efforts of Egil Lindberg were revealed to the British public. Lindberg had operated the secret radio transmitter codenamed Vidar, forwarding information on the state of the *Tirpitz*. Sadly, Lindberg died in 1952 due to heart failure at the age of forty-two.

Relics

The capsized hull of the once proud battleship was sold in 1948 to a Norwegian scrap-dealing company, Einar Høvding Skippsupphugging, which paid 120,000 Norwegian kroner for the rights to cut up and dispose of the once mighty battleship. It was a bargain and much of the battleship remained above the water surface. Apart from the scrap metal, many other items of value such as generators (a rare item in post-war Norway), range finders, etc., could be resold with a profit. Smaller items such as binoculars had a ready market. Most of the thick armour plating was exported to the Swedish gun manufacturer Bofors. There was some irony in this as the construction of the *Tirpitz* in all likelihood had involved high-grade iron ore imported from Sweden.

Some of the armour plating was transported to various gunnery ranges around Sweden for use as targets. During the late 1980s, bits and pieces of the battleship were still used by the Swedish Army as artillery and tank targets. A small piece has since been recovered and put on display at the Boden Fortress Museum. Other pieces of armour were sold to Spain. The deck found use nearer to home with part of a quay at Tromsø being built using these planks of teak. None of this is said to remain today.

The effort of cutting up the *Tirpitz*, by both Norwegian and German interests, lasted for nearly ten years, finally ending in 1957. Among the last things to be removed were the 38 cm barrels of the main gun artillery. There was a reason for this as it had been established that all eight of these guns had been loaded and ready to fire during the final raid.

The scrapping of the *Tirpitz* saw the emergence of industrial development in Finnmark. Cutting up the huge battleship and the removal of heavy chunks of armour plate was arduous work and required a large amount of manual labour. Initially, a 20-ton floating crane was used, but it was decided that this was lacking in capacity. As a result, the German salvage company Eisen und Metall of Hamburg became involved from the summer of 1951 and they brought with them a larger and more capable crane. A large floating platform was towed to Tromsø during the early 1950s and this platform can still be found at the site of *Tirpitz*'s last battle.[2]

Some of the metal, apart from the armour plating, recovered from the *Tirpitz* was fed into the local industry and smelted down. Thus, it might be said that during the meagre post-war years, the *Tirpitz* created many job opportunities for the local population with her remains being used to rebuild the ravaged villages and communities of northern Norway.

With the Germans having failed to recover many of their fallen comrades from the *Tirpitz*, many hundreds of Kriegsmarine sailors remained aboard the wreck in 1947. Initially, whenever bodies or parts thereof were found, these were buried close to Håkøya along with unwanted parts of the *Tirpitz*; however, this practice was stopped following strong reactions from a local minister, Artur Berg. Consequently, any German sailor discovered in the wreck was buried ashore.

Small pieces of the *Tirpitz* can be found in several Norwegian museums, including the museums at Alta and Tromsø, and small parts of the battleship can be seen at many museums around the world. For instance, one link from the anchor chain is on display at the Bomber Command Museum at Nanton, Canada. Much of the battleship—particularly the superstructure—still lies scattered on the bottom of the fjord. Due to environmental concerns as well as cost, no plans exist for recovering these remains. An unexploded shell fired from one of the *Tirpitz*'s heavy guns was found half buried in a bog during the 1960s. Apparently, the shell was fired during Operation *Catechism* on 12 November 1944, travelling some 40 km inland. The shell, with its explosive charge removed, has since been placed on display at the site.

Halifax recovery

The RAF raids during the spring of 1942 had an interesting post-war aftermath. In 1973, the wreck of Halifax W1048 was recovered from Lake Hoklingen near Trondheim by a team of British divers led by Peter Cornish. At the time, this was the sole remaining Halifax out of 6,176 built and the iconic bomber can be seen in a largely unrestored state at the RAF Museum in Hendon. The remains of the Halifax are displayed on a bed of sand that imitates a lake bed. Leaving the Halifax in this state, largely unrestored but albeit conserved, is arguably better than restoring the aircraft to mint condition where most of its original structure and parts would be removed.

The fate of midget submarine *X 5* was a lingering mystery for several decades after the war. In 1974 and 1976, diving expeditions led by Cornish attempted to locate *X 5* at Kaa Fjord. During the search for the missing submarine, parts of a Fleet Air Arm Fairey Barracuda, Grumman F6F Hellcat and a single float from one of *Tirpitz*'s Arado Ar 196 floatplanes were discovered. From the wrecked Hellcat, the parachute, machine guns and ammunition were recovered in the summer of 1974. However, the wrecked vessel located by Cornish and another one found in 2003 were both thought to be that of *X 5*. Sadly in both cases, it was not the midget submarine. Instead, it is now thought that the wreck is a German auxiliary vessel sunk on 15 September during Operation *Paravane*. To this day, the exact fate of *X 5* and her crew remains a mystery.

In 2005, the privately-run *Tirpitz* museum at Tromsø opened to the public. Present during the opening ceremony were several survivors from the *Tirpitz* as well as John Lorrimer who had served aboard the midget submarine *X 6*. The *Tirpitz* museum contains the world's largest repository of contemporary documents, photographs and artefacts of the battleship. Here, the complete history of the *Tirpitz*, from its launch in April 1939 until the end of the arduous process of scrapping in 1957, can be found.

The *Tirpitz* bulkhead

Since 12 November 1944, a rivalry has been raging between IX(B) and 617 Squadrons. The question is which squadron delivered the final blow to the Beast? A part of the *Tirpitz*'s bulkhead changed hands between the squadrons for decades, usually by various devious and cloak and dagger means, and the background to this story is interesting. Roger Audis of the IX(B) Squadron Association has the following to say on *Tirpitz*'s bulkhead:

> There were a number of raids during October and November of 1944, but the raid that finally sank the battleship was mounted on 12 November 1944 from RAF Lossiemouth in Scotland. The ship was hit by a number of Tallboys delivered by both squadrons, causing it to capsize and come to rest in the shallows. The final and decisive bomb was delivered by Dougie Tweddle of IX Squadron.
>
> In 1947, former IX Squadron rear gunner, 'Jeep' Jepson, and now a fisherman, was working in the Tromsø area and became friendly with its people, including the town watchmaker and his daughter. 'Jeep' told them of the IX Squadron raids against the famous ship and the watchmaker's daughter mentioned that she would contact the mayor of Tromsø. At the time, a Norwegian company was salvaging the *Tirpitz* for scrap and salvage workers discovered that the German crew had painted a representation of the ship on one of the propeller shaft bulkheads. The 1.5 cm thick bulkhead, weighing over 100 kg and measuring 1,200 mm by 1,000 mm, had been previously removed from the ship. 'Jeep' mentioned that if the bulkhead became available it would be much appreciated by IX Squadron at RAF Binbrook. Therefore, Tromsø's mayor passed the story to the Norwegian Government. In November 1949, the bulkhead was presented to the RAF in Norway by the Norwegian Government and was accepted by the RAF Air Historical Branch. It was dispatched from Tromsø and arrived in the UK on 1 December 1949. The bulkhead was presented formally to the C in C, Royal Air Force Bomber Command, on 16 February 1950 by the C in C, Royal Norwegian Air Force, in commemoration of the friendship and co-operation during the Second World War.
>
> It was planned to display the new trophy at RAF Binbrook, the airfield from where IX and 617 Squadrons were then based. Soon after the trophy arrived at RAF Binbrook, IX Squadron removed it from its official home and placed it in their squadron building. In due course, 617 Squadron responded by raiding IX Squadron and moving the bulkhead to a wall in their building. This started an intense rivalry between the two squadrons that still exists today. Indeed, it is an unofficial crime to mention the Squadron's numbers to a member of IX Squadron.
>
> The raids carried on for many years with each squadron trying to retain ownership of the great trophy. The most famous raid was launched by the ever alert IX Squadron when stationed at Cyprus in 1971 and the junior squadron was stationed at Scampton. IX Squadron sent a Vulcan bomber on a UK ranger to RAF Waddington. The bulkhead was stolen, loaded in the back of a large van and driven to RAF Wittering down the A1; the IX Squadron Vulcan was searched by members of 617 Squadron before it took off from Waddington, but nothing was found. However, just after take-off, the captain declared an inflight emergency and diverted without permission to Wittering. Bemused air traffic controllers watched as the van containing the bulkhead was positioned next to the Vulcan bomb bay and the bulkhead was quickly transferred. The Vulcan returned to Cyprus and the crew were the toast of IX Squadron.

In 1981, it was announced that both squadrons would re-equip with the Tornado, therefore a truce was called and the bulkhead was moved to the RAF Museum Hendon. The following year, just as IX Squadron became the world's first operational Tornado squadron, historian Alan Cooper found the bulkhead on the floor in the Bomber Command room at the RAF Museum. He phoned IX Squadron who immediately sent a team to recover the bulkhead that was put on display in the crew room at RAF Honington. In 1986, IX Squadron moved to RAF Bruggen in Germany and the bulkhead was remounted on the crew room wall. IX Squadron had owned the trophy for nine years and a few postings of aircrew from the senior to the junior squadron reignited interest in the bulkhead.

In June 1991, 617 Squadron were on exercise in nearby Holland and a team of aircrew, disguised as workmen, broke into the IX Squadron crew room and removed the bulkhead, loaded it in the back of a van and used the Channel ferry to return it to RAF Marham. It was set deep in the crew room floor with extra cross beams at the back and permanently fixed in concrete. (According to Sqn Ldr Dick James of IX(B) Squadron: '617 Squadron then became very unsporting. They mounted the bulkhead in 30 cm of special concrete and alarmed the room at RAF Marham where it was kept. IX Squadron made an attempt to rescue it a few months later, but it was immovable.') A year later, a few crews from IX Squadron were told to do some Tornado trials work with 617 Squadron. The IX Squadrons crews were followed everywhere. However, one of the IX Squadron crews memorised the key numbers to 617 Squadron's headquarters and managed to take some pictures of the bulkhead mounting. Back at Bruggen, a plan was hatched to return the bulkhead to its rightful owners. Everything was considered, including the use of dynamite to blow the bulkhead out of the floor. In the end, power tools were hired but to no avail. After eight hours of overnight work, the bulkhead was still secure in the concrete.

A few years later, 617 Squadron was moved to RAF Lossiemouth and it reportedly took four expert workmen several days to extricate the bulkhead from the floor. Aware of the likely attempts to remove it from the Lossiemouth crew room, an elaborate security system was purchased and installed by the aircrew, and the bulkhead was fixed into place using huge bolts. In 2001, it was decided to return the bulkhead to the RAF Museum at RAF Hendon so it could be seen by the general public. On 8 November 2002, the bulkhead was formally handed back to the RAF Museum for safekeeping. The presentation was watched by twenty IX Squadron aircrews and over 100 members of the IX Squadron Association, and a handful of 617 Squadron Association members.

Sqn Ldr Ian Wood of 617 Squadron stated, 'We hope that it provides an item of interest, not just for its provenance but also as an illustration of how *esprit de corps* and friendly rivalry has been part of the history of two of the RAF's premier bomber squadrons for more than 50 years.'[3]

The bulkhead was not the only part of the *Tirpitz* presented to a former RAF crewmembers that had sunk her. Also in 1949, part of the armoured deck was sent to the United States and Hubert Knilans. (Knilans had participated in Operation *Paravane* before returning to his native America.)[4]

The intense rivalry between 9 and 617 Squadrons regarding the sinking of the *Tirpitz* led to a re-enactment of Operation *Catechism*. This was held at the RAF Wainfleet Air-Weapons Range in Wiltshire on 12 November 2009, sixty-five years to the day after the sinking of the *Tirpitz*. The event lasted the whole day and 617 Squadron was victorious.[5] The raids against the *Tirpitz* have been recognised by the Battle of Britain Memorial Flight (BBMF), which operates an airworthy Avro Lancaster. For the 2013 season, the Lancaster has been marked as DV385 (code letters KC-A) that flew on two *Tirpitz* raids—Operation *Obviate* and Operation *Catechism*—by Flt Lt Castagnola, who had also taken part in the first raid flying Lancaster PB415. This particular Lancaster flew some fifty operational sorties with 617 Squadron and also carried nose art and the name 'Thumper' after the Disney cartoon character.

'Easy Elsie'

The wreck of 'Easy Elsie' remained at the crash site near Porjus. Lancaster, NF920, was built at Baginton by Armstrong Whitworth as part of its fourth production batch of 400 bombers (delivered to the RAF in July 1944 and completed in February 1945). NF920 was the fourteenth Lancaster of the batch and was delivered to the RAF on 12 August 1944. The Lancaster was assigned to 617 Squadron and remained on charge with the squadron for its entire service life. The forced landing at Porjus on 29 October meant the end of the road for NF920. On 30 October, the comment 'CAT E/burnt' was inscribed on the individual aircraft record card for NF920 and the Lancaster was formally struck off RAF charge on 2 November. The Lancaster had enjoyed a life span of just over two-and-a-half months.

Soon after the crash, two serviceable Merlin engines as well as the tyres were removed and sold locally. The engines were removed by sled. Allegedly, the buyer had purchased the engines to gain access to oil in the tanks; however, not much oil remained, which—also according to uncorroborated information—was so disappointing that he gave the engines away. Exactly where the engines ended up is not known.

Twentieth anniversary of 'Easy Elsie's arrival

The twentieth anniversary of the unscheduled arrival of 'Easy Elsie' at Porjus was recognised in November 1964 in a special issue of the local newspaper *Norrländska Socialdemokraten* (NSD). The tail gunner, Gerry Witherick, was interviewed by an NSD reporter saying that before reaching the *Tirpitz*, they had flown for eight hours. Witherick continued:

> The right engine was hit by flak on our first pass. We dropped our bomb on the third pass, which hit the water beside the battleship. We were busy trying to avoid being hit again by the German flak to see exactly where the bomb landed. However, we were hit

yet again, forcing us to seek refuge in Sweden. We threw everything that was loose out of the Lanc, trying to trade loss of weight for an increase in altitude. After about one hour, we noticed a large lake, completely surrounded by forest and a small village. We decided to take the chance and set down the Lanc. The hydraulics had been shot to pieces, which meant that the undercarriage, flaps and bomb-bay doors were all in the down position. This made things difficult. During the landing, Carey injured his knee and we had to carry him from the aircraft.

For the most part of the 1960s and early 1970s, the resting place for 'Easy Elsie' remained largely undisturbed. Apart from the front fuselage, which had been completely burnt out after the forced landing in 1944 and the removal of the Merlin engines, the old bomber was in fair condition. Also, not many people ventured a visit to the wreck and this was mainly due to Porjus being located in a remote and sparsely populated part of Sweden. Interest in the old bomber seemed almost non-existent, particularly regarding its importance to aviation history. This attitude towards the wrecked bomber might be understood when considering that the war was still present in the memories of many people. Thousands of people had been killed during operations on the Arctic Front with large parts of Finland and Norway having suffered near and complete devastation at the hands of German forces. Even though Sweden had not been actively involved, the country and its people had suffered indirectly during the war. Thus, there seemed to be no need to recover and preserve any relic from the war.

However, a local scrap merchant, Ernst Öhman, did cut up large parts of the remaining wreckage with the intention of selling them for smelting. Öhman went to work on the Lancaster with a heavy axe, cutting through the aluminium sheet metal of the fuselage and wings. Having cut up the Lancaster into smaller and more manageable pieces, the scrap merchant then proceeded to leave the wreck in situ, considering it too difficult to move the parts to the nearest road.

Revival of interest

When the wreck of Hampden AE436 was discovered in the Swedish mountains in August 1976, public interest in other remaining Second World War aircraft wrecks in the area increased substantially. This particular Hampden had crashed into the Tsatsa Mountain during the night of 5 September 1942 during a ferry flight to Russia during Operation *Orator*. The Swedish national press even printed special inserts covering the histories behind these wrecks. A number of the surviving aircrew were traced and interviewed. Although most of the Hampden's remains were recovered and returned to Britain for restoration, 'Easy Elsie' remained at Porjus. There were several Lancasters preserved in Britain, including one in airworthy condition, which may be one way of explaining the apparent lack of interest in recovering 'Easy Elsie'. The warbird movement of preserving Second World War aircraft, preferably in flying condition, was in its infancy; however, as no Hampden remained in existence, the wreck of AE436 was recovered and returned to Britain.

Sadly, Bill Carey lost his life in a car accident in 1981, never being able to make a return visit to Porjus. His widow and son were to later visit Porjus (related below). By the early 1980s, the remains of the wrecked Lancaster received some attention through a local exhibition, including a scale model of 'Easy Elsie' built by Pär Erixon, detailing the raid on the *Tirpitz* and eventual arrival in Sweden of Lancaster NF920 and her crew. The fact that the remains of a Lancaster bomber, one that had taken part in the final raid on the mighty battleship *Tirpitz*, was good news for the local tourist trade. Tentative attempts of having the wreck recovered and preserved elsewhere were made, but without success.

Nothing more came of this until late 1984 when the tail section, including stabiliser and both fins, was recovered by Wing F 21 on behalf of the Flygvapenmuseum (Swedish Air Force Museum). Also recovered at the same time was the wreck of a Hawker Osprey as well as small parts of a de Havilland DH 60T Moth Trainer and Messerschmitt Bf 109G. No effort was made to restore or display parts of 'Easy Elsie' by the Flygvapenmuseum. With Flygvapenmuseum's primary function being to present and display the history of Flygvapnet and the aircraft it has operated, there existed little interest in the Lancaster remains.

One might have argued that the wreck of 'Easy Elsie' could have been put on display as a physical reminder of the 350 or so foreign aircraft which for various reasons ended up in neutral Sweden during the war. With Flygvapnet being very active in intercepting the foreign intruders, either to turn them away or escort them to a safe landing, the Lancaster could have been incorporated into a full-scale diorama telling the story of these aircraft, but it was not to be.

In the early 1990s, a small bridge was built, making it possible to walk from the road to the crash site and was officially inaugurated on 14 June 1992. Following a request by the Porjus Archival Committee, the Lancaster parts that had been recovered almost ten years previously were returned to Porjus. The return of the parts also secured additional storage space at the Flygvapenmuseum.

Carey's widow and son were present when the tail section was lowered to the ground by a Flygvapnet Agusta-Bell AB 204 helicopter, both being visibly moved by the event. The author remembers watching the event on television, being struck by the human suffering that had been brought on by the war could still, decades later, evoke such strong feelings. Carey, and other participants of the raids against the *Tirpitz*, had to receive their overdue share of honour. The wreck site has since then been managed by the Porjus Archival Committee that opened the bog for visitors in 1992. Spreading the word to the public about 'Easy Elsie' included putting brief information—and travel directions on milk cartons—as part of promoting various tourist sightseeing locations in northern Sweden. Incredibly, it is still possible to make out the name 'Easy Elsie' on the wreckage of the forward fuselage.

Alex McKie visits 'Easy Elsie'

Alex McKie, the original navigator from the bomber, visited 'Easy Elsie' in late June 2002. The Swedish aviation historian John Bryggman had corresponded with McKie for some time and McKie wrote about his wish to pay a visit to his old aeroplane. In the event, McKie's sons presented him with the trip to Sweden as an eightieth birthday present. Upon arriving at Gällivare Airport, McKie casually mentioned that during his earlier visit to Porjus, he and the crew (apart from Carey) had spent the night at the local jail. This time around, McKie hoped that the accommodation would be of a higher standard!

McKie's visit was hosted by John Bryggman with the local press in attendance and McKie reminisced about his wartime experiences. Having trained as a navigator in Canada, he initially served with 106 Squadron, participating in thirty raids. McKie was later posted to 617 Squadron and took part in Operation *Paravane* on 15 September. During the briefing for the second raid on the *Tirpitz*, one of the crew asked if Swedish fighters or flak would fire against the Lancasters. The briefing officer smiled craftily saying that he really did not think so. In McKie's opinion, some form of tacit agreement existed between the British and Swedish Governments regarding crossing into Swedish airspace.

The visit to 'Easy Elsie' was, understandably, very emotional for McKie. Standing by the wreck, he remained quiet for several minutes. Apart from McKie, nearly forty people, including members of the press and the chairman of Jokkmokk County, Kent Ögren, were present. A visit to the former Porjus police station, now converted into a tourist information office, was also part of the trip. The cells had been kept just as they were in 1944. Pulling the iron hasp of the cell door, McKie smiled and said: 'I still recall this sound!' Sadly, McKie passed away in 2008 and was the last survivor from the crew of 'Easy Elsie'.

On 5 June 2011, a Swedish aviation and amateur telegraphic radio enthusiast visited 'Easy Elsie'. He subsequently sent several messages while sitting on what had been the wireless operator's station aboard the Lancaster. Due to the poor weather conditions, it was decided to repeat the event the following year. Following intense preparations, a group of Swedish radio amateurs travelled to the wreck site of the Lancaster. Telegraphic radio messages were subsequently sent to the RAF Amateur Radio Society as well as several aviation museums, other organisations and radio amateurs. The broadcast took place during the weekend of 16–17 June.

The future for 'Easy Elsie'

The remains of 'Easy Elsie' have slowly but surely been picked clean by visiting tourists and thoughtless souvenir hunters. It is more than likely that within the next five years and if decisive action is not taken, the remains of this Lancaster will succumb to nature and souvenir hunters. Efforts to have the remains of NF920 recovered and returned to the UK have not been successful. With the hulk of the *Tirpitz* having been scrapped, the 617 Squadron Lancaster is the largest surviving relic of the many operations conducted by British forces against the huge battleship. It is to be hoped that at least some parts of this most historic Lancaster can be preserved for posterity, either in Sweden, Norway or the UK. Displaying the remains of 'Easy Elsie' in a post-crash diorama, not unlike the presentation of Halifax W1048 at the RAF Museum, could be one way of securing the Lancaster for posterity. In 2008, parts of the Lancaster—in all likelihood removed by souvenir hunters—were offered for sale on eBay.

Less than twenty Lancasters out of the 7,377 built are in existence. Only two of these are airworthy. A number of substantial Lancaster wrecks can still be found around the world, particularly in Canada. The remains of 'Easy Elsie' are a unique remainder, not only of a historically important Avro Lancaster, but also of one of the most well-known operations during the Second World War.

APPENDIX 1

Avro Lancaster B. Mk I Specification and Data

Span: 31.088 m (102 feet)
Length: 21.14 m (69 feet 4 inches)
Height: 5.97 m (20 feet 6 inches)
Wing area: 120.5 m² (1,297 square feet)
Maximum speed: 440 kph (287 mph)
Cruise speed: 322 kph (200 mph)
Maximum range: 4,070 km (2,530 miles)

APPENDIX 2

RAF raids against the *Tirpitz* 1940-1942

9–10 July 1940	Wilhelmshaven	Eleven Hampdens	No damage
20–21 July 1940	Wilhelmshaven	Fifteen Hampdens	No damage
24–25 July 1940	Wilhelmshaven	Fourteen Whitleys	No damage
5–6 August 1940	Wilhelmshaven	Seventeen Hampdens	No damage
8–9 October 1940	Wilhelmshaven	Seventeen bombers	No damage
10–11 October 1940	Wilhelmshaven	Forty Wellingtons/ thirty-five Hampdens	No damage
20–21 October 1940	Wilhelmshaven	Seven Wellingtons	No damage
25–26 November 1940	Wilhelmshaven	Five Whitleys	No damage
8–9 January 1941	Wilhelmshaven	Thirty-two bombers	No damage
15 January 1941	Wilhelmshaven	Ninety-six bombers	No damage
16 January 1941	Wilhelmshaven	Eighty-one bombers	No damage
29–30 January 1941	Wilhelmshaven	Thirty-four bombers	No damage
9 February 1941	Wilhelmshaven	Thirteen Hampdens	No damage
27–28 February 1941	Wilhelmshaven	Thirty Wellingtons	No damage
28 February–March 1941	Wilhelmshaven	116 bombers	No damage
28–29 March 1941	Kiel	Fourteen bombers	No damage
20–21 June 1941	Kiel	115 bombers	No damage
7 September 1941	Kiel	N/A	N/A
29–30 January 1942	Fætten Fjord	Sixteen bombers	No damage
10 March 1942	Fætten Fjord	Twelve Beauforts	Cancelled
29–30 March 1942	Fætten Fjord	Thirty-eight bombers	No damage
30–31 March 1942	Fætten Fjord	Thirty-four bombers	No damage
27–28 April 1942	Fætten Fjord	Forty-four bombers	No damage
28/29 April 1942	Fætten Fjord	Twenty-three bombers	No damage

APPENDIX 3

Fleet Air Arm raids against the *Tirpitz* 1942–1944

9 March 1942	Lofoten Islands	Twelve Fairey Albacore torpedo bombers	N/A
3 April 1944	Kaa Fjord	Operation *Tungsten*/ Ninety-three aircraft	Substantial damage
24 April 1944	Kaa Fjord	N/A	Cancelled due to poor weather
14 May 1944	Kaa Fjord	Operation *Brawn*/ Sixty-three aircraft took off	Raid abandoned due to low-cloud base
28 May 1944	Kaa Fjord	N/A	Cancelled due to poor weather
17 July 1944	Kaa Fjord	Operation *Mascot*/ Ninety-two aircraft	No damage
22 August 1944	Kaa Fjord	Operation *Goodwood*/ Eighty-four aircraft	No damage
22 August 1944	Kaa Fjord	Fourteen aircraft	No damage
24 August 1944	Kaa Fjord	Seventy-seven aircraft	No damage
29 August 1944	Kaa Fjord	Sixty-seven aircraft	No damage
18 October 1944	Håkøya	Seven Firefly fighter-bombers	No damage

APPENDIX 4

Operation *Paravane*
15 September 1944

No. IX(B) Squadron Lancasters and crews

LM715
Wg Cdr J. M. Bazin
Flt Lt A. M. Richie
Flt Lt E. F. A. Jones
Plt Off. J. M. Gran (Can)
FS R. Collins
FS C. Cameron

W4964
Plt Off. S. E. Evans
Flt Lt J. D. Melrose
FS E. Selfe
Plt Off. R. W. Moore (Aus)
Plt Off. S. A. Morris
Plt Off. R. G. Woolf (Aus)
FS E. Hoyle
FS E. E. Stalley

PB289
Plt Off. B. Taylor
FS D. J. Doherty
FS A. L. Cunningham
FS A. M. Holmes (Can)
FS K. A. Burns
FS G. C. Freeman (Can)
FS G. M. Young (Can)

LM448
Fg Off. A. F. Jones (Aus)
FS A. E. W. Biles

FS S. Scott
Fg Off. R. L. Blunsdon
FS R. L. Birch (Aus)
FS R. Glover
FS J. Acheson (Aus)

LL914
Fg Off. W. D. Tweddle
FS C. G. Heath
FS E. Shields
FS J. W. Singer (Can)
FS A. Carson
FS J. A. Foot
FS K. Mallinson

LM548
Fg Off. J. J. Dunne (Aus)
FS A. F. Grant
FS M. J. Thain
Fg Off. C. L. Philpott
FS J. W. Knight
FS J. T. Rose (Can)
FS J. F. Jordan

LL845
Sqn Ldr H. R. Pooley
FS S. Bloom
FS C. L. Griffiths
Fg Off. F. Sowerby
Flt Lt R. W. Cook

FS A. J. Williams
FS N. Smith

LL901
Fg Off. M. Scott
FS J. E. Simkin
FS L. A. Harding
FS J. W. Langley
FS E. M. Hayward
FS F. A. Saunders
FS L. J. Hambly

NF925
Fg Off. J. E. Stowell
FS C. R. Spalding

FS J. C. Taylor
FS R. S. Liversedge
FS F. Millington
FS R. G. Hicker
FS M. W. A. Allsopp

LM713
Fg Off. D. MacIntosh
FS R. V. Cosser
FS N. Hawkins
FS P. J. Ramwell
FS P. E. Tetlow
FS J. A. Wood
FS G. Owen

No. 617 Squadron Lancasters and crews

EE146
Wg Cdr J. B. Tait
FS A. W. Gallagher
Fg Off. B. R. Bayne
Fg Off. W. W. Daniel (Can)
Fg Off. A. J. Ward
W/op M. D. Vaughan

LM489
Fg Off. J. Gingles
FS W. Mason
FS R. Johnson
FS L. Hazell
W/op J. Riley
Flt Lt R. F. Scott-Kiddie
FS R. W. Hunnisette

ME434
Fg Off. I. S. Ross (Aus)
FS W. Walter
FS A. Jackson
FS E. G Tilby
FS K. Jenkinson

FS R. D. Griffiths
Plt Off. A. P. McKellar

NF920
Fg Off. D. W. Carey
FS L. Franks
Plt Off. W. M. McKie
Plt Off. D. H. McLennan (Can)
FS A. E. Young
Fg Off. G. A. Witherick
FS A. E. Sharp

ME554
Flt Lt T. T. Iveson
FS J. D. Phillips
Fg Off. J. D. Harrison
FS P. H. Chance
Fg Off. A. Tittle
FS A. L. Smith
FS E. A. Wass

PD233
Flt Lt M. Hamilton
FS J. P. Rooke

Plt Off. J. T. Jackson
Fg Off. F. C. Atkinson (Can)
FS R. C. Thompson
FS J. A. Dadge
FS D. Hamilton

PD238
Sqn Ldr J. V. Cockshott
FS R. C. Fryer
FS L. E. Gosling
Plt Off. E. Booth
FS A. S. Bates
FS G. R. Bradbury
W/op L. J. Birch (Aus)

DV405
Sqn Ldr G. L. Fawke
FS A. W. Cherrington
Fg Off. T. Bennett
Flt Lt R. E. Woods (Can)
Plt Off. M. Ellwood
Plt Off. R. M. Heggie
Fg Off. P. H. Martin (Aus)

ME562
Plt Off. J. Sanders
FS T. H. Nutley
Plt Off. J. B. Barron
Plt Off. H. G. Allen (Can)
FS A. Ward
FS R. A. Briars
FS R. Maghin

NF923
Flt Lt C. J. G. Howard
FS F. C. Hawkins
Flt Lt T. J. Tate
Plt Off. L. Hartley
Plt Off. R. D. Lucan
W/op J. Cods
FS J. Clarke

LM483
Fg Off. F. H. A. Watts
FS H. Luck
Plt Off. C. H. Housden
Plt Off. M. L. McKay (Can)
Plt Off. D. Cooper
FS G. Matthews
FS T. J. Trebilcock

DV391
Flt Lt R. E. Knights
Plt Off. E. Twells
Plt Off. T. J. Hayford
Fg Off. A. Walker
Plt Off. L. J. Hosie (NZ)
W/op W. H. Pengelly
Plt Off. P. W. Denham

LM402
Plt Off. A. E. Kell (Aus)
Plt Off. J. Soilleur
Fg Off. J. L. Hager (Aus)
Fg Off. K. C. Morteson (Aus)
FS A. M. Lovatt (Aus)
Fg Off. K. S. Jewell

ME561
Flt Lt C. S. Stout
Plt Off. E. Benting
Plt Off. O. E. M. Graham
Fg Off. W. A. Rupert (Can)
Fg Off. R. J. Allen
FS Whittaker
Plt Off. R. H. Petch

PB415
Fg Off. J. Castagnola
FS S. J. Henderson
Fg Off. T. J. Gorringe
FS N. Evans
FS W. T. Eaves
FS R. E. Salter
FS J. K. Ronald

DV246
Flt Lt H. J. Pryor
Plt Off. R. J. Telper
Fg Off. R. L. Pinder (Can)
Fg Off. G. Hoyland
Plt Off. A. Hepworth
Plt Off. A. J. Patterson
FS A. J. Colyer

PB416
Fg Off. F. Levy
FS P. W. Groom
Fg Off. O. L. Fox
FS E. E. S. Peck
FS G. M. McGuire
Plt Off. A. F. McNally (Can)
FS D. G. Thomas

LM492
Lt H. C. Knilans (USA)
Flt Lt K. J. Nyall
Fg Off. D. A. Bell (Can)

Fg Off. C. G. Rogers
Flt Lt L. W. Curtis
FS J. J. Blanche
Fg Off. R. A. Learmonth

ME559
Sqn Ldr D. H. Wyness
Fg Off. J. S. Naylor
Flt Lt R. H. Williams
Plt Off. H. W. Honig
Fg Off. D. C. Shea
FS T. Horrocks
Plt Off. G. E. Camsell

ED763
Flt Lt D. J. Grael
FS R. P. Haywood
Plt Off. D. R. Brand (Can)
Plt Off. J. H. Cole (Can)
Plt Off. A. Dicken
Fg Off. D. T. Watkins
FS D. P. Peirson

463 Squadron Lancaster and crew

LM587
Flt Lt B. A. Buckham
FS W. Sinclair
Plt Off. R. W. Board
FS L. J. Manning
Fg Off. E. J. Holden

Fg Off. H. H. Giersch
Fg Off. D. M. Procter
Flt Lt J. Loftus (Film Unit)
Fg Off. Kimberly (Film Unit)
Mr Guy Byams (BBC)
Mr W. E. West (Press Association)

APPENDIX 5

Operation *Obviate* 29 October 1944

No. IX(B) Squadron Lancasters and crews

PB377
Wg Cdr J. M. Bazin
Plt Off. J. McDonnell
Sqn Ldr F. G. Rumbles
Plt Off. K. L. Lewis
FS R. Collins
Flt Lt C. J. Campbell (Aus)
Plt Off. S. Evans

NF929
Flt Lt G. C. Camsell (Can)
FS W. Andrews
FS P. R. Aslin
FS R. J. Gran (Can)
FS D. Beevers
FS A. E. Boon (Can)

NG220
Fg Off. W. D. Tweddle
FS C. G. Heath
FS E. Shields
FS J. W. Singer (Can)
FS A. Carson
FS K. Mallinson

ME198
Fg Off. R. J. Harris
FS T. R. Andrew
FS J. T. Adair
Plt Off. H. F. C. Parsons

FS P. Newman
FS S. Sanders

ME809
Fg Off. R. F. Adams
FS L. A. Brown
FS H. R. Lynam
FS P. F. Jackson
FS R. F. Faucheux
FS F. Whitfield

LM448
Fg Off. A. F. Jones (Aus)
FS A. E. W. Biles
Plt Off. S. Scott
Fg Off. R. L. Blunsdon
FS R. L. Birch (Aus)
FS J. Acheson (Aus)

NN722
Fg Off. A. L. Keeley
FS A. E. Wotherspoon
FS W. Chorny (Can)
FS L. W. Tanner
FS S. D. Chambers
FS J. E. Johnson

NG235
Fg Off. Laws
FS W. E. Harrison

FS H. I. Middleton
Fg Off. D. M. MacDonald (Can)
W/op. G. G. Charlton
FS J. R. Charlton

NG252
Fg Off. K. S. Arnwell (Aus)
FS P. H. Jones
FS P. E. Campbell (NZ)
Fg Off. H. W. Porter
FS R. Meads
FS L. J. Richards

PB368
Sqn Ldr L. A. G. Williams
FS G. V. Prettejohns
Fg Off. R. C. Harvey
FS A. H. Horry
FS P. A. Morgan
FS A. B. Watt

NG206
Flt Lt D. Melrose
FS E. Selfe
Plt Off. J. W. Moore (Aus)
Fg Off. S. A. Morris
Fg Off. R. G. Woolf (Aus)
FS E. E. Stalley

NG845
Flt Lt A. M. Morrison
FS A Aitkenhead
Flt Lt E. F. A. Jones
FS R. Watt
FS L. L. Westrope
W/op F. Black (Aus)
FS F. Hooper

NF937
Flt Lt J. J. Dunne (Aus)
FS A. F. Grant
FS M. J. Thain
Fg Off. C. L. Philpott

FS J. W. Knight
FS J. E. Jordan

NG242
Fg Off. D. Macintosh
FS R. V. Cosser
FS N. Hawkins
FS P. J. Ramwell
FS P. E. Tetlow
FS G. Owen

PD213
Fg Off. B. Taylor
FS D. J. Doherty
FS A. L. Cunningham
FS A. M. Holmes (Can)
FS K. A. Burns
FS G. M. Young (Can)

NG223
Fg Off. A. F. Williams (Aus)
FS W. C. Lewis
FS J. Lockerbie
FS J. B. Gold
FS L. S. J. Stenner
FS J. M. Reilly

PA172
Fg Off. L. E. Marsh
FS C. L. Harrison
Plt Off. A. Brown
Fg Off. J. A. Carr (Can)
W/op C. I. G. Davis
FS F. R. Riches

NG220
Fg Off. J. E. Stowell
FS C. R. Spalding
FS J. G. Taylor
FS R. S. Liversedge
FS F. Millington
FS M. W. A. Allsopp

NG249
Fg Off. C. R. Redfern
FS J. W. Williams
FS R. W. Cooper
Fg Off. O. P. Hill
FS L. G. Roberts
FS D. Winch

PB696
Fg Off. R. C. Lake
FS R. W. Baird
Plt Off. J. A. Peterson (Can)
W/op G. B. Watts (Can)
Fg Off. D. Cooper
Flt Lt W. T. G. Gabriel

No. 617 Squadron Lancasters and crews

NG180
Wg Cdr J. B. Tait
FS A. E. Gallagher
Plt Off. H. Ellis
Plt Off. W. A. Daniel (Can)
Fg Off. A. J. Ward
W/op H. D. Vaughan

PD233
Flt Lt M. D. Hamilton
FS L. S. Rooke
Plt Off. J. T. Jackson
Plt Off. E. Booth
FS J. T. Thompson
FS D. Hamilton

DV405
Sqn Ldr G. E. Fawke
FS A. W. Cherrington
Fg Off. T. Bennett
Fg Off. C. G. Rogers
Fg Off. M. Ellwood
Plt Off. R. M. Heggie

LM492
Flt Lt H. J. Pryor
FS A. L. Winston
Fg Off. R. L. Pinder (Can)
Plt Off. G. Hoyland
Plt Off. A. Hepworth
FS M. A. Colyer

ME554
Sqn Ldr T. G. Iveson
FS J. D. Phillips
Fg Off. J. D. Harrison
FS F. R. Chance
Fg Off. A. Tittle
FS A. L. Smith
Plt Off. M. B. Flatman (passenger)

DV402
Flt Lt J. L. Sayers (Aus)
Plt Off. V. L. Johnson
Fg Off. E. O. Strom (Aus)
Plt Off. E. W. Weaver (Aus)
Plt Off. F. E. Howkins
Plt Off. R. P. Barry (Aus)

ED763
Flt Lt D. J. Gram
FS R. P. Haywood
Plt Off. F. R. Brand (Can)
Plt Off. J. B. Cole (Can)
W/opW/op J. B. Forshaw
FS D. P. Peirson

PB415
Flt Lt R. E. Knights
Fg Off. E. Twells
Fg Off. T. R. J. Playford
Fg Off. A. B. Walker
FS A. S. Bates
W/op W. H. Pengelly

Operation Obviate 29 October 1944

DV391
Flt Lt I. M. Marshall
FS F. Cholerton
Fg Off. K. Newby
Fg Off. J. L. Rumgay
Fg Off. H. J. Riding
Fg Off. D. W. Bale

DV380
Flt Lt B. A. Gumbley (NZ)
Fg Off. A. E. Barnett
Fg Off. M. Gill
Fg Off. J. C. Randon
Plt Off. S. V. Grimes
FS G. Bell

EE131
Flt Lt L. S. Goodman
FS W. Burnett
Fg Off. H. Watkinson
Fg Off. H. A. Hayward
FS H. J. G. Booth
FS A. S. Hulbert

LM489
Fg Off. J. Gingles
FS W. Johnson
FS H. Johnson
W/op W/op L. J. Hazell
W/op W/op G. H. Riley
Flt Lt R. F. Scott-Kiddie

DV385
Fg Off. J. Castagnola
FS S. J. Henderson
Fg Off. F. J. Gorringe
Plt Off. H. Evans
FS W. T. Eaves
Plt Off. J. K. Ronald

PD238
Fg Off. Martin (Aus)
FS J. Blagbrough

FS A. Jackson
FS D. A. Day
Plt Off. G. M. Lovatt (Aus)
FS H. Mayoh

ME462
Fg Off. J. A. Sanders
FS T. H. Nutley
Plt Off. J. B. Barron
Plt Off. H. G. Allen (Can)
FS A. Ward
FS R. A. Briars

ME561
Fg Off. A. W. Joplin (NZ)
FS F. L. Tilley
FS C. D. R. Fish
FS L. Hebbard (NZ)
FS G. Cooke
Fg Off. R. B. Yates

LM695
Fg Off. F. H. A. Watts
Flt Lt K. J. Ryall
Plt Off. C. R. Housden
Plt Off. M. L. Mackay (Can)
Plt Off. D. Cooper
FS G. Matthews
Fg Off. J. H. Leavitt (passenger)

NG181
Fg Off. A. E. Kell
Plt Off. J. Soilleaux
FS L. E. Gosling
Flt Lt G. K. Astbury (Aus)
Fg Off. D. E. Freeman
Plt Off. R. Wikinson

NF920
Fg Off. D. W. Carey (Aus)
FS L. Franks
Fg Off. A. M. McKie
Plt Off. D. H. McLennan (Can)

FS A. E. Young
Fg Off. G. A. Witherick

No. 463 Squadron Lancasters and crew (film aircraft)

PD329
Flt Lt B. A. Buckham
FS W. Sinclair
Plt Off. R. W. Egard
FS L. J. Manning

APPENDIX 6

Operation *Catechism* 12 November 1944

No. IX(B) Squadron Lancasters and crews

PB696
Flt Lt R. C. Lake
FS R. W. Baird
Plt Off. J. A. Peterson (Can)
W/opW/op G. B. Watts (Can)
FS G. E. Parkinson
FS J. S. Parkes

PB368
Sqn Ldr A. G. Williams
FS G. V. Prettejohns
Fg Off. R. C. Harvey
FS A. H. Horry
FS P. A. Morgan
FS A. B. Watt

LM220
Fg Off. W. B. Tweddle
FS C. G. Heath
Plt Off. E. Shields
Fg Off. D. A. Nolan
FS A. Carson
FS K. Mallinson

NF999
Fg Off. E. Jeffs
FS C. V. Higgins
FS K. C. Mousley
FS H. A. Fisher

FS C. M. McMillan
FS G. J. Symonds

NG242
Fg Off. D. Macintosh
FS R. V. Cosser
FS N. Hawkins
FS P. J. Ramwell
FS P. E. Tetlow
FS G. Owen

PA172
Flt Lt L. E. Marsh
FS C. L. Harrison
Plt Off. A. Brown (Can)
Plt Off. J. A. Carr (Can)
W/opW/op C. I. G. Davies
FS F. R. Riches

NF929
Flt Lt G. C. Camsell (Can)
FS W. Andrews
FS P. R. Aslin
Plt Off. R. J. Gran (Can)
FS D. Beevers
FS A. E. Boon

NG249
Fg Off. C. E. Redfern
FS J. W. Williams

FS R. W. Cooper
Fg Off. D. Mitchell
FS L. G. Roberts
FS D. Winch

NN722
Fg Off. M. L. T. Harper (NZ)
FS A. Whitworth
Fg Off. J. G. Home
FS D. Williams
FS G. H. Irwin
FS J. J. Meagher

PD198
Flt Lt H. Watkins
FS F. W. Jowett
Flt Lt E. F. A. Jones
Fg Off. A. E. Jones (Aus)
Plt Off. J. Ware
Flt Lt W. T. G. Gabriel

NG252
Fg Off. O. C. Newton (Can)
FS W. Gregory
FS F. Grant
FS R. Flynn (Can)
FS L. G. Kelly
FS R. S. Stevens (Can)

NG220
Fg Off. Stowell
FS C. R. Spalding
FS J. G. Taylor
FS R. S. Liversedge
FS F. Millington
FS M. W. A. Allsopp

LM448
Fg Off. Coster (NZ)
FS J. C. Pinning
FS C. W. Black (NZ)
FS J. H. Boag (NZ)
FS H. G. East
FS W. J. Jones

No. 617 Squadron Lancasters and crews

EE146
Wg Cdr J. E. Tait
FS A. E. Gallagher
Fg Off. H. Ellis
Fg Off. W. A. Daniel (Can)
Fg Off. A. J. Ward
W/opW/op H. D. Vaughan

ME554
Sqn Ldr T. G. Iveson
FS J. D. Phillips
Fg Off. J. D. Harrison
FS E. R. Chance
Plt Off. A. Tittle
FS E. A. Wass
Flt Lt H. V. Gavin (Aus) (passenger)

LM492
Flt Lt J. L. Sayers (Aus)
Plt Off. V. L. Johnson
Fg Off. E. G. Strom (Aus)
Plt Off. E. W. Weaver (Aus)
Plt Off. P. E. Howkins
Plt Off. B. P. Kent

DV391
Flt Lt I. M. Marshall
FS P. Cholerton
Fg Off. K. Newby
Plt Off. H. Booth
Fg Off. H. J. Riding
Fg Off. D. W. Bale

Operation Catechism 12 November 1944

PD371
Flt Lt B. J. Dobson
Plt Off. A. T. McKenzie
W/opW/op S. R. Anderson
Plt Off. A. K. Johnstone
Plt Off. R. J. Edge (Aus)
Plt Off. W. J. Dry (Can)

ED763
Flt Lt S. A. Anning
FS F. J. Snedker
W/opW/op F. Cardwell (NZ)
Fg Off. R. Valentine
Fg Off. J. Slater
FS D. E. Retter

PB415
Flt Lt R. E. Knights
Fg Off. E. Twells
Fg Off. T. H. Playford
Fg Off. A. B. Walker
Fg Off. R. L. Hayter
W/op. W. H. Pengelly

DV405
Flt Lt B. A. Gumbley (NZ)
Fg Off. E. A. Barnett
Fg Off. K. Gill
Fg Off. J. C. Randon
Fg Off. S. V. Grimes
FS J. Penswick

NG181
Plt Off. A. E. Kell (Aus)
Plt Off. J. Soilleux
FS L. E. Gosling
Flt Lt C. K. Astbury (Aus)
Plt Off. D. E. Freeman
Fg Off. R. Wilkinson

LM489
Fg Off. J. Gingles
FS H. W. Felton

FS H. Johnson
W/op. L. J. Hazell
W/op. G. H. Riley
FS A. D. Tirel

PD233
Fg Off. M. B. Flatman
FS R. M. Ross
Fg Off. G. Mackie
Fg Off. G. E. Kelly
FS A. S. Harwood
Plt Off. K. C. Kirk

ME555
Fg Off. I. S. Ross (Aus)
FS R. C. Fryer
Fg Off. T. O'Brien
Plt Off. E. G. Tilby
Fg Off. M. Ellwood
Fg Off. A. P. McKellar

ME561
Fg Off. A. W. Joplin (NZ)
FS F. L. Tilley
FS C. D. R. Fish
FS L. Hebbard (NZ)
FS G. Cooke
Fg Off. R. B. Yates

DV385
Fg Off. J. Castagnola
FS S. J. Henderson
Fg Off. F. J. Gorringe
Plt Off. N. Evans
FS W. T. Eaves
Plt Off. J. K. Ronald

LM485
Plt Off. F. H. A. Watts
FS A. W. Cherrington
Plt Off. C. H. Housden
Plt Off. M. L. McKay (Can)

FS H. J. C. Booth
FS G. Matthews

ME562
Fg Off. J. A. Sanders
FS T. H. Nutley
Plt Off. J. B. Barron
Plt Off. H. G. Allen (Can)
FS A. Ward
FS R. Machin

DV393
Fg Off. J. H. Leavitt

FS H. Griffin
Fg Off. R. F. Withams
FS D. A. Oldman
FS G. Cole
FS P. Goldie

DV380
Fg Off. W. R. Lee (Aus)
FS W. Johnson
Fg Off. H. Watkinson
Plt Off. G. Hoyland
W/op. A. J. Lammas
Fg Off. J. Watson

No. 463 Squadron Lancasters and crew (film aircraft)

PD329
Bruce Buckham
John Loftus

Endnotes

Chapter One: A Background History

1. The work of recovering the scuttled German warships continued well into the 1930s. German companies were also involved, which saw tugboats flying the Nazi flag operating between Scapa Flow and the Firth of Forth.
2. The 1939 edition of *Jane's Fighting Ships* states that two additional battleships, referred to as *H* and *I* respectively, were under construction. It was believed that *H* and *I* would have a displacement of 40,000 tons. Neither of these battleships was completed.
3. Holmberg and Korva (2006), p. 8.
4. Sweetman (2004), p. 4.
5. Even larger battleships were planned. In early 1936, a future battleship codenamed *H41* was to have a displacement of 64,000 tonnes. This remained on the drawing board as did the subsequent projects *H42*, *H43* and *H44*. The latter was to have a displacement of 122,000 tonnes and a length of no less than 345 metres. None of these grandiose projects were proceeded with, but it is interesting to speculate on the cost, materials and manpower needed in developing, building and operating such naval behemoths. For instance, the infrastructure of the port naval facilities to service these battleships would have to be considerably expanded. Also, the operational value of such huge battleships would have been questionable. See Holmberg and Korva (2006), p. 8, for a brief discussion on these projected vessels.
6. In the event, the surface warship fleets of Britain and Germany only clashed once in a major naval battle: the inconclusive Battle of Jutland in 1916. On the other hand, the German submarine fleet was a major success sinking so many merchant vessels that Britain was almost brought to her knees in 1917.
7. Holmberg and Korva (2006), p. 9.
8. Moyle (1989), p. 20.
9. These words were included in a speech held before the House of Commons on 20 August.
10. Holmberg & Korva (2006), p. 11.
11. On 8 July, the Swedish naval attaché in Berlin received word from German Admiral Frick that the Kriegsmarine wished to incorporate captured Soviet naval vessels into their service. Because of this, the Germans were considering letting Soviet ships slip through the German lines so that they could be interned in Sweden. Following this,

the Kriegsmarine would put forward a request for the ships to be handed over from Swedish custody. The Swedish naval attaché replied most strongly that Sweden did not desire any Soviet naval vessels to be interned and if any such vessels crossed into Swedish territorial waters, they would be fired upon. The naval attaché then suggested that if the Kriegsmarine desired to press into service any Soviet naval vessels, they would have to capture such warships by themselves.
12. During the northward cruise, the Flygvapnet (Swedish Air Force) kept a close eye on the Tirpitz and Baltenflotte. Reportedly, several aerial-reconnaissance photographs were taken of the battleship. However, a careful check of the Swedish Military Archives has so far failed to reveal any such images.
13. *These battleships had been completed in January 1914 and January 1915, and originally served with the Imperial Russian Navy as Petropavlovsk and Gangut respectively. Considering their age and inferior armament, neither could match the firepower of Tirpitz or any other Kriegsmarine major warship.*
14. Tarrant (1996), p. 126.
15. It must be remembered that the Bismarck had been disabled by carried-based Fairey Swordfish torpedo bombers, thus clearly showing the vulnerability of large warships to aerial attacks.
16. On 17 January, Kapitän zur See Topp had observed 'high-flying aircraft' above Fætten Fjord. Sweetman (2004), p. 19.

Chapter Two: Sink the Beast!

1. Smith, Nigel, Tirpitz: The Halifax Raids (Air Research Publications 2003), p. 46.
2. Two of the six Beauforts of 217 Squadron failed to arrive at Sumburgh, one having to land at Arbroath due to engine trouble and the other crashing near Montrose.
3. Interestingly, of the seventy Messerschmitt Bf 109T fighters built for operations from the Graf Zeppelin, the majority were initially delivered in mid-1941 to two Luftwaffe fighter units in Norway, I./JG 77 and Jagdgruppe.
4. The Fw 200 Condor had been developed from a successful pre-war airliner. It became well known to Allied sailors. On one occasion, a Condor had circled a convoy on and off for four days. An annoyed captain sent the signal, 'Please circle the other way. You are making me dizzy.' The Condor pilot duly complied.
5. Bishop, Patrick, Target Tirpitz: X-Craft, Agents and Dambusters—The Epic Quest to Destroy Hitler's Mightiest Warship, p. 217. The lack of petroleum, oil and lubricants would severely hamper the German war effort. By 1944, the constant lack of fuel forced a reduction of Luftwaffe, Kriegsmarine and Wehrmacht operations. When Romania changed sides in August 1944, work on producing synthetic fuel was already well underway in Germany.
6. It is unclear if the story of the British airman sitting on top of the downed Albacore is accurate. In his book, Tirpitz: Hunting the Beast, historian John Sweetman refers to it as a 'legend', p. 31.
7. Quoted in Smith, Nigel, Tirpitz: The Halifax Raids, p. 116.

8. Sergeant Ben Gibbons of 10 Squadron quoted in Nigel Smith's Tirpitz: The Halifax Raids, p. 188.
9. It would appear that Bennett's claim that he had been captured and escaped was a fabrication, intended to earn him an early repatriation back to the UK.
10. A detailed discussion about these proposed air raids can be found in Sweetman (2004), p. 63-69.
11. Sweetman (2004), p. 70.
12. One of the Sunderlands converted for the mission was JM715 and is currently preserved at Solent Sky in Southampton. Trials in using aeroplanes as carriers for human torpedoes continued until the end of the war.
13. During the Second World War, German U-boats sunk around 2,900 merchant ships with a displacement of 14.6 million tons. Twenty U-boat commanders sank just over 20 per cent out of these ships. The Kriegsmarine heavy surface vessels did not come close to these numbers.
14. Jacobsen (2007), p. 11.
15. The Spitfire is currently under long-term rebuild to airworthiness in Sweden.
16. Barracuda LS580 of 829 Squadron by Sub-Lt (A) E. C. Bowles crashed into the sea shortly after being catapulted off HMS *Victorious*. The two Barracudas shot down were LS551 of 829 Squadron flown by Sub-Lt (A) H. H. Richardson and LS569 of 830 Squadron flown by Sub-Lt (A) T. C. Bell.
17. Jacobsen, Alf R., *Dödligt angrepp*, p. 232.
18. Holmberg and Korva (2006), p. 23. There remains some uncertainty about the actual date that Operation *Planet was due to take place*.
19. The Kriegsmarine was by early May 1944 still a force to be reckoned with. In all, twenty-four destroyers, sixty-nine torpedo boats and 126 Schnellboote (small and fast torpedo boats) and 449 submarines (of which only 162 were operational, the rest mainly undergoing trials or used for training in the Baltic Sea) remained in service. However, in comparison, Allied naval power was overwhelming with no less than 286 Allied destroyers, frigates and anti-submarine vessels made available for Operation Overlord. In addition, a number of aircraft carriers, battleships and cruisers were available to the Allies. See Tarrant (1996), p 16
20. Tarrant (1996), p. 130.
21. This was LS653 of 826 Squadron. The pilot, Sub-Lt (A) E. S. Falwasser and his crew, were picked up by a destroyer.
22. Tarrant (1996), p. 131.
23. Tarrant (1996), p. 135.

Chapter Three: Operation Paravane

1. The *New Oxford Dictionary of English* (Oxford University Press, 2001) describes the noun Paravane as 'A device towed behind a boat at a depth regulated by its vanes or planes, so that the cable to which it is attached can cut the moorings of submerged mines.'

2. A Mosquito was first landed aboard a carrier, HMS Indefatigable, on 25 March 1944. No. 618 Squadron was subsequently deployed to the Pacific where, equipped with the Highball anti-shipping mine, they were to operate from British carriers to attack Japanese shipping. However, no operational sorties were flown.
3. These rotating mines were colloquially called bouncing bombs and codenamed Upkeep.
4. Sweetman (2004), p. 143.
5. Cooper (2013), p. 109.
6. Sweetman (2004), p. 155. The tree branch was later sent to Australia.
7. www.467463raafsquadrons.com/TrueTales/sink_the_tirpitz.htm: 22/04/2013.
8. www.lancaster-archive.com/bc_tirpitz2.htm: 22/08/2011.
9. Sweetman (2004), p. 161.
10. 617 Squadron newsletter in *Après Moi*, summer 2010, p. 16.
11. *Operation Paravane* became Knilans' 31st and last sortie with 617 Squadron. When he returned to his native USA, Knilans joined the USAAF, flying the Northrop P-61 night fighter. However, the war ended before Knilans unit entered frontline service. Knilans resigned from the USAAF with the rank of major.
12. http://ktsorens.tihlde.org/flyvrak/syningen.html: 22/04/2013.
13. Cooper (2013), p. 120.
14. Jacobsen, Alf R., *Dödligt angrepp*, p. 234.
15. Cooper (2013), p. 123.
16. Jacobsen, Alf R., *Dödligt angrepp*, p. 238.

Chapter Four: Operation *Obviate*

1. Tamelander and Zetterling (2006), p. 306.
2. Jacobsen, Alf R., *Dödligt angrepp*, p. 242.
3. The German retreat from northern Norway contained one fascinating episode. On 25 October, Junkers Ju 52/3M floatplanes of II/.TGr 20 were ordered to fly north from Trondheim to assist in the evacuation of wounded soldiers and material. With the take-off being delayed due to poor weather conditions, the pilot and wireless operator aboard Ju 52, 7U+IK, decided to take the chance to defect. Carrying a full load of fuel, the Ju 52 took off and headed for Iceland; however, incessant poor weather meant that they strayed off course. Instead of reaching Iceland, the two Luftwaffe fliers had to put down on the open sea due to a lack of fuel. They were soon rescued by a Scottish trawler, having put down some 48 km off Aberdeen. See Pegg (2006), p. 163, for more details on this little-known event.
4. Sweetman (2004), p. 188.
5. Sweetman (2004), p. 196.
6. Sweetman (2004), p. 196.
7. Sweetman (2004), p. 201. However, this cannot be verified with surviving documentation in Swedish military archives. Thus, Carey's remark was possibly made after his return to Britain.

8. Sweetman (2004), p. 197-203.
9. Sweetman (2004), p. 202.

Chapter Five: Operation *Catechism*

1. Sweetman (2004), p. 206.
2. Sweetman (2004), p. 206.
3. An excellent chronicle of the events on 12 November 1944 can be found in Asmussen and Aakra's *Tirpitz: Hitlers siste slagskip* (2006), p. 170.
4. www.vannasberget.se/ormanget.html: 27/08/2013
5. Girbig (2010), p. 261. Incidentally, both Girbig and John Sweetman make reference to Gayko shooting down a Swedish military aircraft prior to the 12 November sortie. Great diplomatic anger ensued, it is said. The incident that is referred to occurred in 1943, not in 1944, and involved a Flygvapnet Saab S 17B reconnaissance aeroplane which was slightly damaged, but not shot down.
6. Asmussen and Aakra (2006), p. 210.
7. www.bombercommandmuseum.ca/s,tweddle.html: 08/07/2013.
8. Cooper (2013), p. 138.
9. Bishop (2013), p. 397.
10. Bishop (2013), p. 397.
11. Arthur Ward. In 617 Squadron's newsletter, *Après Moi*, summer 2010, p. 18.
12. Zuba, Alfred, *TIRPITZ—A German Sailor's Eye Witness Report*. In *Après Moi*, winter 2009-10, p. 23-29. Submitted to *Après Moi* by Tom Bennett. Reproduced by permission.
13. Sweetman (2004), p. 216.
14. Asmussen and Aakra (2006), p. 169.
15. Cooper (2013), p. 230.
16. Sweetman (2004), p. 242.

Chapter Six: Aftermath

1. Cooper (2013), p. 197.
2. Asmussen and Åkra (2006), p. 217.
3. *Available on http://ixb.org.uk/history/tirpitz-bulkhead/: 18/06/2013. Sadly, Roger Audis died in June 2013. Sqn Ldr Wood's statement was originally published by Lynnews 'End of battle of Tirpitz bulkhead' on 12 November 2002.*
4. Cooper (2013), p. 159.
5. The RAF Wainfleet Air-Weapons Range closed on 3 December 2009 as a MoD cost-saving measure. 617 Squadron was no stranger to Wainfleet with the Barnes Wallis 'Bouncing Bomb' used during the dam raids in May 1943 being tested there.

Bibliography

Unprinted sources

National Archives, Kew
Operational Record Books: IX(B) Squadron, 44 Squadron, 97 Squadron, 463 Squadron and 617 Squadron
AIR 27/128
AIR 27/449
AIR 27/766
AIR 27/1922
AIR 27/2128
AIR 27/2129

RAF Museum, Hendon
Individual aircraft record cards for Lancasters LM448 and NF920

Swedish National War Archives
Reports regarding violations of Swedish airspace by British aircraft, September-November 1944

Swedish National Military Archives
Interrogation reports for Fg Off. D. W. Carey and Fg Off. D. A. Coster
Secret report on condition of Lancaster LM448

Holmberg, Andreas and Korva, Niklas, *Easy Elsie och Nordens ensamma drottning* (Master's thesis for the Department of History, Luleå Technical University, 2006)

Internet

www.lancaster-archive.com/bc_tirpitz2.htm: 22/08/2011
http://ixb.org.uk/2012/history/sep-1939-1945: 18/06/2013
http://ixb.org.uk/2012/history/tirpitz-bulkhead: 18/06/2013

http://weimar.facinghistory.org/content/political-parties-weimar-germany: 10/06/2013
www.vannasberget.se/ormanget.html: 31/03/2013
www.churchillarchive.com: 05/04/2013
www.467463raafsquadrons.com/TrueTales/sink_the_tirpitz.htm: 22/04/2013
www.historysite.co.uk/tirpitz.htm: 31/01/2013
www.bismarck-class.dk/tirpitz/tiroperationalhist.html: 31/01/2013
www.bombercommandmuseum.ca/s,tweddle.html: 08/07/2013
www.bombercommandmuseum.ca/tirpitz.html: 08/07/2013
www.sm2tos.se/easyelsie/swe/html/historia.html: 21/10.2013
www.tirpitz-museum.no: 31/01/2013
http://ktsorens.tihlde.org/flyvrak/syningen.html: 22/04/2013

Printed books and articles

Après Moi, The 617 Squadron Aircrew Association Newsletter (winter 2009-2010, summer 2010 and December 2011 issues)

Asmussen, John and Aakra, Kjetil, *Tirpitz: Hitlers siste slagskip* (Midt-Troms Museum, Norway, 2006)

Backer, Steve, *Bismarck and Tirpitz* (Seaforth Publishing, UK, 2011) (reprint)

Bishop, Patrick, *Uppdrag Tirpitz Så sänktes Hitlers största slagskepp* (Fischer & Co., 2013)

Brickhill, Paul, *Vi flyger i natt (Dam Busters)* (Natur och Kultur, Sweden, 1952)

Cooper, Alan W., *From the Dams to the Tirpitz: The Later Operations of 617 Squadron* (Pen & Sword Aviation, UK, 2013)

Geust, Carl-Fredrik & Petrov, Gennadiy, *Red Stars 4: Lend-Lease Aircraft in Russia* (Apali Oy, Finland 2002)

Girbig, Werner, *Chronik Jagdgeschwader 5 'Eismeerjäger'* (Motorbuchverlag, Germany, 2010)

Heeley, Howard, *Sinking the Mighty Tirpitz* (*Aeroplane*: November 2004)

Hore, Peter, *The World Encyclopedia of Battleships: An Illustrated History of Battleships and their Evolution* (Hermes House, UK, 2010)

Kotelnikov, Vladimir, *From Roundels to Red Stars* (*Aeroplane*: January 2007)

Linder, Jan and Lundberg, Lennart, *Ofredens hav Östersjön 1939-1992* (Infomanager Förlag Jan Linder, 2002)

Moyle, Harry, *The Hampden File* (Air-Britain Ltd, UK, 1989)

Moyes, Philip J. R., *Bomber Squadrons of the R.A.F. and their Aircraft* (Macdonald & Co., UK, 1964)

Pegg, Martin, *Luftwaffe Transport Units 1943-1945* (Classic, Ian Allan Publishing, UK, 2006)

Robertson, Bruce, *Lancaster—The Story of a Famous Bomber* (Harleyford Publications Limited, UK, 1964)

Schofield, Ernest and Nesbit, Roy Conyers, *Arctic Airmen: The RAF in Spitsbergen and*

North Russia, 1942 (Spellmount Limited, UK, 2005)
Smith, Nigel, *Tirpitz: The Halifax Raids* (Air Research Publications, UK, 2003)
Sturtivant, Ray, *Barracuda in Action* (*Aeroplane*: March 1981)
Sweetman, John, *Tirpitz: Hunting the Beast* (Sutton, UK, 2004)
Tamelander, Michael and Zetterling, Niklas, *Slagskeppet Tirpitz: Kampen om norra Ishavet* (Norstedts, 2006)
Tarrant, V.E., *The Last Year of the Kriegsmarine May 1944-May 1945* (Arms & Armour Press, UK, 1996)
Wegmann, Rolph, *Brittiska nödlandare 1940-1945* (Air Historic Research AB, Nässjö, 2008)
Williamson, Gordon, *German Battleships 1939-45* (Osprey, UK, 2008)

Index

Aaland Islands, 30
Aasen Fjord, 47
Abisko, 112
Adams, Flt Lt, 86
Adams, Fg Off, 89, 113
Admiral Hipper, 47, 48, 53, 59, 60, 148
Admiral Scheer, 17, 30, 46, 51, 66
Akrotiri, 151
Alta Fjord, 49, 60-62, 75, 92, 107, 124, 141, 148
Arado Ar 196, 22, 38, 40, 59, 61, 63, 72, 106, 155
Archangel, 33, 56, 79, 84, 91, 93
Armstrong Whitworth Whitley, 23, 25, 26
Arthur (fishing boat), 57
Audis, Roger, 10, 156
Avro Manchester, 77
Avro Lancaster, 13-15, 35, 42-51, 60, 64, 76-91, 94-98, 100-103, 107, 108, 111-125, 127-136, 142-147, 150, 153, 158-162
Avro Lincoln, 150, 151, 153
Avro Vulcan, 151, 153, 156

Banak, 72, 126
Bardney, 80, 85, 86, 89, 94, 101, 108
Bardufoss, 106, 122, 126, 128-131, 134, 149
Barentsburg, 13, 61
Bazin, James Michael, 97, 112, 113
Beech 18R, 87
Bell, T.C., 181n
Bell P-39 Airacobra, 32
Bennett, Donald, 46, 48, 49, 181n
Berchtesgarten, 150
Berg, Artur, 154
Bergen, 27
Berlin, 38, 78, 149, 150, 152, 179n
Bielefeld viaduct, 152
Binbrook, 151, 156
Bismarck, Otto von, 20
Bismarck, 12, 13, 20-22, 25, 27-29, 32, 75, 180n

Bjørnøya, 39, 52, 53
Björnstierna, Carl, 52
Black, Cliff, 146
Blanchet, Pierre, 48, 49, 90
Blohm & Voss Bv 138, 53, 72
Blücher, 24
Boag, Jim, 146
Boden, 87, 154
Bodø, 65, 71, 128
Boehm, Hermann, 27
Bogen Fjord, 48, 50-52, 57-59
Bos Fjord, 64
Boeing B-17 Flying Fortress, 64, 65, 84, 101
Braunschweig, 17
Brickhill, Paul, 9, 78, 118, 128
Bristol Blenheim, 23, 26, 112
Bristol Beaufort, 36, 37, 180n
Bristol Beaufighter, 45, 50, 51
Brünner, Adalbert, 134
Bruno Heinemann, 34
Bryggman, John, 119, 160, 161
Buckham, Bruce, 91, 97, 98, 111, 116, 133
Bygren, Karl-Gunnar, 146

Camsell, Fg Off, 90, 112, 133
Capsey, 86
Carey, Daniel William, 101, 112, 116-120, 159-161
Cheshire, Leonard, 81, 83
Churchill, Winston, 12, 24, 25, 32, 35, 36, 40, 45, 51, 63, 65, 74, 107, 144
Ciliax, Otto, 38-40
Cochrane, Ralph, 78, 81, 83, 103, 107, 122, 124
Colgan, J., 48, 49
Consolidated B-24 Liberator, 29, 76, 86, 89, 91, 92, 101, 112
Consolidated PBY-5 Catalina, 54
Cooper, Alan, 157
Cornish, Peter, 155

Coster, David, 131, 145-147
Coton, Flt Lt, 43
Cottesmore, 151
Cunningham, Andrew, 107

Dallachay, 132, 136, 142
Daniels, W. A., 96
Denham, Henry, 52
Deutschland/Lützow, p. 17, 19, 26, 149, 152
DH 60T Moth Trainer, 160
DH 98 Mosquito, 42, 43, 56, 60, 70, 75, 76, 81, 85, 92, 94, 104, 106, 107, 123, 124, 142, 148, 182n
Dietl, Eduard, 27, 32
Digri, 152
Dixon, John, 62, 66
Dodd, Sqn Ldr, 148
Dollart, 68
Dönitz, Karl, 59-61, 104, 105, 149
Dornier Do 217, 44
Douglas C-47 Skytrain, 90, 110
Dunne, Flt Lt, 98, 112
Dvina, 79, 91
Dyce, 50

East, Harry, 146
Ehrler, Heinrich, 125, 126, 130, 131, 149
Eisenhower, Dwight D., 76
Elsass, 17
Elvebakken, 126
Emden, 26, 30
English Electric Canberra., 151, 153
Eriksson, Mauritz, 127
Erixon, Pär, 160
Evans, Plt Off, 96

Fairey Swordfish, 28, 38, 41, 54, 65, 180n
Fairey Albacore, 12, 13, 37-41, 59, 65
Fairey Barracuda, 14, 65, 67, 68, 70-73, 75, 82, 106, 123, 155, 181n
Fairey Firefly, 70-73, 106
Fairhurst, Edward A. 'Tim', 56
Fauquier, J. E., 152
Fane, Flt Lt, 43
Fearn, 50
FFVS J 22, 87
Filey Bay, 42
Finucane, 'Paddy', 107
Fjällbacka, 100
Focke-Wulf Fw 190, 113, 126, 130
Focke-Wulf Fw 200, 29, 38, 180n
Forbes, C. R., 48, 49
Fox, Charles Lawrence, 100

Franks, Les, 117, 118
Fraser, Bruce, 69
Frick, Admiral, 179n
Friedrich Eckholt, 50
Frostviken, 86, 112
Furniss, Donald R. M., 56, 66

Gavin, Flt Lt, 124
Gibson, Guy, 25, 60, 80, 81
Gingles, Fg Off, 97, 142
Gneisenau, 18, 34, 148
Gotenhafen, 26, 27, 31, 148
Gothenburg, 100, 101
Grael, Flt Lt, 96
Graf Spee, 17, 19
Graf Zeppelin, 29, 38, 180n
Grasnaya, 54
Greif, 60
Grimstad Fjord, 27
Groom, Peter William, 100
Grumman F4F Wildcat, 67
Grumman F6F Hellcat, 67, 70-73, 155
Grumman TBF/TBM Avenger, 54, 72, 73
Gumbley, Flt Lt, 114, 115, 142
Göring, Hermann, 29, 149

Håkøya, 14, 106, 108, 109, 113, 122, 124, 126, 129, 130, 136, 137, 142, 148, 154
Hallows, Flt Lt, 43
Halmstad, 100
Hamilton, Flt Lt, 96, 114
Hammerfest, 64
Handley Page Heyford, 80
Handley Page Hampden, 23, 25, 26, 50, 54, 55, 159
Handley Page Halifax, 35, 36, 42-49, 76, 155, 162
Hannover, 17
Harris, Arthur, 49, 65, 74, 78, 143
Harris, Fg Off, 91, 92
Hassel, Ilse von, 23
Hawker Hart, 87
Hawker Osprey, 87, 160
Hawkr Hurricane, 32, 54
Heg Bay, 64
Heinkel He 111, 52, 53, 55
Heinkel He 115, 55, 72, 106
Heligoland, 24, 77
Herbert, Sgt, 36
Hesketh, 105
Hessen, 17, 18, 29
Hewitt, I., 48, 49
Hill, Plt Off, 48
Hitler, Adolf, 18, 19, 23, 27, 29-31, 33, 38, 41, 59, 60, 70, 109, 149, 150, 152

Hjärpe, Yngve, 146
HMS *Achates*, 54, 59
HMS *Achilles*, 19
HMS *Ajax*, 19
HMS *Amazon*, 54
HMS *Anson*, 66
HMS *Ark Royal*, 28
HMS *Avenger*, 54, 55
HMS *Belfast*, 63
HMS *Berwick*, 110
HMS *Duke of York*, 38, 63, 66
HMS *Emperor*, 66, 67
HMS *Exeter*, 19
HMS *Fencer*, 66
HMS *Formidable*, p. 71, 72
HMS *Furious*, 65-67, 70, 71
HMS *Hood*, 28
HMS Implacable, 106
HMS *Indefatigable*, 71, 72, 182n
HMS *Jamaica*, 63
HMS *Malcolm*, 54
HMS *Nabob*, 71, 73
HMS *Nairana*, 110
HMS *Norfolk*, 63
HMS *Prince of Wales*, 28, 41
HMS *Pursuer*, 66, 67
HMS *Renown*, 38
HMS *Searcher*, 66, 67
HMS *Seawolf*, 38
HMS *Trumpeter*, 71, 73
HMS *Unshaken*, 53
HMS *Victorious*, 38-40, 53, 66, 67, 70, 181n
Höganäs, 100
Hopps, F. R., 54
Horta Fjord, 108, 125
Howard, Flt Lt, 96
Høvding, Einar, 154

Ilyushin Il-4, 13, 64
Innerträsket, 145
Ivan Kalyev, 93
Iveson, Tony, 84, 90, 92, 97, 113, 114, 142
Izhora, 39

Jaguar, 60
James, 'Dicky', 157
Jepson, 'Jeep', 156
Jokkmokk, 118, 161
Jones, Taffy, 146
Junge, Wolf, 69, 73, 95, 96, 98, 106, 124
Junkers Ju 52/3m, 130, 182n
Junkers Ju 87, 88
Junkers Ju 88, 55, 130

Junkers Ju 290, 29

K21, 53
Kaa Fjord, 13, 14, 60, 62-65, 67, 69, 70, 72, 73, 75, 76, 78, 85, 94-97, 105, 106, 109, 110, 126, 134, 155
Käinntjägge, 117
Kaldadammen, 46
Kalixfors, 87
Karl Geister, 60
Karlstad, 101
Karlsruhe, 24
Karungi, 87
Kautokeino, 95
Kegostrov, 89, 91, 92
Kehrwieder, 104
Kell, Arthur, 96, 115, 129, 142
Kennedy, Ludovic, 14
Kenwright, Roy, 62
KHZ-57, 104
Kiel, 26, 32, 34, 40, 148
Kinloss, 44, 50
Kirkenes, 64, 110
Köln, 30
Königsberg, 24
Krause, Max, 62
Kummavuopio, 113
Kungsbacka, 100

Laine, Finnish Master Pilot, 30
Lake, Fg Off, 86, 114
Lake Akkojaure, 127, 129
Lake Hoklingen, 155
Lake Lakhta, 54
Laks River, 64
Larsen, C.A., 68
Leavitt, Fg Off, 114-116, 124, 125, 142
Leipzig, 30
Levy, Frank, 86, 100
Lie Jonas, 109
Liinahamari, 64
Lille Grindøya, 106, 109
Lindberg, Egil, 108, 109, 122, 142, 153
Lindeman, Grant M., 55
Lippestad, Johan, 109
Litza, 32
Lockheed Hudson, 45
Lockheed Lodestar, 49
Lockheed Martin F-35B, 153
Loftus, John, 86, 97, 153
Loginov, Colonel, 92
London, 24, 110, 143
Lorrimer, John, 155

Lossiemouth, 35, 36, 42-45, 47, 50, 55, 77, 84-86, 98, 101, 107, 112-116, 123, 126, 132, 133, 136, 142, 156, 157
Lothringen, 17
Luleå, 87, 110
Lusitania, 20, 21
Lützow/Deutschland, 19, 24, 60, 65, 66, 148, 152

Macintosh, Fg Off, 97
MacIntyre, D. P., 48, 49
Marat, Jean Paul, 31
Marat, 31
Marham, 31
Matthodie, Lt, 71
McGuire, George Muir, 100
McKie, Alex, 7, 118, 119, 121, 160, 161
McNally, Allan Frank, Melrose, Flt Lt, 100
Messerschmitt Bf 109, 24, 42, 126, 131, 160, 180n
Messerschmitt Bf 110, 55
Messerschmitt Me 262, 149
Meyer, Hans, 60, 66-68, 95
Miller, Tommy, 40
Molotovskij Fjord, 27
Moore, Sir Henry, 67, 75, 105
Moscow, 69, 88, 103
Mosjøen, 128
Munro, Les, 83
Murmansk, 27, 32, 33, 52, 55, 56, 91, 110
Musashi, 21
Naisjärv, 145
Nanton, 155
Narvik, 24, 27, 30, 37, 48, 50, 52, 55, 57, 59, 71
Naylor, James Frazer, 100
Neumark, 66
Nicholson, Plt Off, 66
Nord 29, 104
Northrop 8A-1, 87
Nürnberg, 30
Nymphe, 106

Ögren, Kent, 161
Öhman, Ernst, 159
Oktiabraskaya Revolutia, 31
Olav, Crown Prince of Norway, 144
Onega, 89-92
Orlowski, Heinz, 130
Osborn, W/Op, 47
Ostfriesland, 18

Panavia Tornado, 151
Parsons, Plt Off, 92
Paul Jacobi, 34
Peck, Eric Edward Stephen, 100

Perry, D. L., 48, 49
Persson, Bert, 7
Petersen, Torstein, 61, 63, 70
Petlyakov Pe-8/TB-7, 64, 95
Pinning, Jim, 145, 147
Polikarpov Po-2, 90
Porjus, 108, 117, 119-121, 158-161
Pound, Dudley, 51, 52
Preussen, 17
Prinz Eugen, 26, 28, 34, 47, 48, 60, 66, 149, 152
Pryor, Flt Lt, 86, 96, 114, 117, 143

Raeder, Erich, 19, 27-30, 32, 33, 38, 39, 41, 53, 59, 60
RAF BE 2C, 79
RAF RE 8, 79
Redfern, Fg Off, 112, 114, 133
Reidel, Otto, 20
Rendulic, Lothar, 88
Republic EP-106, 87
Richard Beitzen, 34
Richardson, Archibald, 72, 73
Richardson, H. H., 181n
Robertsfors, 87
Robinson, F. A., 62
Roosevelt, Franklin Delano, 144
Ross, Plt Off, 92, 142
Ruhr River, 151
Ryeng, Tordis, 124
Ryeng, Vidar, 124

Savage, E. G., 40
Saxnäs, 86
Scampton, 80, 153, 156
Scapa Flow, 17, 28, 38, 52, 65, 67, 73, 74, 110, 179n
Scharnhorst, 18, 34, 60, 61, 63, 66
Schlesien, 17, 18, 60
Schleswig-Holstein, 17, 18, 20, 60
Searle, Fg Off, 66
Senje, Sigurd, 127
Shea, Denis Charles, 100
Sheppard, Don, 68
Shilling Roads, 24
Shinano, 21
Short Sunderland, 57, 153, 181n
Short Stirling, 35, 36, 42, 76, 101
Skattøra, 52, 106
Slessor, Sir John, 60
Smith, J. M., 43
Solovkin, Senior Lieutenant, 62
Stalin, Josef, 32, 63, 144
St Nazaire, 28, 42

Index

Stockholm, 52, 100, 118, 121
Stout, Flt Lt, 96
Stowell, Fg Off, 95, 97
Suckling, Michael, Fg Off, 27
Sumburgh, 37, 45, 50, 56, 62, 115, 142, 180n
Suorva, 108, 112, 117, 127
Supermarine Seafire, 67, 70-73
Supermarine Spitfire, 24, 28, 35, 43, 54-57, 60, 62, 64, 66, 130, 133, 181n
Sweetman, John, 10, 118, 144, 180n

Tain, 43, 44, 50
Tait, James Brian, 81, 90, 94, 96, 103, 112, 114, 115, 125, 128, 129, 131, 132, 134-136, 142, 143, 152, 153
Tamelander, Mikael, 7, 10
Tärna, 112
Tautra, 57
Terboven, Josef, 109
Thetis, 106
Thomas, Daniel Gorowny, 100
Thompson, George, 150
Tirpitz, Alfred von, 10, 20, 21, 23
Tirpitz, Marie von, 23
Tirpitz
Operation *Catechism*, 9, 14, 15, 108, 123-147, 155, 158
Operation *Obviate*, 9, 14, 15, 107-122, 123, 124, 136, 158
Operation *Paravane*, 7-9, 14, 15, 49, 75-106, 107, 111, 123, 135, 136, 155, 157, 161
Operation *Polar Night*, 34
Operation *Rösselsprung*, 53, 57
Operation *Sicily*, 13, 60, 61
Operation *Sportpalast*, 38, 39, 43
Ordnance expended, 61, 72, 73
Performance characteristics, 21-22
RAF photo reconnaissance sorties against, 23, 14, 35, 37, 38, 42, 43, 45, 48, 54-57, 60, 62, 64-66, 68, 70, 72, 73, 85, 106, 123, 124, 142, 148
RAF 1939-1940 bombing campaign, 24-26
RAF 1942 bomb raids, 35-37, 41-51
Sea trials of, 26, 32, 66, 67
X-Craft attack, 10, 62-64
Tirpitzøya, 21
Topp, Friedrich Karl, 26, 27, 33, 42, 60
Tovey, John, 28, 34, 38, 40, 52, 53
Tromsø, 7, 14, 52, 56, 105-108, 110, 113, 122, 127-129, 131, 134, 135, 141, 142, 154-156
Trondheim, 33-37, 42, 43, 45, 51, 85, 155, 182n
Tupolev Tu-4, 101
Turowsky, Bernhard, 58, 59

U-253, 54
U-354, 73
U-965, 72
Urft Dam, p.151
USS *Iowa*, 21
USS *Missouri*, 21.
USS *New Jersey*, 21
USS *Ranger*, 65
USS *Wisconsin*, 21

Værnes, 42, 43, 50, 77
Vännäsberget, 145-147
Vaskovo, 90, 92, 103
Vickers Vimy, 80
Vickers Virginia, 80

Walker, Gavin William 'Sleepy', 56
Wallis, Barnes, 81-83, 183n
Walmsley, H., 48, 49
Ward, Artur, 8,10, 93, 135
Weber, Robert 124, 128, 132, 136
Wibe, Gunvor, 130
Wick, 35, 50, 110
Wig Bay, 57
Wilhelmshaven, 12, 20, 23-26, 34, 63, 81
Williams, Sqn Ldr, 133
Wilson, R. H., 48, 49
Wilson, Woodrow, 21
Witherick, Gerry, 88, 116-118, 158
Wittering, 156
Woodhall Spa, 43, 83, 91, 108, 112, 121-124, 143
Wyness, Sdn Ldr, 91, 92

X 5, 62, 155
X 6, 62, 155
X 7, 62

Yagodnik, 79, 85, 86-93, 95-98, 100-104
Yamato, 21
Young, Flt Sgt, 116, 118

Z 14 Friedrich Ihn, 39
Z 29, 34, 61
Z 33, 61
Z 38, 68
Zuba, Alfred, 7, 10, 137
Z 38, 68
Zuba, Alfred, 7, 10, 137